ASP.NET Core 2 High Performance

Second Edition

Learn the secrets of developing high performance web applications using C# and ASP.NET Core 2 on Windows, Mac, and Linux

James Singleton

BIRMINGHAM - MUMBAI

ASP.NET Core 2 High Performance

Second Edition

First published: June 2016

Second edition: October 2017

Production reference: 1061017

Published by Packt Publishing Ltd.
Livery Place
35 Livery Street
Birmingham
B3 2PB, UK.
ISBN 978-1-78839-976-0

www.packtpub.com

Credits

Author
James Singleton

Reviewer
Vidya Vrat Agarwal

Commissioning Editor
Merint Mathew

Acquisition Editor
Aiswarya Narayanan

Content Development Editor
Vikas Tiwari

Technical Editor
Madhunikita Sunil Chindarkar

Copy Editor
Muktikant Garimella

Project Coordinator
Ulhas Kambali

Proofreader
Safis Editing

Indexer
Tejal Daruwale Soni

Production Coordinator
Shraddha Falebhai

Foreword

"The most amazing achievement of the computer software industry is its continuing cancellation of the steady and staggering gains made by the computer hardware industry."

– Henry Petroski

We live in the age of distributed systems. Computers have shrunk from room-sized industrial mainframes to embedded devices that are smaller than a thumbnail. However, at the same time, the software applications that we build, maintain, and use every day have grown beyond measure. We create distributed applications that run on clusters of virtual machines scattered all over the world, and billions of people rely on these systems, such as email, chat, social networks, productivity applications, and banking, every day. We're online 24 hours a day, seven days a week, and we're hooked on instant gratification. A generation ago, we'd happily wait until after the weekend for a cheque to clear, or allow 28 days for delivery. Today, we expect instant feedback, and why shouldn't we? The modern web is real-time, immediate, on-demand, and built on packets of data flashing around the world at the speed of light, and when it isn't, we notice. We've all had that sinking feeling... you know, when you've just put your credit card number into a page to buy some expensive concert tickets, and the site takes just a little too long to respond. Performance and responsiveness are a fundamental part of delivering a great user experience in the distributed age. However, for a working developer trying to ship your next feature on time, performance is often one of the most challenging requirements. How do you find the bottlenecks in your application performance? How do you measure the impact of those problems? How do you analyze them, design and test solutions and workarounds, and monitor them in production so that you can be confident that they won't happen again? This book has the answers. Inside, James Singleton presents a pragmatic, in-depth, and balanced discussion of modern performance optimization techniques, and how to apply them to your .NET and web applications. Starting from the premise that we should treat performance as a core feature of our systems, James shows how you can use profiling tools such as Glimpse, MiniProfiler, Fiddler, and Wireshark to track down the bottlenecks and bugs that cause your performance problems. He addresses the scientific principles behind effective performance tuning, monitoring, instrumentation, and the importance of using accurate and repeatable measurements when you make changes to a running system to try and improve performance.

This book goes on to discuss almost every aspect of modern application development: database tuning, hardware optimisations, compression algorithms, network protocols, and object-relational mappers. For each topic, James describes the symptoms of common performance problems, identifies the underlying causes of those symptoms, and then describes the patterns and tools that you can use to measure and fix these underlying causes in your own applications. There's an in-depth discussion of high-performance software patterns such as asynchronous methods and message queues, accompanied by real-world examples showing you how to implement these patterns in the latest versions of the .NET framework. Finally, James shows how you can not only load test your applications as a part of your release pipeline, but you can continuously monitor and measure your systems in production, letting you find and fix potential problems long before they start upsetting your end users.

When I worked with James here at Spotlight, he consistently demonstrated a remarkable breadth of knowledge, from ASP.NET to Arduinos and from Resharper to resistors. One day, he'd build reactive frontend interfaces in ASP.NET and JavaScript; the next day, he'd create build monitors by wiring microcontrollers into Star Wars toys, or working out how to connect the bathroom door lock to the intranet so that our bicycling employees could see from their desks when the office shower was free. After James moved on from Spotlight, I've been following his work with Cleanweb and Computing 4 Kids Education. He's one of those rare developers who really understands the social and environmental implications of technology; whether it's delivering great user interactions or just saving electricity, improving your systems' performance is a great way to delight your users. With this book, James has distilled years of hands-on lessons and experience into a truly excellent all-round reference for .NET developers who want to understand how to build responsive and scalable applications. It's a great resource for new developers who want to develop a holistic understanding of application performance, but the coverage of cutting-edge techniques and patterns means it's also ideal for more experienced developers who want to make sure they're not getting left behind. Buy it, read it, share it with your team, and let's make the web a better place.

Dylan Beattie
Systems architect REST evangelist, technical speaker
Co-organizer of the London .NET User Group

About the Author

James Singleton is a British software developer, engineer, and entrepreneur, who has been writing code since the days of the BBC Micro. His formal training is in electrical and electronic engineering, yet he has worked professionally in .NET software development for nearly a decade. He is active in the London start-up community and helps organize Cleanweb London events for environmentally conscious technologists. He runs Cleanweb Jobs (`https://cleanwebjobs.com/`), which aims to help get developers, engineers, managers, and data scientists into roles that can help tackle climate change and other environmental problems. He also does public speaking and has presented talks at many local user groups, including at the Hacker News London meet up. James holds a first class degree (with honors) in electronic engineering with computing, and has designed and built his own basic microprocessor on an FPGA, along with a custom instruction set to run on it. James contributes to, and is influenced by, many open source projects, and he regularly uses alternative technologies such as Python, Ruby, and Linux. He is enthusiastic about the direction that Microsoft is taking with .NET, and their embracing of open source practices. He is particularly interested in hardware, environmental, and digital rights projects, and is keen on security, compression, and algorithms. When not hacking on code, or writing for books and magazines, he enjoys walking, skiing, rock climbing, traveling, brewing, and craft beer. James has gained varied skills by working in many diverse industries and roles, from high performance stock exchanges to video encoding systems. He has worked as a business analyst, consultant, tester, developer, and technical architect. He has a wide range of knowledge, gained from big corporates to start-ups, and lots of places in between. He has first-hand experience of the best, and the worst, ways of building high-performance software. You can read his blog at `https://unop.uk/`.

I would like to thank all of my friends and family for being so supportive while I was working on this book. I would especially like to thank my mum and dad for getting me into science and technology at a young age, and Lou for her limitless enthusiasm and positivity. I would also like to thank Dylan for writing the foreword to this book. Writing a book is much harder work than most people probably imagine, and I couldn't have done it without the constant encouragement. Many sacrifices have been made, and I thank everyone for their understanding. Sorry for all the events I've had to miss and to anyone who I've forgotten to thank here.

About the Reviewer

Vidya Vrat Agarwal is a software technology enthusiast, Microsoft MVP, C# Corner MVP, TOGAF Certified Architect, Certified Scrum Master (CSM), and a published author. He has presented sessions at various technical conferences and code camps in India and the USA. He lives in Redmond, WA, with his wife, Rupali, and two daughters, Pearly and Arshika. He is passionate about .NET and works as Principal Architect, Systems, with T-Mobile USA. He blogs at `http://www.MyPassionFor.NET` and can be followed on Twitter at `@DotNetAuthor`.

www.PacktPub.com

For support files and downloads related to your book, please visit www.PacktPub.com. Did you know that Packt offers eBook versions of every book published, with PDF and ePub files available? You can upgrade to the eBook version at www.PacktPub.com and as a print book customer, you are entitled to a discount on the eBook copy. Get in touch with us at service@packtpub.com for more details. At www.PacktPub.com, you can also read a collection of free technical articles, sign up for a range of free newsletters and receive exclusive discounts and offers on Packt books and eBooks.

https://www.packtpub.com/mapt Get the most in-demand software skills with Mapt. Mapt gives you full access to all Packt books and video courses, as well as industry-leading tools to help you plan your personal development and advance your career.

Why subscribe?

- Fully searchable across every book published by Packt
- Copy and paste, print, and bookmark content
- On demand and accessible via a web browser

Customer Feedback

Thanks for purchasing this Packt book. At Packt, quality is at the heart of our editorial process. To help us improve, please leave us an honest review on this book's Amazon page at https://www.amazon.com/dp/1788399765. If you'd like to join our team of regular reviewers, you can email us at customerreviews@packtpub.com. We award our regular reviewers with free eBooks and videos in exchange for their valuable feedback. Help us be relentless in improving our products!

Table of Contents

Preface

Microsoft has released the second major version of its open source and cross-platform web application framework, ASP.NET Core. This runs on top of .NET Core, which is also open and is now, likewise, at version 2. ASP.NET Core is primarily used with the C# programming language, but F# and VB.NET can also be used. You are no longer tied to using Windows with ASP.NET, and you can now develop on a Mac and deploy to Linux. The new platform also offers much higher performance.

Version 2 is what version 1 should have been, as the first stable release was not really production ready. Major changes were made very late in the release candidate stage. Thankfully, things have stabilized with the new tooling, and you can now use ASP.NET Core in earnest.

In today's world, a web application that only performs well on a developer's workstation and fails to deliver high performance in production is unacceptable. The way that web applications are now deployed at scale has changed, and development practices must adapt to take advantage of this. By reading this book, you'll learn about the modern way of making high-performance web applications, and how to do this with ASP.NET Core.

This is a high-level book that provides performance tips that are applicable to web application development with any programming stack. However, it focuses specifically on C# and ASP.NET Core. The reader should already know how to build a web app, though not necessarily in .NET Core.

This book addresses web application performance improvement techniques, from both a general standpoint (HTTP, HTTPS, HTTP/2, TCP/IP, database access, compression, I/O, asset optimization, caching, message queuing, and other concerns) and from a C#, ASP.NET Core, and .NET Core perspective. This includes delving into the details of the latest frameworks and demonstrating software design patterns that improve performance.

Common performance pitfalls will be highlighted, which can often occur unnoticed on developer workstations, along with strategies to detect and resolve these issues early. By understanding and addressing the challenges upfront, any nasty surprises can be avoided when it comes to live deployment.

Many performance improvements will be introduced, along with the trade-offs they entail. We will strike a balance between premature optimization and inefficient code by taking a scientific and evidence-based approach, focusing on the big problems, and avoiding changes that have little impact.

We assume that you understand the importance of the performance for web applications, but we will recap why it's crucial. However, you may not have had any specific or actionable advice, or much experience of performance problems occurring in the wild.

By reading this book, you'll understand what problems can occur when web applications are deployed at scale to distributed infrastructure, and you will know how to avoid or mitigate these issues. You will gain experience of how to write high-performance applications without having to learn about issues the hard way, possibly late at night.

You'll see what's new in ASP.NET Core, why it's been rebuilt from the ground up, and what this means for performance. You will understand the future of .NET Core and how you can now develop and deploy on Windows, macOS, and Linux. You'll appreciate the performance of new features in ASP.NET Core, including updates to the Razor view engine, and you will be aware of cross-platform tools such as Visual Studio Code.

What this book covers

Chapter 1, *What's New in ASP.NET Core 2*, summarizes the significant changes between ASP.NET Core 1.0 and ASP.NET Core 2.0. We will also go into the history of the project to show why it was such a moving target. We will take a look at some of the new features in C# 6.0 and C# 7.0 to see how they can make your life easier. We will also cover .NET Standard 2.0 and how this improves library portability.

Chapter 2, *Why Performance Is a Feature*, discusses the basic premise of this book and shows why you need to care about the performance of your software. Responsive applications are vital and it's not simply enough to have functionalities work; they also needs to be quick. Think of the last time you heard someone complaining about an app or website, and it's likely that they were unhappy with the performance. Poor performance doesn't only make users unhappy, it also affects your bottom line. There's good data to suggest that fast performance increases engagement and improves conversion rates, which is why it's rewarded by search engines.

Chapter 3, *Setting Up Your Environment*, shows how to get started with the latest tooling on your operating system of choice. It is no longer a case of having to use Visual Studio on Windows if you want to develop with .NET. We will cover VS 2017 and the new integrated tooling for .NET Core and ASP.NET Core. We will also cover Visual Studio for Mac (previously called Xamarin Studio) and the multi-platform VS Code editor (built using TypeScript and web technologies). We will show how to use Docker containers to make cross-platform development easy and consistent. We will also take a look at the dotnet command-line tooling.

Chapter 4, *Measuring Performance Bottlenecks*, shows that the only way you can solve performance problems is by carefully measuring your application. Without knowing where a problem lies, your chance of solving it is extremely slim, and you won't even know if you've improved matters or made things worse. We will highlight a few ways of manually monitoring performance and some helpful tools you can use for measuring statistics. You'll see how to gain insights into the database, application, HTTP, and network levels of your software, so you know what is going on internally. We'll also show you how to build your own basic timing code and cover the importance of taking a scientific approach to the results.

Chapter 5, *Fixing Common Performance Problems*, looks at some of the most frequent performance mistakes. We'll show how to fix simple issues across a range of different application areas—for example, how to optimize media with image resizing or encoding, select N+1 problems, and asynchronous background operations. We will also talk a little about using hardware to improve performance once you know where the bottlenecks lie. This approach buys you some time and allows you to fix things properly at a reasonable pace.

Chapter 6, *Addressing Network Performance*, digs into the networking layer that underpins all web applications. We'll show how remote resources can slow down your app, and we'll demonstrate what you can do about measuring and addressing these problems. We will look at internet protocols, including TCP/IP, HTTP, HTTP/2, and WebSockets, along with a primer on encryption and how all of these can alter the performance. We'll cover the compression of textual and image assets, including some exotic image formats. Finally, we will introduce caching at the browser, server, proxy, and Content Delivery Network (CDN) levels, showing some of the basics.

Chapter 7, *Optimizing I/O Performance*, focuses on input/output and how this can negatively affect performance. We will look at disks, databases, and remote APIs, many of which use the network, particularly if virtualized. We'll cover batching your requests and optimizing database usage with aggregates and sampling, aiming to reduce the data and time required. Due to networking's ubiquity in cloud environments, we'll spend considerable time on network diagnostics, including pinging, route tracing and looking up records in the domain name system. You'll learn how latency can be driven by physical distance, or geography, and how this can cause problems for your application. We'll also demonstrate how to build your own network information gathering tools using .NET.

Chapter 8, *Understanding Code Execution and Asynchronous Operations*, jumps into the intricacies of C# code and looks at how its execution can alter performance. We'll look at the various open source projects that make up ASP.NET Core and .NET Core, including Kestrel, a high-performance web server. We will examine the importance of choosing the correct data structures and see various examples of different options, such as lists and dictionaries. We'll also look at hashing and serialization, and perform some simple benchmarking. You will learn some techniques that can speed up your processing by parallelizing it, such as Single Instruction Multiple Data (SIMD) or parallel extensions programming with the Task Parallel Library (TPL) and Parallel LINQ (PLINQ). You'll also see some practices that are best to avoid due to their performance penalties, such as reflection and regular expressions.

Chapter 9, *Learning Caching and Message Queuing*, initially looks at caching, which is widely regarded to be difficult. You'll see how caching works from a HTTP perspective in browsers, web servers, proxies, and CDNs. You will learn about cache busting (or breaking) for forcing your changes and using the new JavaScript service workers in modern browsers for gaining a finer control over caching.

Additionally, we'll examine caching at the application and database levels within your infrastructure. We will see the benefits of in-memory caches such as Redis and how these can reduce the load on your database, lower latency, and increase the performance of your application.

We will investigate message queuing as a way to build a distributed and reliable system. We'll use an analogy to explain how asynchronous message passing systems work, and we'll show some common styles of message queuing, including unicast and publish/subscribe.

We will also show how message queuing can be useful to an internal caching layer by broadcasting cache invalidation data. You'll learn about message brokers, such as RabbitMQ, and various libraries for interacting with them from .NET.

Chapter 10, *The Downsides of Performance-Enhancing Tools*, concentrates on the negatives of the techniques that we have covered, as nothing comes for free. We'll discuss the virtues of the various methods for reducing complexity, using frameworks, and designing distributed architecture. We will also cover project culture and see how high performance is not simply about code but about people too.

We'll look into the possible solutions for tackling the problem of distributed debugging and see some available technologies for centrally managing application logging. We'll have a brief introduction to statistics to make sense of your performance metrics, and we'll touch upon managing caches.

Chapter 11, *Monitoring Performance Regressions*, again looks at measuring performance but, in this case, from an automation and Continuous Integration (CI) perspective. We'll reiterate the importance of monitoring and show how you can build this into your development workflow in order to make it routine and almost transparent. You will see how it is possible to automate almost any type of testing, from simple unit testing to integration testing and even complex browser User Interface (UI) testing.

We'll show how you can make your tests more realistic and useful by using techniques such as blue-green deployment and feature switching. You will discover how to perform A/B testing of two versions of a web page, with some very basic feature switching, and a few options for fun hardware to keep people engaged in the test results. We'll also cover DevOps practices and cloud hosting, both of which make CI easier to implement and complement it nicely.

Chapter 12, *The Way Ahead*, briefly sums up the lessons of the book and then takes a look at some advanced topics that you may want to read more about. We will also try to predict the future for the .NET Core platforms and give you some ideas to take further.

What you need for this book

You will need a development environment to follow the code examples in this book—Visual Studio 2017, Visual Studio Mac, or VS Code. You could also use your text editor of choice and the dotnet command-line tool. If you're using Visual Studio, then you should still install the latest .NET Core SDK to enable the tooling.

For some of the chapters, you will also need SQL Server 2016, although you could use 2017. However, you could also use Azure and run against a cloud database.

There are other tools that we will cover, but we will introduce these as they are used. The detailed software/hardware list is available along with the code files.

Who this book is for

This book is aimed at web application developers who want to increase the performance of their software and discover what requires consideration when hosting in the cloud. It will be most useful to ASP.NET and C# developers, but developers familiar with other open source platforms will also find much of it informative.

You should have some experience of working with a framework for web application development, and you should be looking to deploy applications that will perform well on live production environments. These could be virtual machines or hosted by a cloud service provider such as AWS or Azure.

Conventions

In this book, you will find a number of text styles that distinguish between different kinds of information. Here are some examples of these styles and an explanation of their meaning. Code words in text, database table names, folder names, filenames, file extensions, pathnames, dummy URLs, user input, and Twitter handles are shown as follows: "The update command is different to the upgrade command, but they are often used together."

A block of code is set as follows:

```
#import packages into the project
from bs4 import BeautifulSoup
from urllib.request import urlopen
import pandas as pd
```

Any command-line input or output is written as follows:

```
sudo apt-get install docker-ce
```

New terms and **important words** are shown in bold. Words that you see on the screen, for example, in menus or dialog boxes, appear in the text like this: "Right-click on your web application project in **Solution Explorer** and select **Manage NuGet Packages...** to open the graphical package manager window."

Warnings or important notes appear like this.

Tips and tricks appear like this.

Reader feedback

Feedback from our readers is always welcome. Let us know what you think about this book-what you liked or disliked. Reader feedback is important for us as it helps us develop titles that you will really get the most out of. To send us general feedback, simply email feedback@packtpub.com, and mention the book's title in the subject of your message. If there is a topic that you have expertise in and you are interested in either writing or contributing to a book, see our author guide at www.packtpub.com/authors.

Customer support

Now that you are the proud owner of a Packt book, we have a number of things to help you to get the most from your purchase.

Downloading the example code

You can download the example code files for this book from your account at http://www.packtpub.com. If you purchased this book elsewhere, you can visit http://www.packtpub.com/support and register to have the files emailed directly to you. You can download the code files by following these steps:

1. Log in or register to our website using your email address and password.
2. Hover the mouse pointer on the **SUPPORT** tab at the top.
3. Click on **Code Downloads & Errata**.
4. Enter the name of the book in the **Search** box.
5. Select the book for which you're looking to download the code files.
6. Choose from the drop-down menu where you purchased this book from.
7. Click on **Code Download**.

Once the file is downloaded, please make sure that you unzip or extract the folder using the latest version of:

- WinRAR / 7-Zip for Windows
- Zipeg / iZip / UnRarX for Mac
- 7-Zip / PeaZip for Linux

The code bundle for the book is also hosted on GitHub at `https://github.com/PacktPublishing/ASPdotNET-High-Performance`. We also have other code bundles from our rich catalog of books and videos available at `https://github.com/PacktPublishing/`. Check them out!

Errata

Although we have taken every care to ensure the accuracy of our content, mistakes do happen. If you find a mistake in one of our books-maybe a mistake in the text or the code-we would be grateful if you could report this to us. By doing so, you can save other readers from frustration and help us improve subsequent versions of this book. If you find any errata, please report them by visiting `http://www.packtpub.com/submit-errata`, selecting your book, clicking on the **Errata Submission Form** link, and entering the details of your errata. Once your errata are verified, your submission will be accepted and the errata will be uploaded to our website or added to any list of existing errata under the Errata section of that title. To view the previously submitted errata, go to `https://www.packtpub.com/books/content/support` and enter the name of the book in the search field. The required information will appear under the **Errata** section.

Piracy

Piracy of copyrighted material on the internet is an ongoing problem across all media. At Packt, we take the protection of our copyright and licenses very seriously. If you come across any illegal copies of our works in any form on the internet, please provide us with the location address or website name immediately so that we can pursue a remedy. Please contact us at `copyright@packtpub.com` with a link to the suspected pirated material. We appreciate your help in protecting our authors and our ability to bring you valuable content.

Questions

If you have a problem with any aspect of this book, you can contact us at `questions@packtpub.com`, and we will do our best to address the problem.

1
What's New in ASP.NET Core 2?

There are many things that have changed in version 2 of the ASP.NET Core framework. There have been a lot of improvements in some of its supporting technologies as well. Now is a great time to give it a try, as its code has been stabilized and the pace of change has settled down a bit.

There were significant differences between the original release candidate and version 1 of ASP.NET Core and further alterations between version 1 and version 2. Some of these changes have been controversial, particularly ones related to tooling; however, the scope of .NET Core has grown massively, and this is a good thing.

One of the high-profile differences between version 1 and version 2 is the change (some would say regression) from the new **JavaScript Object Notation** (**JSON**)-based project format back to the **Extensible Markup Language** (**XML**)-based csproj format. However, it is a simplified and stripped-down version, compared to the format used in the original .NET Framework.

There has been a move toward standardization between the different .NET Frameworks, and .NET Core 2 has a much larger API surface as a result. The interface specification, known as .NET Standard 2, covers the intersection between .NET Core, the .NET Framework, and Xamarin. There is also an effort to standardize **Extensible Application Markup Language** (**XAML**) into the XAML standard, which will work across **Universal Windows Platform** (**UWP**) and Xamarin.Forms apps.

C# and .NET can be used on a huge range of diverse platforms and in a large number of different use cases, from server-side web applications to mobile apps and even games (using game engines such as Unity 3D). In this book, we'll focus on web application programming and, in particular, on general ways to make web apps perform well. This means that we will also cover client-side web browser scripting with JavaScript and the performance implications involved.

This book is not just about C# and ASP.NET. It takes a holistic approach to performance and aims to educate you about a wide range of relevant topics. We don't have the space to take a deep dive into everything, so the idea here is to help you discover some useful tools, technologies, and techniques.

In this chapter, we will go through the changes between version 1 and version 2 of both .NET Core and ASP.NET Core. We will also look at some new features of the C# language. There have been many useful additions and a plethora of performance improvements too.

In this chapter, we will cover the following topics:

- What's new in .NET Core 2.0
- What's new in ASP.NET Core 2.0
- Performance improvements
- .NET Standard 2.0
- New C# 6.0 features
- New C# 7.0 features
- JavaScript considerations

What's new in Core 2

There are two main products in the Core family. The first is .NET Core, which is a low-level framework that provides basic libraries. It can be used to write console applications, and it is also the foundation for higher level application frameworks.

The second is ASP.NET Core, which is a framework for building web applications that run on a server and service clients (usually web browsers). This was originally the only workload for .NET Core until it grew in scope to handle a more diverse range of scenarios.

We'll cover the differences in the newer versions separately for each of these frameworks. The changes in .NET Core will also apply to ASP.NET Core, unless you are running it on top of the .NET Framework, version 4.

What's new in .NET Core 2

The main focus of .NET Core 2 is the huge increase in scope. There are more than double the number of APIs included, and it supports .NET Standard 2 (covered later in this chapter). You can also reference .NET Framework assemblies with no recompilation required. This should just work as long as the assemblies only use APIs that have been implemented in .NET Core.

This means that more NuGet packages will work with .NET Core. Finding whether your favorite library was supported or not was always a challenge in the previous version. The author set up a repository listing package compatibility to help with this. You can find the **ASP.NET Core Library and Framework Support (ANCLAFS)** list at `https://anclafs.com/` and `https://github.com/jpsingleton/ANCLAFS`. If you want to make a change, then please send a pull request. Hopefully, in future, all the packages will support Core, and this list will no longer be required.

There is now support in .NET Core for Visual Basic, and more Linux distributions. You can also perform live unit testing with Visual Studio 2017 (Enterprise Edition only), much like the old NCrunch extension. We'll talk more about tooling in `Chapter 3`, *Setting Up Your Environment*, where we will also cover containerization.

Performance improvements

Some of the more interesting changes in .NET Core 2.0 are performance improvements over the original .NET Framework. There have been tweaks to the implementations of many framework data structures. Some of the classes and methods that have seen speedy improvements or memory reduction include:

- `List<T>`
- `Queue<T>`
- `SortedSet<T>`
- `ConcurrentQueue<T>`
- `Lazy<T>`
- `Enumerable.Concat()`
- `Enumerable.OrderBy()`
- `Enumerable.ToList()`
- `Enumerable.ToArray()`
- `DeflateStream`

- SHA256
- BigInteger
- BinaryFormatter
- Regex
- WebUtility.UrlDecode()
- Encoding.UTF8.GetBytes()
- Enum.Parse()
- DateTime.ToString()
- String.IndexOf()
- String.StartsWith()
- FileStream
- Socket
- NetworkStream
- SslStream
- ThreadPool
- SpinLock

We won't go into specific benchmarks here because benchmarking is hard and the improvements you see will clearly depend on your usage. The thing to take away is that lots of work has been done to increase the performance of .NET Core. Many of these changes have come from the community, which shows one of the benefits of open source development. Some of these advances will probably work their way back to a future version of the regular .NET Framework too.

There have been improvements made to the RyuJIT Just In Time compiler for .NET Core 2 as well. As just one example, `finally` blocks are now almost as efficient as not using exception handling at all, which is beneficial in a normal situation where no exceptions are thrown. You now have no excuses not to liberally use `try` and `using` blocks, for example, by the `checked` arithmetic to avoid integer overflows.

What's new in ASP.NET Core 2

ASP.NET Core 2 takes advantage of all the improvements to .NET Core 2, if that is what you choose to run it on. It will also run on .NET Framework 4.7, but it's best to run it on .NET Core if you can. With the increase in scope and support of .NET Core 2, this should be less of a problem than it was previously.

.NET Core 2 includes a new metapackage, so you only need to reference one NuGet item to get all the things. However, it is still composed of individual packages, if you want to pick and choose. They haven't reverted to the bad old days of having one huge `System.Web` assembly. A new package-trimming feature ensures that if you don't use a package, then its binaries won't be included in your deployment, even if you use a metapackage to reference it.

There is also a sensible default for setting up a web host configuration. You don't need to add logging, Kestrel, and IIS individually anymore. Logging has also gotten simpler and, as it is built in, you have no excuses not to use it from the start.

A new feature is support for controllerless Razor Pages. This is exactly what it sounds like, and it allows you to write pages with just a Razor template. It is similar to the Web Pages product, not to be confused with Web Forms. There is talk of Web Forms making a comeback; if this happens, then hopefully, the abstraction will be thought out more and it won't carry so much state around with it.

There is a new authentication model that makes better use of dependency injection. ASP.NET Core Identity allows you to use OpenID and OAuth 2 and get access tokens for your APIs. You may also want to investigate the Identity Server 4 project that provides a lot of similar functionality.

A nice time saver is that you no longer need to emit anti-forgery tokens in forms (to prevent Cross-Site Request Forgery) with attributes to validate them on post methods. This is all done automatically for you, which should prevent you from forgetting to do this and leaving a security vulnerability.

Performance improvements

There have been additional increases to performance in ASP.NET Core that are not related to the improvements in .NET Core, which also help. The start-up time has been reduced by shipping binaries that have already been through the Just In Time compilation process.

Although not a new feature in ASP.NET Core 2, output caching is now available. In 1.0, only response caching was included, which simply sets the correct HTTP headers. In 1.1, an in-memory cache was added, and today, you can use local memory or a distributed cache kept in SQL Server or Redis.

Standards

Standards are important; that's why we have so many of them. The latest version of the .NET Standard is version 2, and .NET Core 2 implements this. A good way to think about .NET Standard is it's an interface that a class would implement. The interface will define an abstract API, but the concrete implementation of this API will be left to the classes that inherit from it. Another way to think about this is like the HTML5 standard that is supported by different web browsers.

Version 2 of the .NET Standard was defined by looking at the intersection of the .NET Framework and Mono. This standard was then implemented by .NET Core 2, which is why it contains more APIs than version 1. Version 4.6.1 of the .NET Framework also implements .NET Standard 2, and there is work to support the latest versions of the .NET Framework, UWP, and Xamarin (including Xamarin.Forms).

There is also the new XAML Standard that aims to find a common ground between Xamarin.Forms and UWP. Hopefully, it will include **Windows Presentation Foundation (WPF)** in future. As this is a book about web applications, we won't go into XAML and native user interfaces.

If you create libraries and packages that use these standards, then they will work on all the platforms that support them. As a developer who simply consumes libraries, you don't need to worry about these standards. It just means that you are more likely to be able to use the packages that you want on the platforms you are working with.

New C# features

It's not just the frameworks and libraries that have been worked on. The underlying language also had some nice new features added. We will focus on C# here as it is the most popular language for the **Common Language Runtime (CLR)**. Other options include Visual Basic and the functional programming language F#.

C# is a great language to work with, especially when compared to a language such as JavaScript. Although JavaScript is great for many reasons (such as its ubiquity and the number of frameworks available), the elegance and design of the language is not one of them. We will cover JavaScript later in the book.

Many of these new features are just syntactic sugar, which means they don't add any new functionality. They simply provide a more succinct and easier-to-read way of writing code that does the same thing.

C# 6

Although the latest version of C# is 7, there are some very handy features in C# 6 that often go underused. Also, some of the new additions in 7 are improvements on features added in 6 and would not make much sense without any context. We will quickly cover a few features of C# 6 here, in case you are unaware of how useful they can be.

String interpolation

String interpolation is a more elegant and easier-to-work-with version of the familiar string format method. Instead of supplying the arguments to embed in the string placeholders separately, you can now embed them directly in the string. This is far more readable and less error-prone.

Let's demonstrate this with an example. Consider the following code that embeds an exception in a string:

```
catch (Exception e)
{
    Console.WriteLine("Oh dear, oh dear! {0}", e);
}
```

This embeds the first (and in this case only) object in the string at the position marked by zero. It may seem simple, but it quickly gets complex if you have many objects and want to add another at the start. You then have to correctly renumber all the placeholders.

Instead, you can now prefix the string with a dollar character and embed the object directly in it. This is shown in the following code that behaves the same as the previous example:

```
catch (Exception e)
{
    Console.WriteLine($"Oh dear, oh dear! {e}");
}
```

The `ToString()` method on an exception outputs all the required information, including the name, message, stack trace, and any inner exceptions. There is no need to deconstruct it manually; you may even miss things if you do.

You can also use the same format strings as you are used to. Consider the following code that formats a date in a custom manner:

```
Console.WriteLine($"Starting at: {DateTimeOffset.UtcNow:yyyy/MM/dd
HH:mm:ss}");
```

When this feature was being built, the syntax was slightly different. So, be wary of any old blog posts or documentation that may not be correct.

Null conditional

The null conditional operator is a way of simplifying null checks. You can now place an inline check for null rather than use an if statement or ternary operator. This makes it easier to use in more places and will hopefully help you avoid the dreaded null reference exception.

You can avoid doing a manual null check, as in the following code:

```
int? length = (null == bytes) ? null : (int?)bytes.Length;
```

This can now be simplified to the following statement by adding a question mark:

```
int? length = bytes?.Length;
```

Exception filters

You can filter exceptions more easily with the `when` keyword. You no longer need to catch every type of exception that you are interested in and then filter it manually inside the `catch` block. This is a feature that was already present in VB and F#, so it's nice that C# has finally caught up.

There are some small benefits to this approach. For example, if your filter is not matched, then the exception will still be caught by other catch blocks in the same `try` statement. You also don't need to remember to rethrow the exception to avoid it from being swallowed. This helps with debugging, as Visual Studio will no longer break as it would when you use `throw`.

For example, you could check to see whether there is a message in the exception and handle it differently, as shown here:

```
catch (Exception e) when (e?.Message?.Length > 0)
```

When this feature was in development, a different keyword (`if`) was used. So be careful of any old information online.

One thing to keep in mind is that relying on a particular exception message is fragile. If your application is localized, then the message may be in a different language to what you expect. This holds true outside of exception filtering too.

Asynchronous availability

Another small improvement is that you can use the `await` keyword inside `catch` and `finally` blocks. This was not initially allowed when this incredibly useful feature was added to C# 5. There is not a lot more to say about this. The implementation is complex, but you don't need to worry about this unless you're interested in the internals. From a developer's point of view, it just works, as in this simple example:

```
catch (Exception e) when (e?.Message?.Length > 0)
{
    await Task.Delay(200);
}
```

This feature has been improved in C# 7, so read on. You will see `async` and `await` used a lot throughout this book. Asynchronous programming is a great way of improving performance and not just from within your C# code.

Expression bodies

Expression bodies allow you to assign an expression to a method or getter property using the lambda arrow operator (=>), which you may be familiar with from fluent LINQ syntax. You no longer need to provide a full statement or method signature and body. This feature has also been improved in C# 7, so see the examples in the next section.

For example, a getter property can be implemented like so:

```
public static string Text => $"Today: {DateTime.Now:o}";
```

A method can be written in a similar way, such as the following example:

```
private byte[] GetBytes(string text) => Encoding.UTF8.GetBytes(text);
```

C# 7

The most recent version of the C# language is 7, and there are yet more improvements to readability and ease of use. We'll cover a subset of the more interesting changes here.

Literals

There are a couple of minor additional capabilities and readability enhancements when specifying literal values in code. You can specify binary literals, which means you don't have to work out how to represent them using a different base anymore. You can also put underscores anywhere within a literal to make it easier to read the number. The underscores are ignored but allow you to separate digits into convention groupings. This is particularly well suited to the new binary literal as it can be very verbose, listing out all those zeros and ones.

Take the following example that uses the new `0b` prefix to specify a binary literal that will be rendered as an integer in a string:

```
Console.WriteLine($"Binary solo! {0b0000001_00000011_000000111_00001111}");
```

You can do this with other bases too, such as this integer, which is formatted to use a thousands separator:

```
Console.WriteLine($"Over {9_000:#,0}!"); // Prints "Over 9,000!"
```

Tuples

One of the big new features in C# 7 is support for tuples. Tuples are groups of values, and you can now return them directly from method calls. You are no longer restricted to returning a single value. Previously, you could work around this limitation in a few suboptimal ways, including creating a custom complex object to return, perhaps with a **Plain Old C# Object** (**POCO**) or **Data Transfer Object** (**DTO**), which are the same thing. You could have also passed in a reference using the `ref` or `out` keyword, which are still not great although there are improvements to the syntax.

There was `System.Tuple` in C# 6, but it wasn't ideal. It was a framework feature, rather than a language feature, and the items were only numbered and not named. With C# 7 tuples, you can name the objects and they make a great alternative to anonymous types, particularly in LINQ query expression lambda functions. As an example, if you only want to work on a subset of the data available, perhaps when filtering a database table with an O/RM, such as Entity Framework, then you could use a tuple for this.

The following example returns a tuple from a method. You may need to add the `System.ValueTuple` NuGet package for this to work:

```
private static (int one, string two, DateTime three) GetTuple()
{
    return (one: 1, two: "too", three: DateTime.UtcNow);
}
```

You can also use tuples in string interpolation and all the values will be rendered, as shown here:

```
Console.WriteLine($"Tuple = {GetTuple()}");
```

Out variables

If you want to pass parameters to a method for modification, then you always need to declare them first. This is no longer necessary, and you can simply declare the variables at the point you pass them in. You can also declare a variable to be discarded, using an underscore. This is particularly useful if you don't want to use the returned value, for example, in some of the try parse methods of the native framework data types.

Here, we parse a date without declaring the `dt` variable first:

```
DateTime.TryParse("2017-08-09", out var dt);
```

In this example, we test for an integer, but we don't care what it is:

```
var isInt = int.TryParse("w00t", out _);
```

References

You can now return values by reference from a method as well as consume them. This is a little like working with pointers in C but safer. For example, you can only return references that were passed to the method, and you can't modify references to point to a different location in memory. This is a very specialist feature, but in certain niche situations, it can dramatically improve performance.

Consider the following method:

```
private static ref string GetFirstRef(ref string[] texts)
{
    if (texts?.Length > 0)
    {
        return ref texts[0];
    }
    throw new ArgumentOutOfRangeException();
}
```

You could call this method like so, and the second console output line would appear differently (one instead of 1):

```
var strings = new string[] { "1", "2" };
ref var first = ref GetFirstRef(ref strings);
Console.WriteLine($"{strings?[0]}"); // 1
first = "one";
Console.WriteLine($"{strings?[0]}"); // one
```

Patterns

The other big addition is you can now match patterns in C# 7 using the `is` keyword. This simplifies testing for null and matching against types, among other things. It also lets you easily use the cast value. This is a simpler alternative to using full polymorphism (where a derived class can be treated as a base class and override methods). However, if you control the code base and are able to make use of polymorphism properly, then you should still do this and follow good **object-oriented programming** (**OOP**) principles.

In the following example, pattern matching is used to parse the type and value of an unknown object:

```
private static int PatternMatch(object obj)
{
    if (obj is null)
    {
        return 0;
    }
    if (obj is int i)
    {
        return i++;
    }
    if (obj is DateTime d ||
        (obj is string str && DateTime.TryParse(str, out d)))
    {
        return d.DayOfYear;
```

```
    }
    return -1;
}
```

You can also use pattern matching in the case of a `switch` statement, and you can switch on non-primitive types, such as custom objects.

More expression bodies

Expression bodies are expanded from the offering in C# 6, and you can now use them in more places, for example, as object constructors and property setters. Here, we extend our previous example to include the setting up of the value on the property we were previously just reading:

```
private static string text;
public static string Text
{
    get => text ?? $"Today: {DateTime.Now:r}";
    set => text = value;
}
```

More asynchronous improvements

There have been some small improvements to what `async` methods can return and, although small, they could offer big performance gains in certain situations. You no longer have to return a task which can be beneficial if the value is already available. This can reduce the overhead of using `async` methods and creating a task object.

JavaScript

You can't write a book on web applications without covering JavaScript. It is everywhere.

If you write a web app that does a full page load on every request and it's not a simple content site, then it will feel slow. However, users expect responsiveness.

If you are a backend developer, then you may think that you don't have to worry about this. However, if you are building an API, then you may want to make it easy to consume with JavaScript, and you will need to make sure that your JSON is correctly and quickly serialized.

Even if you are building a **Single-Page Application** (**SPA**) in JavaScript (or TypeScript) that runs in the browser, the server can still play a key role. You can use SPA services to run Angular or React on the server and generate the initial output. This can increase performance as the browser has something to render immediately. For example, there is a project called React.NET that integrates React with ASP.NET, and it supports ASP.NET Core.

If you have been struggling to keep up with the latest developments in the .NET world, then JavaScript is on another level. There seems to be something new almost every week, and this can lead to framework fatigue and a paradox of choice. There is so much to choose from that you don't know what to pick.

We will cover some of the more modern practices later in the book and show the improved performance that they can bring. We'll look at service workers and show how they can be used to move work into the background of a browser to make it feel more responsive to the user.

Summary

In this introductory chapter, you saw a brief but high-level summary of what has changed in .NET Core 2 and ASP.NET Core 2, compared to previous versions. Now, you are also aware of .NET Standard 2 and what it is for.

We showed examples of some of the new features available in C# 6 and C# 7. These can be very useful in letting you write more with less and in making your code more readable and easier to maintain.

Finally, we touched upon JavaScript as it is ubiquitous, and this is a book about web apps after all. Moreover, this is a book on general web application performance improvements, and many of the lessons are applicable regardless of the language or framework used.

In the next chapter, you'll see why performance matters and learn how the new .NET Core stack fits together. We will also see the tools that are available and learn about hardware performance with a graph.

2
Why Performance Is a Feature

This is an exciting time to be a C# developer. Microsoft is in the middle of one of the biggest changes in its history and it is embracing open source software. The ASP.NET and .NET Frameworks have been rebuilt from the ground up so they are componentized, cross platform, and fully open source. Many of the recent improvements have come from the community.

ASP.NET Core 2 and .NET Core 2 embrace other popular open source projects, including Linux. The ASP.NET **Model View Controller** (**MVC**) web application framework, which is part of ASP.NET Core, borrows heavily from **Ruby on Rails**, and Microsoft is keen on promoting tools, such as **Node.js**, **Grunt**, **gulp**, and **Yeoman**. Support for React, Redux, and Angular **Single Page Apps** (**SPAs**) is also inbuilt. You can write these in **TypeScript**, which is a statically typed version of JavaScript that is developed by Microsoft.

By reading this book, you will learn how to write high performance software using these new .NET Core technologies. You'll be able to make your web applications responsive to input and scalable to demand.

We'll focus on the latest Core versions of .NET. Yet, many of these techniques also apply to previous versions, and they will be useful for web application development in general (in any language or framework).

Understanding how all of these new frameworks and libraries fit together can be a bit confusing. We'll present the various options available while using the newest technology, guiding you down the path to high-speed success and avoiding performance pitfalls.

After finishing this book, you will understand what problems can occur when web applications are deployed at scale (to distributed infrastructure) and know how to avoid or mitigate these issues. You will gain experience in how to write high performance applications without learning about issues the hard way.

In this chapter, we will cover the following topics:

- Performance as a feature
- The common classes of performance issues
- Basic hardware knowledge
- Microsoft tools and alternatives
- New .NET naming and compatibility

Performance as a feature

You may have previously heard about the practice of treating performance as a first-class feature. Traditionally, performance (along with things such as security, availability, and uptime) was only considered a **non-functional requirement** (**NFR**) and usually had some arbitrary made-up metrics that needed to be fulfilled. You may have heard the term *performant* before. This is the quality of performing well and is often captured in requirements without quantification, providing very little value. It is better to avoid this sort of corporate jargon when corresponding with clients or users.

Using the outdated waterfall method of development, these NFRs were inevitably left until the end and dropped from an over budget and late project in order to get the functional requirements completed. This resulted in a substandard product that was unreliable, slow, and often insecure (as reliability and security are also often neglected NFRs). Think about how many times you're frustrated at software that lags behind in responding to your input. Perhaps, you used a ticket-vending machine or a self-service checkout that is unresponsive to the point of being unusable.

There is a better way. By treating performance as a feature and considering it at every stage of your **agile** development process, you can get users and customers to love your product. When software responds quicker than a user can perceive, it is a delight to use because it doesn't slow them down. When there is a noticeable lag, users need to adjust their behavior to wait for the machine instead of working at their own pace.

Computers have incredible amounts of processing power today, and they now possess many more resources than they did even just a few years ago. So, why do we still have software that is noticeably slow at responding when computers are so fast and can calculate much quicker than people can? The answer to this is poorly written software that does not consider performance. Why does this happen? The reason is that often the signs of poor performance are not visible in development, and they only appear when deployed. However, if you know what to look for, then you can avoid these problems before releasing your software to the production environment.

This book will show you how to write software that is a joy to use and never keeps the user waiting or uninformed. You will learn how to make products that users will love instead of products that frustrate them.

Common classes of performance problems

Let's take a look at some common areas of performance problems and see whether they matter or not. We will also learn why we often miss these issues during development. We will look at programming language choice, latency, bandwidth, computation, and when you should consider performance.

Language considerations

People often focus on the speed of the programming language that is used. However, this often misses the point. This is a very simplistic view that glosses over the nuances of technology choices. It is easy to write slow software in any language.

With the huge amounts of processing speed that is available today, relatively *slow* interpreted languages can often be fast enough and the increase in development speed is worth it. It is important to understand the arguments and the trade-offs involved, even if after reading this book you decide to use C# and .NET.

The way to write the fastest software is to get down to the metal and write in assembly language (or even machine code). This is complex to develop, debug, and test, which requires expert knowledge. We rarely do this these days, except for very niche applications (such as virtual reality games, scientific data crunching, and sometimes embedded devices) and usually only for a tiny part of the software.

A higher level of abstraction is writing in a language such as Go, C, or C++ and compiling the code to run on the machine. This is still popular for games and other performance-sensitive applications, but you often have to manage your own memory (which can cause memory leaks or security issues, such as buffer overflows). The .NET Native project, which is currently in development, promises a lot of performance benefits of this ahead-of-time compilation without the downsides, similar to Go.

A level above is software that compiles to a hardware-agnostic **Intermediate Language (IL)** or bytecode and runs on a **Virtual Machine (VM)**. Examples of this are **Java**, **Scala**, **Clojure** (bytecode on the Java VM), and, of course, C# (IL on the Common Language Runtime). Memory management is normally taken care of, and there is usually a **Garbage Collector (GC)** to tidy up unused references (Go and the .NET Native CoreRT also have a GC). These applications can run on multiple platforms, and they are safer. However, you can still get near native performance in terms of execution speed, although startup speed can suffer.

Above these are interpreted languages, such as Ruby, Python, and JavaScript. These languages are not usually compiled, and they are run line by line by an interpreter. They usually run slower than a compiled language, but this is often not a problem. A more serious concern is catching bugs when using dynamic typing. You won't be able to see an error until you encounter it, whereas many errors can be caught at compile time when using statically typed languages.

It is best to avoid generic advice. You may hear an argument against using Ruby on Rails, citing the example of Twitter having to migrate to Java for performance reasons. This may well not be a problem for your application, and indeed, having the popularity of Twitter would be a nice problem to have. A bigger concern when running Rails may be the large memory footprint, making it expensive to run on cloud instances.

This section is only to give you a taste, and the main lesson is that normally language doesn't matter. It is not usually the language that makes a program slow, it's poor design choices. C# offers a nice balance between speed and flexibility that makes it suitable for a wide range of applications, especially server-side web applications.

Types of performance problems

There are many types of performance problems and most of them are independent of the programming language that is used. A lot of these result from how the code runs on the computer, and we will cover the impact of this later on in the chapter.

We will briefly introduce common performance problems here and will cover them in more detail in later chapters of this book. Issues that you may encounter will usually fall into a few simple categories, including the following:

- Latency:
    - Memory latency
    - Network latency
    - Disk and I/O latency
    - Chattiness/handshakes

- Bandwidth:
    - Excessive payloads
    - Unoptimized data
    - Compression
- Computation:
    - Working on too much data
    - Calculating unnecessary results
    - Brute forcing algorithms
- Responsiveness:
    - Synchronous operations that could be done offline
    - Caching and coping with stale data

When writing software for a platform, you are usually constrained by two resources. These are the computation processing speed and accessing remote (to the processor) resources. Processing speed is rarely a limiting factor these days, and this can be traded for other resources, for example, compressing some data to reduce the network transfer time. Accessing remote resources, such as the main memory, disk, and network, will have various time costs. It is important to understand that speed is not a single value and it has multiple parameters. The most important of these parameters are bandwidth and, crucially, **latency**.

Latency is the lag in time before the operation starts, whereas bandwidth is the rate at which data is transferred once the operation starts. Posting a hard drive has a very high bandwidth, but it also has very high latency. This would make it very slow to send lots of text files back and forth, but perhaps, it is a good choice to send a large batch of 3D videos (depending on the Weissman score). A mobile phone data connection may be better for text files. Although this is a contrived example, the same concerns are often applicable to every layer of the computing stack with similar orders of magnitude in time difference. The problem is that the differences are too quick to perceive, and we need to use tools and science to see them.

The secret to solving performance problems is gaining a deeper understanding of the technology and knowing what happens at lower levels. You should appreciate what the framework is doing with your instructions at the network level. It's also important to have a basic grasp of how these commands run on the underlying hardware and how they are affected by the infrastructure that they are deployed to.

When performance matters

Performance is not always important in every situation. Learning when performance does and doesn't matter is an important skill to acquire. A general rule of thumb is that if the user has to wait for something to happen, then it should perform well. If this is something that can be performed asynchronously, then the constraints are not as strict, unless an operation is so slow that it takes longer than the time window for it, for example, an overnight batch job on an old financial services mainframe.

A good example from a web application standpoint is rendering a user view versus sending an email. It is a common, yet naive, practice to accept a form submission and send an email (or worse, many emails) before returning the result. Yet, unlike a database update, an email is not something that needs to happen instantly. There are many stages over which we have no control that will delay an email in reaching a user. Therefore, there is no need to send an email before returning the result of the form. You can do this in the background and asynchronously, after the result of the form submission is returned.

The important thing to remember here is that it is the perception of performance that matters and not absolute performance. It can be better to not perform some demanding work (or at least defer it until later) rather than speed it up.

This may be counter-intuitive, especially considering how individual computational operations can be too quick to perceive. However, the multiplying factor is scaled. One operation may be relatively quick, but millions of them may accumulate to a visible delay. Optimizing these will have a corresponding effect due to the magnification. Improving code that runs in a tight loop or for every user is better than fixing a routine that runs only once a day.

Slower is sometimes better

In some situations, processes are designed to be slow, and this is essential to their operation and security. A good example of this, which may be a hit in profiling, is **password hashing** or **key stretching**. A secure password hashing function should be slow so that the password, which (despite being bad practice) may have been reused on other services, is not easily recovered.

We should not use generic hashing functions, such as **MD5**, **SHA1**, and **SHA256**, to hash passwords because they are too quick. Some better algorithms that are designed for this task are **PBKDF2** and **bcrypt** or even **Argon2** for new projects. Always remember to use a unique salt per password too. We won't go into any more details here, but you can clearly see that speeding up password hashing would be bad, and it's important to identify where to apply optimizations.

Why issues are missed

One of the main reasons that performance issues are not noticed in development is that some problems are not perceivable on a development system. Issues may not occur until latency increases. This may be because a large amount of data was loaded into the system and retrieving a specific record takes longer. This may also be because each piece of the system is deployed to a separate server, increasing network latency. When the number of users accessing a resource increases, then the latency will also increase.

For example, we can quickly insert a row into an empty database or retrieve a record from a small table, especially when the database is running on the same physical machine as the web server. When a web server is on one virtual machine and the big database server is on another, then the time taken for this operation can increase dramatically.

This will not be a problem for one single database operation, which appears just as quick to a user in both cases. However, if the software is poorly written and performs hundreds or even thousands of database operations per request, then this quickly becomes slow.

Scale this up to all the users that a web server deals with (and all the web servers) and this can be a real problem. A developer may not notice that this problem exists if they're not looking for it as the software performs well on their workstation. Tools can help in identifying these problems before the software is released.

Measuring

The most important takeaway from this book is the importance of measuring. You need to measure problems or you can't fix them. You won't even know when you have fixed them. Measurement is the key to fixing performance issues before they become noticeable. Slow operations can be identified early on and then they can be fixed.

However, not all operations need optimizing. It's important to keep a sense of perspective, but you should understand where the choke points are and how they will behave when magnified by scale. We'll cover measuring and profiling in later chapters.

The benefits of planning ahead

When you consider performance from the very beginning, it is cheaper and quicker to fix issues. This is true for most problems in software development. The earlier you catch a bug, the better. The worst time to find a bug is once it is deployed and then being reported by your users.

Performance issues are a little different when compared to functional bugs because often they only reveal themselves at scale, and you won't notice them before a live deployment unless you go looking for them. You can write integration and load tests to check performance against your specific quantified goals, which we will cover later in this book.

Understanding hardware

Remember that there is a computer in computer science. It is important to understand what your code runs on and the effects that this has; this isn't magic.

Storage access speeds

Computers are so fast that it can be difficult to understand which operation is a quick operation and which one is slow. Everything appears instant. In fact, anything that happens in less than a few hundred milliseconds is imperceptible to humans. However, certain things are much faster than others are, and you only get performance issues at scale when millions of operations are performed in parallel.

There are various different resources that can be accessed by an application and a selection of these are listed as follows:

- CPU caches and registers:
    - L1 cache
    - L2 cache
    - L3 cache
- RAM
- Permanent storage:
    - Local **Solid State Drive (SSD)**
    - Local **Hard Disk Drive (HDD)**
- Network resources:
    - **Local Area Network (LAN)**
    - Regional networking
    - Global internetworking

Virtual Machines (**VMs**) and cloud infrastructure services may simplify deployment but could add more performance complications. The local disk that is mounted on a machine may in fact be a shared network disk and respond much slower than a real physical disk that is attached to the same machine. You may also have to contend with other users for resources.

In order to appreciate the differences in speed between the various forms of storage, consider the following graph. This shows the time taken to retrieve a small amount of data from a selection of storage mediums:

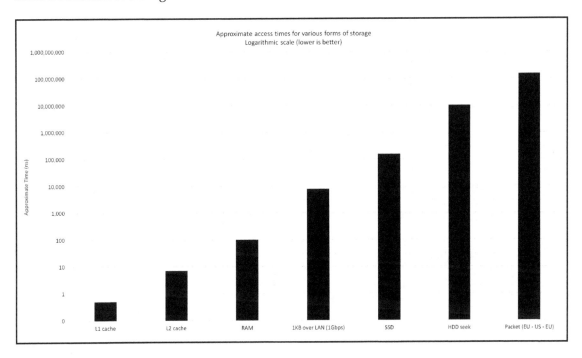

This graph has been made for this book and it uses averages of latency data found online. It has a logarithmic scale, which means that the differences are very large. The top of the graph represents one second or one billion nanoseconds. Sending a packet across the Atlantic Ocean and back takes roughly 150 milliseconds (ms) or 150 million nanoseconds (ns), and this is mainly limited by the speed of light. This is still far quicker than you can think about, and it will appear instantaneously. Indeed, it can often take longer to push a pixel to a screen than to get a packet to another continent.

The next largest bar is the time that it takes a physical HDD to move the arm into position to start reading data (10 ms). Mechanical devices are slow.

The next bar down is how long it takes to randomly read a small block of data from a local SSD, which is about 150 microseconds. These are based on Flash memory technology, and they are usually connected in the same way as an HDD.

The next value is the time taken to send a small datagram of 1 KB (1 kilobyte or 8 kilobits) over a gigabit LAN, which is just under 10 microseconds. This is typically how servers are connected in a data center. Note how the network itself is pretty quick. The thing that really matters is what you are connecting to at the other end. A network lookup to a value in memory on another machine can be much quicker than accessing a local drive (as this is a log graph, you can't just stack the bars).

This brings us to the main memory or RAM. This is fast (about 100 ns for a lookup), and this is where most of your program will run. However, this is not directly connected to the CPU, and it is slower than the on die caches. RAM can be large, often large enough to hold all your working datasets. However, it is not as big as disks can be, and it is not permanent. It disappears when the power is lost.

The CPU itself will contain small caches for data that are currently being worked on, which can respond in less than 10 ns. Modern CPUs may have up to three or even four caches of increasing size and latency. The fastest (less than 1 ns to respond) is the level 1 (L1) cache, but this is also usually the smallest. If you can fit your working data into these few MB or KB of data in caches, then you can process it very quickly.

Scaling approach changes

For many years, the speed and processing capacity of computers increased at an exponential rate. The observation that *the number of transistors in a dense integrated circuit doubles approximately every two years* is known as Moore's Law, named after Gordon Moore of Intel. Sadly, this era is no "Moore" (sorry). Although transistor density is still increasing, single-core processor speeds have flattened out, and these days increases in processing ability come from scaling out to multiple cores, multiple CPUs, and multiple machines (both virtual and physical). Multithreaded programming is no longer exotic; it is essential. Otherwise, you cannot hope to go beyond the capacity of a single core. Modern CPUs typically have at least four cores (even on mobile devices). Add in a technology such as **hyper-threading** and you have at least eight logical CPUs to play with. Naive programming will not be able to fully utilize these.

Traditionally, performance and redundancy was provided by improving the hardware. Everything ran on a single server or mainframe, and the solution was to use faster hardware and duplicate all components for reliability. This is known as vertical scaling, and it has reached the end of its life. It is very expensive to scale this way and impossible beyond a certain size. The future is in distributed and horizontal scaling, using commodity hardware and cloud computing resources. This requires that we write software in a different manner than we did previously. Traditional software can't take advantage of this scaling as it can easily use the extra capabilities and speed of an upgraded computer processor.

There are many trade-offs that have to be made when considering performance, and it can sometimes feel like more of a black art than science. However, taking a scientific approach and measuring results is essential. You will often have to balance memory usage against processing power, bandwidth against storage, and latency against throughput.

An example is deciding whether you should compress data on the server (including what algorithms and settings to use) or send it raw over the wire. This will depend on many factors, including the capacity of the network and the devices at both ends.

Tools and costs

Licensing of Microsoft products has historically been a minefield of complexity. You can even sit for an official exam on it and get a qualification. Microsoft's recent move toward open source practices is very encouraging, as the biggest benefit of open source is not the free monetary cost but that you don't have to think about licensing costs. You can also fix issues, and with a permissive license (such as **MIT**), you don't have to worry about much. The time costs and cognitive load of working out licensing implications now and in future can dwarf the financial sums involved (especially for a small company or startup).

Tools

Despite the new .NET Framework being open source, many of the tools are not. Some editions of Visual Studio and SQL Server can be very expensive. With the new licensing practice of subscriptions, you will lose access if you stop paying, and you are required to sign in to develop. Previously, you could keep using existing versions licensed from a **Microsoft Developer Network** (**MSDN**) or BizSpark subscription after it expired and you didn't need to sign in.

With this in mind, we will try to stick to the free (community) editions of Visual Studio and the Express version of SQL Server, unless there is a feature that is essential to the lesson, which we will highlight when it occurs. We will also use as many free and open source libraries, frameworks, and tools as possible.

There are many alternative options for lots of the tools and software that augments the ASP.NET ecosystem, and you don't just need to use the default Microsoft products. This is known as the **alternative .NET (ALT.NET)** movement, which embraces practices from the rest of the open source world.

Looking at some alternative tools

For version control, Git is a very popular alternative to **Team Foundation Version Control (TFVC)**. Git is integrated into many tools (including Visual Studio) and services, such as GitHub or GitLab. Mercurial (Hg) is also an option, although Git has gained the most developer mind share. **Visual Studio Team Services (VSTS)** and **Team Foundation Server (TFS)** both allow you to use either Git (including GitHub and Bitbucket integration) or legacy TFVC.

PostgreSQL is a fantastic open source relational database, and it works with many **Object Relational Mappers (O/RMs)**, including **Entity Framework (EF)** and **NHibernate**. Now, it is also available on Azure along with MySQL. Dapper is a great tool that provides a high performance, alternative to EF and other bloated O/RMs. There are plenty of NoSQL options that are available too, for example, Redis and MongoDB.

Other code editors and **Integrated Development Environments (IDEs)** are available, such as Visual Studio Code by Microsoft, which also works on Apple OS X/macOS. ASP.NET Core 2 runs on Linux (on Mono and CoreCLR). Therefore, you don't need Windows (although Nano Server may be worth investigating).

RabbitMQ is a brilliant open source message queuing server that is written in Erlang (which WhatsApp also uses). This is far better than **Microsoft Message Queuing (MSMQ)**, which comes with Windows. Hosted services are readily available, for example, CloudAMQP.

I've been a long time Mac user (since the PowerPC days), and I've run Linux servers well before this. It's positive to see OS X become popular and observe the rise of Linux on Android smartphones and cheap computers, such as the Raspberry Pi. You can run Windows 10 on a Raspberry Pi 2 or 3, but this is not a full operating system and is only meant to run **Internet of Things (IoT)** devices. Having used Windows professionally for a long time, developing and deploying with Mac and Linux and seeing what performance effects this brings is an interesting opportunity.

Although not open source (or always free), it is worth mentioning JetBrains products. TeamCity is a very good build and **Continuous Integration (CI)** server that has a free tier. ReSharper is an awesome plugin for Visual Studio, which will make you a better developer. There is also their new C# IDE called Rider that's based on ReSharper and IntelliJ (the platform that powers Android Studio and their other IDEs).

There is a product called Octopus Deploy, which is extremely useful for the **continuous deployment** of .NET and .NET Core applications, and it has a free tier. TFS also offers CI builds / CD releases, and there are cloud solutions, such as AppVeyor and VSTS.

Regarding cloud services, **Amazon Web Services (AWS)** is an obvious alternative to Azure. Even if AWS Windows support leaves something to be desired, this is less of a problem now that Core is available and runs on Linux. There are many other hosts available, and dedicated servers can often be cheaper for a steady load if you don't need the dynamic scaling of the cloud.

Much of this is beyond the scope of this book, but it would be wise to investigate some of these tools. The point is that there is always a choice about how to build a system from the huge range of components available, especially with the newer version of ASP.NET.

The new .NET

The new ASP.NET and the .NET Framework that it relies upon were rewritten to be open source and cross-platform in Core version 1. The packages were also split up, which although done with admirable intentions has caused confusion. ASP.NET Core 2 is now included in the .NET Core 2 installation package along with **Entity Framework Core**. This means that you no longer need to ship the ASP.NET Core framework with your app when you deploy. The project known as **.NET Native** has been postponed (outside of **UWP**) and will hopefully arrive within the next year.

All these different names can be perplexing, but naming things is hard. A humorous variation of Phil Karlton's famous quote goes like this:

> *"There are only two hard things in Computer Science: cache invalidation, naming things, and off-by-one errors."*

We've looked at naming here, and we'll get to caching later on in this book.

It can be a little confusing understanding how all of these versions fit together. This is best explained with a diagram like the following, which shows how the layers interact:

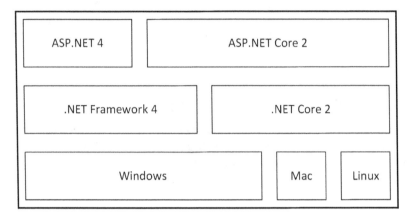

ASP.NET Core 2 can run against the existing .NET Framework 4.7 or the new .NET Core 2 framework. Similarly, .NET Core can run on Windows, OS X / macOS, and Linux, but the old .NET only runs on Windows.

There is also the Mono framework, which has been omitted for clarity. This was a previous project that allowed .NET to run on multiple platforms. Mono was acquired by Microsoft, and it was open sourced (along with other Xamarin products). We are now starting to see the convergence of these different platforms, driven by the .NET Standard.

Core is not as feature filled as the existing .NET Framework, although the gap has shrunk significantly in version 2. If you write graphical desktop applications, perhaps using **Windows Presentation Foundation** (**WPF**), then you should stick with .NET 4. There is no plan to port these Windows-specific APIs to Core as then it wouldn't be cross-platform.

As this book is mainly about web-application development, we will use the latest Core versions of all the software. We will investigate the performance implications of various operating systems and architectures. This is particularly important if your deployment target is a computer, such as the Raspberry Pi, which uses a processor with an ARM architecture. It also has limited memory, which is important to consider when using a managed runtime that includes a garbage collection, such as .NET.

Summary

Let's sum up what we covered in this chapter and what we will cover in the next chapter. We introduced the concept of treating performance as a feature, and we covered why this is important. We also briefly touched on some common performance problems and why we often miss them in the software development process. We'll cover these in more detail later on in this book.

We showed the performance differences between various types of storage hardware. We highlighted the importance of knowing what your code runs on and, crucially, what it will run on when your users see it. We talked about how the process of scaling systems has changed from what it used to be, how scaling is now performed horizontally instead of vertically, and how you can take advantage of this in the creation of your code and systems. We showed you the tools that you can use and the licensing implications of some of them. We also explained the new world of .NET and how these latest frameworks fit in with the stable ones. We touched upon why measurement is vitally important.

In the next chapter, we will show you how to get started with ASP.NET Core 2 when using Windows, Mac, or Linux. We will also demonstrate how to use Docker containers to build and run your app.

3
Setting Up Your Environment

One of the main benefits of .NET Core is that it is cross-platform, which means that it runs on a wide variety of operating systems. You no longer need a dependency on the Windows OS to host or even develop your .NET application. Although this was technically possible before, it is now easier than ever and actively encouraged by Microsoft. They even provide Linux servers on Azure and premade Docker images on which you can build and host your code.

In this chapter, we will show you how to get started with the latest tooling on the OS of your choice. We'll cover the process of setting up a development environment on Windows, macOS (previously OS X), and Linux. Each system has a preferred solution, but there is cross-platform tooling available that will work on any of them.

We will also discuss the modern DevOps way of developing applications and deploying them, using containers. In particular, we will cover how to work with Docker. Containers are a great way of packaging your application and its dependencies so that you can deploy more consistently and with fewer nasty surprises. By shipping your app as a standard unit, you can worry less about configuring a live production server or setting up a new developer workstation.

To get you started, we will cover the following topics in this chapter:

- Windows
- macOS
- Linux
- Visual Studio 2017
- Visual Studio for Mac
- Visual Studio Code
- .NET Core SDK

- Command-line tooling
- Containerization
- Docker

Feel free to skip to the step-by-step guide that is relevant to you. Or, read them all if you are interested in what the other side looks like. Although we won't be covering Visual Studio Code, command-line, and Docker in relation to every OS, these are applicable to all platforms. We would lose focus if we go over all the possible permutations in this book, and it would be a very long, repetitive read. Check out my blog at `https://unop.uk/` for more varied tutorials. As Linux lacks an official .NET IDE and these command-line tools fit better into the Unix philosophy (many simple tools that do one thing well), we'll mostly cover them in the Linux section.

 We won't be covering JetBrains Rider here, but if you're familiar with their other products (such as ReSharper, or Android Studio, which is based on the same IntelliJ platform), then you may want to give it a try. The main application is written in Java, and as such, it runs on most popular operating systems.

There are two main steps to setting things up. Firstly, install some tools to help you work more easily with the code. You could use a simple text editor, but this would not be a great experience. Secondly, install the .NET Core **Software Development Kit** (**SDK**) that now includes ASP.NET Core. This will hook into the tooling to provide templates and will also be usable from the command line. Later, we will use it to build and run our application. Let's get started!

Windows

Windows has traditionally been the primary platform for developing and hosting .NET applications, but this is changing. However, it is still the most feature-rich development environment as the full version of the Visual Studio **Integrated Development Environment** (**IDE**) has a lot of functionality.

Visual Studio 2017

Visual Studio 2017 is the latest version of VS at the time of writing. It supersedes VS 2015 and unfortunately drops support for some versions of Windows. For example, it still supports Windows 7, but the installer will refuse to run on Windows 8. This is because 8.1 is considered a service pack for 8 and you are strongly encouraged by Microsoft to upgrade to 8.1. However, Microsoft will encourage you even more strongly to upgrade to Windows 10, some would say too strongly:

The **Long-Term Service Branch** (**LTSB**) of Windows 10 is similarly listed as not supporting Visual Studio. However, the installer won't actually refuse to run and everything will work fine.

 Windows 10 LTSB is an Enterprise version of Windows 10 that doesn't include many of the annoyances of the regular version (such as forced upgrades, Cortana, and live tiles). You miss out on the Edge browser, but you can, of course, just install Firefox and Chrome, like you would anyway.

In newer versions of VS 2017, the .NET Framework can be shipped separately to the IDE, and you can install additional ones (such as .NET Core 2.0) to enable their use in the IDE. VS 2017 also supports debugging in a container so that you can run your code in a Linux VM while still stepping through it from Windows.

Installing VS

VS 2017 comes with a new installer that lets you manage multiple versions of VS instances installed side by side. It takes care of installing and updating IDE instances. Follow these steps to get started:

1. Open your impartial third-party browser of choice and go to `https://www.microsoft.com/net/core`. You can also use the short URL of `https://dot.net/` and follow the links:

2. Download the Community edition of VS 2017, unless you have a license for the Professional or Enterprise versions. Run the downloaded file to start the installer; it may need to update itself:

3. You can then select the workloads that you want to use. It may be tempting to select everything, but keep an eye on the installation size in the bottom right-hand corner. The more you select, the more disk space you will need and the longer the installation will take:

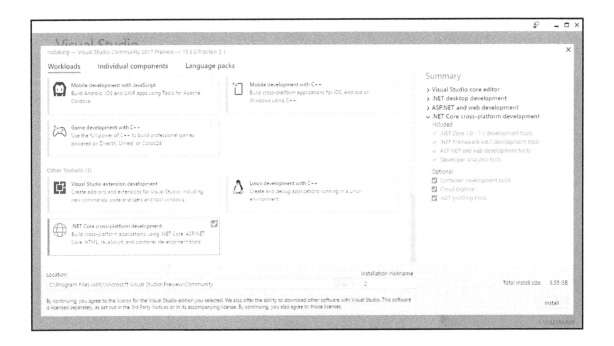

4. Select **.NET Core**, **ASP.NET**, and **.NET Framework**, then **Install**. You can do something else while these workloads are downloaded and installed:

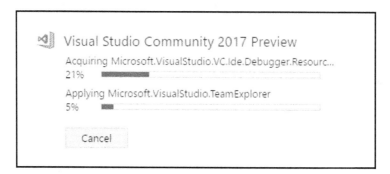

5. When done, you'll be asked to choose your development settings and pick a color theme:

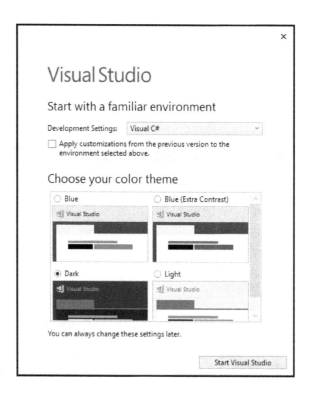

Installing .NET Core 2

If the VS installer does not include the version of .NET Core that you want to work with, then you can install it separately. Download the installer from the Core website and execute it. The reason that the SDK is decoupled from the main VS installation is so that it can be iterated on in a faster way. You will get a stable version shipped with VS, but it may be a little dated:

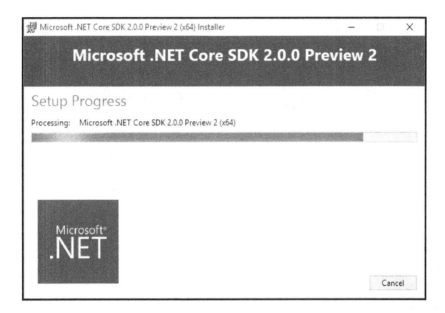

 The .NET Core command-line tools include telemetry turned on by default. This means they report analytics information back to Microsoft, but you can disable this by setting an environment variable. Visual Studio and VS Code also send telemetry by default, but this can be disabled via the UI (or editing the JSON configuration in VS Code).

Creating your first app

Create a new project and select the **ASP.NET Core Web Application** template. You can run this on .NET Core or on .NET Framework (but then it won't run on other platforms). If you wish to create a new Git repository for distributed version control, then check the **Add to Source Control** box:

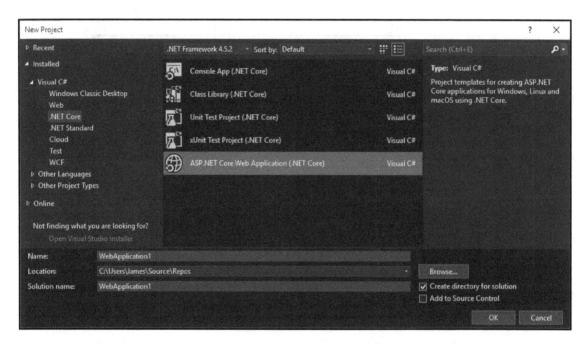

On the next screen, you can select a **Web Application** template. This includes web apps, APIs, and SPA services for Angular and React. The templates are the same as used by command-line tooling and you can create them using either interface. Later in this chapter, we'll see how to use the command-line, as it is almost identical on every platform.

Select the standard **Web Application** template:

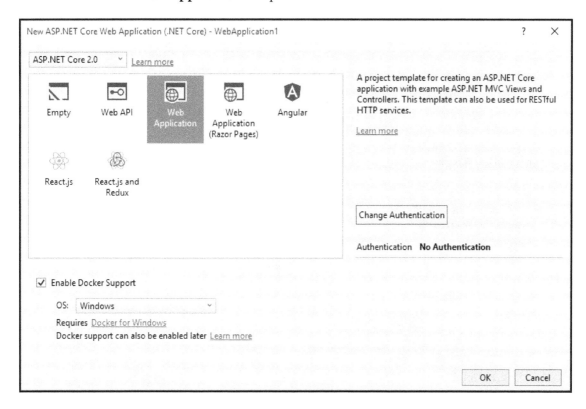

Click on the **Change Authentication** button to alter the way the users log in to your site. Select **Individual User Accounts** but leave the data stored locally. Alternatively, you could connect to cloud services, as shown in the following image, but we won't cover this here:

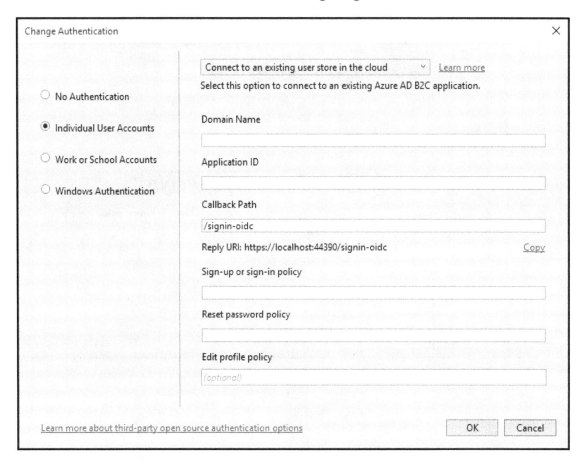

Once you have created your application, VS will restore the NuGet packages in the background. When this is done, press *F5* to build and run your app in the debugger. Your default browser should open containing the ASP.NET Core template site, and VS will show graphs of performance tracing:

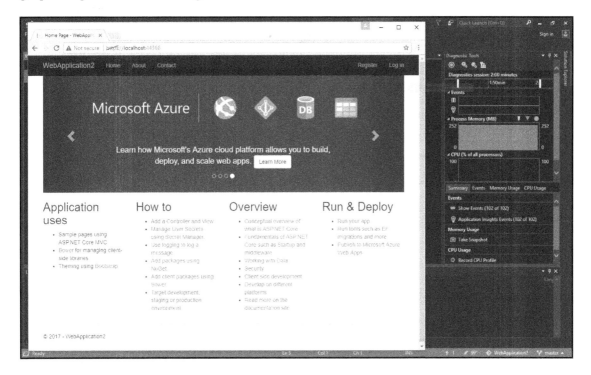

Congratulations! You've just created an ASP.NET Core 2 web app.

Mac

Apple computers have always been desirable and have a price tag to match. They are very popular with developers and web developers in particular. Perhaps this is because they are the only machines that can run all the things on which you might want to test. You can run Windows and Linux in a VM, but Apple's macOS (previously called OS X, pronounced OS ten) won't run on any non-Apple hardware (without some persuasion).

This could also be due to the meteoric rise of iPhone and iPad, along with the ecosystem that goes with them. If you want to develop apps for iOS and Android, then the only reasonable choice is to use a Mac—although, Progressive Web Apps are encroaching on much of the territory that was traditionally occupied by native applications.

Visual Studio for Mac

VS Mac is a rebranding of Xamarin Studio, but it has also been expanded and taken a lot of the features and code from regular VS. It is still best suited for making Xamarin cross-platform mobile and desktop apps, but it also supports .NET Core and ASP.NET web apps.

First, download the files that you'll need. This includes software to build your apps in, such as VS for Mac or VS Code. VS Mac comes as a DMG disk image that contains an installer, whereas VS Code comes as a ZIP file that you can just unpack and run. You will also need the .NET Core SDK, which comes as a PKG file that needs to be installed. You may also want a handy guidebook:

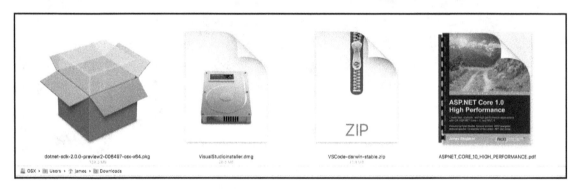

Installing VS Mac

VS for Mac is supported by the latest version of macOS (High Sierra), but it also works on older versions, such as OS X El Capitan (10.11) and macOS Sierra (10.12).

Follow these steps to install Visual Studio for Mac:

1. Open the DMG image that you downloaded, which will mount it as a drive:

2. Open the volume in Finder and run the installer by double-clicking on it:

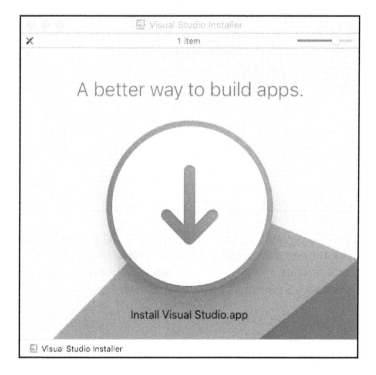

3. Work your way through the installer and do something else while it downloads and installs everything you need:

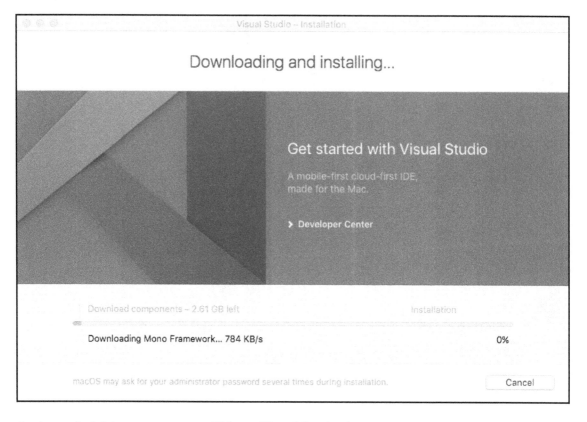

At the end of this process, you will have Visual Studio for Mac installed. While this is going on, you have plenty of time to download and unzip Visual Studio Code. You will probably want to move VS Code to your `Applications` folder, rather than running it from `Downloads`. Then, the two VS editions can sit together and be friends:

Visual Studio Code.app   Visual Studio.app

Installing .NET Core 2

Run the .NET Core SDK package to launch the installer, then follow the wizard:

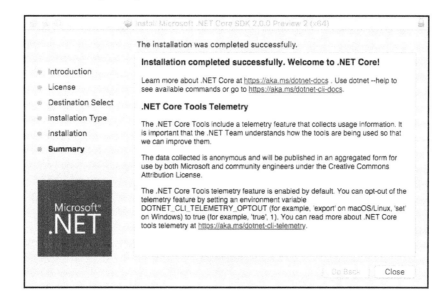

You should now be able to open a terminal and type `dotnet` to use command-line tooling. For example, type `dotnet --version` to see which edition of .NET Core you are using.

 You can use the default shell that comes with the macOS Terminal, or you can use an alternative, such as the Zsh shell. You can manage this with the Oh My Zsh project, which also supports Linux.

Creating your first app

The following steps will show you how to create an ASP.NET Core 2 web application using VS for Mac:

1. Open the Visual Studio app on your Mac and create a new solution and select the **ASP.NET Core Web App** template under the **.NET Core** category:

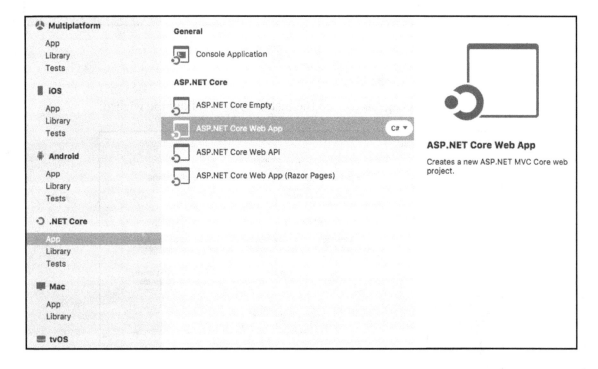

2. On the next screen, select **.NET Core 2.0** as the target framework:

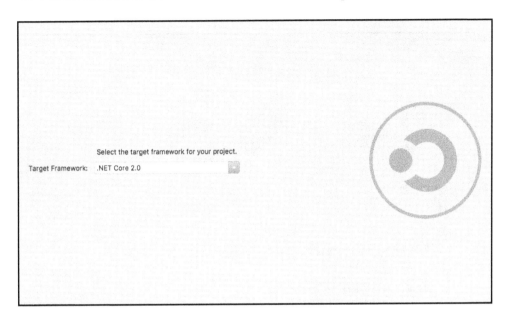

3. Finally, add a project name and finish the wizard:

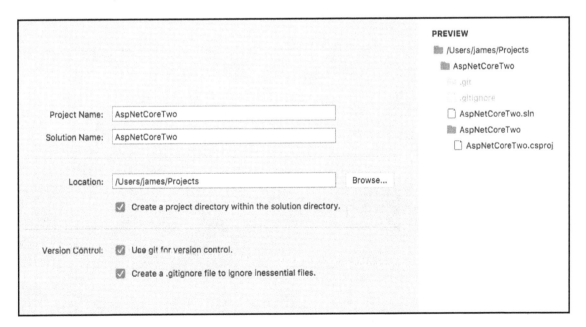

You now have a brand new ASP.NET Core 2 web app. You can click on the Play button to build and run it:

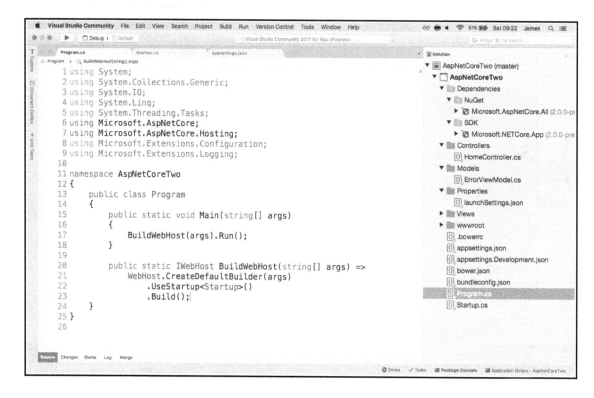

You can also work on this solution in Visual Studio Code by opening the folder containing it:

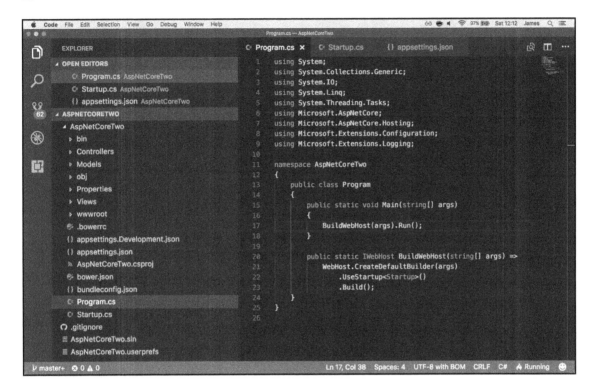

Visual Studio Code

Visual Studio Code runs on Windows, Mac, and Linux. VS Code is more of a text editor than an IDE, but it is a very capable one, and it blurs the line between the editor and full IDE. It supports IntelliSense code completion, building your code, and debugging your app.

It is built using web technologies (TypeScript in particular) and runs in a standalone web browser based app hosting environment. However, it is much quicker than similar Electron desktop apps, such as Atom or Slack. The same engine is used in the Azure web interface for editing code there.

To deal with huge data files, it is better to stick to a native text editor, for example, Notepad++ (on Windows) or Sublime Text.

Linux

Linux is a hugely popular OS outside of the desktop market. Android (the mobile operating system acquired by Google) is based on it, and it runs on most of the world's smartphones. Sometimes it is the main desktop option, if using a computer with specialized hardware, such as the Raspberry Pi. Linux is very popular on embedded devices, in part because it is lightweight and usually much less demanding on resources than a typical Windows or macOS installation.

Linux is also the most popular operating system for web servers, which is what interests us most here. It could be argued that Linux is the most popular operating system on the planet, although many users won't interact with it directly.

 Strictly speaking, Linux only refers to the kernel of the OS. The equivalent part of Windows would be the NT kernel. Many different distributions are built using the Linux kernel at their core, and they bundle it up with many other (often GNU) applications. You can even roll your own stripped-down version, perhaps using something like Buildroot.

Some examples of popular distributions are Ubuntu and CentOS (Community Enterprise OS, a free version of Red Hat Enterprise Linux). Linux distributions can be classified broadly by the type of package management they use. This is useful when trying to find the correct version of software to install, although you can usually get popular applications directly via the distribution's package manager.

 If you've not used a package manager before, then you will be amazed at how much easier it is than manually installing software (or even using an App Store) as you'd normally do on Windows or Mac.

Many distributions are based on Debian and these include Mint, Ubuntu, and Raspbian (the official OS for the Raspberry Pi). These use a Debian-based package format and the APT package manager. The latest version of Debian is called **Stretch** and .NET Core supports it. It also uses it for the official .NET Docker images.

 Debian versions are named after Toy Story characters; the previous version was called Jessie.

Other distributions use a **Red Hat Enterprise Linux** (**RHEL**) RPM package system and the yum package manager. These include CentOS and YellowDog, just to name a couple. There is also **SUSE Linux Enterprise Server** (**SLES**), which is another different distribution, but .NET Core supports it too.

There are many other distributions, far too many to mention here. Linux is not one OS like Windows or Mac. We haven't even covered BSD-based systems, which use a different kernel. These include FreeBSD, OpenBSD, and NetBSD. Even macOS is built on BSD, with its NeXTSTEP heritage (the OS that ran the first web server at CERN).

Most of the instructions here will also work on the command line of Windows and Mac. The tooling is the same; even the graphical tooling in VS uses the same templates as the command-line `dotnet` utility.

Getting started with .NET Core on Linux

We're going to mix things up a little and show how versatile and multiplatform .NET Core is. In the following section, we will demonstrate how to develop a .NET Core app on an Ubuntu Server VM running on Azure, using just the command line and no window manager.

This will be very similar to how you might set things up on any Debian-based distribution, including Ubuntu, Mint, and Raspbian (for Raspberry Pi). The fact that the Raspberry Pi uses a custom ARM processor rather than a traditional Intel x86 CPU does not matter. When Mono was initially ported to the Pi, there were issues with the specialist hardware-based floating-point implementation, but this is no longer an issue with .NET Core.

We will be using a command-line text editor, and it would be foolish to get into the Emacs versus vi debate here, so use whatever you prefer. This setup might make a good workflow if you use a tablet (such as an iPad with a Bluetooth keyboard) to connect to a cloud server over SSH or Mosh. However, if you are working locally and want a graphical editor in your X11/Wayland desktop environment of choice, then you could run VS Code or JetBrains Rider. No doubt you will be using terminal windows a lot too.

Installing .NET Core 2

We're using Ubuntu Server 16.04 LTS in this guide, but these instructions will work on other versions too. Using **Advanced Package Tool** (**APT**), we can install .NET Core very easily, but first we will need to add a custom feed as .NET Core is not in the default repository.

First we need to add the .NET Core package source to the list used by APT. The package source is on Azure, so we write this URL (plus some other info) to a file in the folder of sources used by `apt-get`. We do this by redirecting the standard output of `echo` to it, using the following command:

```
sudo sh -c 'echo "deb [arch=amd64] https://apt-
mo.trafficmanager.net/repos/dotnet-release/ xenial main" >
/etc/apt/sources.list.d/dotnetdev.list'
```

All packages are signed with public key cryptography to verify their integrity (read the later chapters for more on this). We import the public key for the .NET Core packages from the Ubuntu key server with the `apt-key` command:

```
sudo apt-key adv --keyserver hkp://keyserver.ubuntu.com:80 --recv-keys
417A0893
```

We need to update our sources so that the latest changes can be picked up with this simple command:

```
sudo apt-get update
```

The `update` command is different to the `upgrade` command, but they are often used together. While `update` simply refreshes the information that APT holds about packages, `upgrade` allows you to very easily update all of the software on the machine (that hasn't been manually installed) to the latest versions. This can be quite a time-saver.

Now we are in a position to install .NET Core with the following command:

```
sudo apt-get install dotnet-sdk-2.0.0
```

If the SDK package ever makes it to the default list of sources, then this will be all you need to do.

If you are trying out a preview, then the package will have the preview tag suffixed (for example, `-preview2-006497`).

After a wall of text scrolls, assuming you don't get any errors and you see the telemetry notice, you're ready to go. Type `dotnet` to see the usage information and `dotnet --version` to see the current version that you are running.

Creating your first app

Run the following command to create a new console app from a template:

```
dotnet new console -o DotNetCoreTwoHelloWorld
```

Then switch to the directory that was just created and run it with these two commands:

```
cd DotNetCoreTwoHelloWorld
```

```
dotnet run
```

Your console should look something like the following screenshot (if you're using PuTTY on Windows):

With .NET Core 1.0, you needed to call `dotnet restore` before building or running your application with the `dotnet` command. In .NET Core 2.0, this is called on your behalf for `dotnet` commands that require it, and you no longer need to restore NuGet packages manually this way.

Assuming that the basic console application worked, let's create a web app. Run the following commands to move up a level to the parent folder and list the templates:

```
cd ..
```

```
dotnet new
```

Without any additional parameters, the `dotnet new` command will list all the available templates. These are shown in the following screenshot:

Let's make a standard MVC web app like we did in our other previous examples. The next three commands will create a new web app from a template, switch to the folder created, and run the app:

```
dotnet new mvc -o AspNetCoreTwoMvc

cd AspNetCoreTwoMvc

dotnet run &
```

We're executing the app in the background (with `&`) so that we can use the terminal while it is still running. You could connect to your server with a browser on your local machine, but this would require binding the web server to the external IP address and opening ports on the server and cloud firewalls.

Let's very simply test whether our web server is working by downloading the home page with the following command. If you don't have `wget` installed, then you could use `curl` instead:

```
wget localhost:5000
```

This process is shown in the following screenshot:

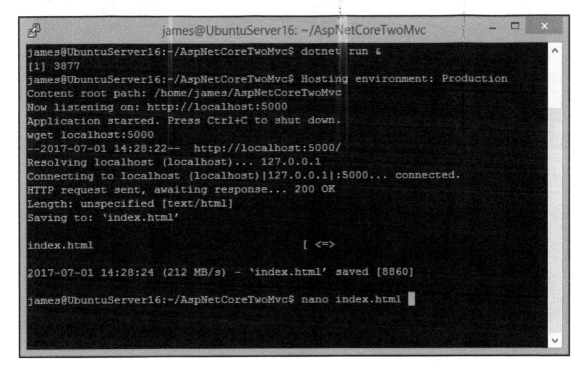

We can view the source of the home page with a command-line text editor, like so:

```
nano index.html
```

You will now see the HTML source of the default home page, as shown here:

To tidy up, we should end the `dotnet` process that is still running. You can use the `kill` command to end the process with the ID shown when you started it. If you can't find the ID, then you can use `ps x` to list the processes that are running.

Containerization with Docker

Docker is an implementation of container technology, which is a lightweight version of VMs. It was originally built on **Linux Containers** (**LXC**), but now it supports many other technologies, including Windows. For the same server, you can run a greater number of containers than traditional VMs as they don't always include a full OS with every image, and they share many resources. For example, if you always use the official Microsoft image, then Docker will share this base between your .NET Core apps while still keeping them separated and sandboxed.

Containers can significantly reduce costs, both in hosting hardware and time saved not configuring and manually security patching the OS yourself. The .NET team saved about $100,000 a year in hosting costs by moving to Docker, although they probably don't pay the market rate on Azure.

The benefits of containers are analogous to those of shipping containers in the real world. By standardizing the unit of transportation and not worrying about the content, costs can be massively reduced. When you separate the concern of how to move containers around from what's inside them, you can share a common infrastructure and scale out much more easily. It also allows much greater scope for automation.

With Docker, you build your application in a container and deploy it. The container takes care of running the app and carries its entire configuration with it. The server you deploy to doesn't need to know anything about your app; it just needs to know how to run containers. This significantly reduces the configuration issues associated with getting an application running. All the main cloud-hosting providers offer a container service for hosting applications packaged in this way.

One of the best reasons for using containers is that they allow you to develop as life like an environment as possible. This means that there should be fewer surprises and difficulties when the time comes to deploy your code to the production infrastructure.

We've all struggled to get a code base working correctly on a new live server or fresh developer workstation. These chores can become a thing of the past. As another benefit, you can be confident that all the environments will have a consistent configuration, which will help cure the headaches associated with promoting releases up the chain of environments to production.

Docker operates a Docker Hub, which hosts images that are ready to use. Microsoft maintains a selection of .NET images published there, and they keep them up to date with patches.

You can pull these images down to get started really easily and quickly, depending on the speed of your Internet connection. There are .NET Core and ASP.NET Core images for both Linux and Windows Nano Server. The Linux images are based on the popular Debian distribution. There are even .NET Framework 3.5 and ASP.NET 4 images for Windows Server, so it's not just limited to the latest cross-platform Core products.

Docker can run on Hyper-V if you have a version of Windows that supports it (for example, Windows 10 Pro, Enterprise, or Education). It requires a 64-bit version with a build number of 10,586 or higher, which unfortunately rules out the LTSB version. To install Docker for Mac, you will need a machine manufactured in 2010 or later, running El Capitan 10.11 or higher.

However, there is an older version of Docker, called Docker Toolbox, which runs on VirtualBox (a cross-platform VM host). This is supported on many more operating systems, including the slightly more mature and stable ones.

 You can start a container from VS when using Visual Studio Tools for Docker, but Docker also allows you to try out .NET without installing anything. If you already have Docker installed, then simply download and run one of the .NET images.

As .NET Core is cross-platform, the simplest way to use Docker is in a Linux VM. It could be hosted on your Mac or Windows system or, as in our examples here, in the cloud.

Let's install Docker Community Edition from the Docker website using the command line and try it out. First we need to add the Docker GPG key to APT. It's a good idea to manually verify the fingerprint of this before going ahead and installing anything.

This process is very similar to the way that we installed .NET earlier in this chapter, but the ordering and syntax are slightly different. First we need to add the Docker GPG public key by downloading it with `curl` and piping it to `apt-key`, using this command:

```
curl -fsSL https://download.docker.com/linux/ubuntu/gpg | sudo apt-key add
-
```

Then, we display the fingerprint of the key that we added with the following command. You should check that this matches the one on the Docker website:

```
sudo apt-key fingerprint 0EBFCD88
```

Next we add the package source to our local list. This command has been split over multiple lines so that it is easier to read:

```
sudo add-apt-repository \
    "deb [arch=amd64] https://download.docker.com/linux/ubuntu \
    $(lsb_release -cs) \
    stable"
```

Then we update our new sources with the following command:

```
sudo apt-get update
```

Now we can install Docker with this simple command:

```
sudo apt-get install docker-ce
```

Assuming you get no errors here, the next step is to test that Docker is working with the following smoke-test container:

```
sudo docker run hello-world
```

You should get an output like the following:

Let's test out .NET Core in Docker with the following command:

```
sudo docker run microsoft/dotnet-samples
```

You should see the .NET bot as ASCII art:

Next, let's upgrade to the latest version of .NET Core and try a web app.

Using ASP.NET Core 2 with Docker

Now that we've checked Docker is working and can run .NET Core, it's time for something a bit more complex. We're going to interactively log in to a container and create an ASP.NET Core 2 app inside.

Run the following command:

```
sudo docker run -it --rm microsoft/aspnetcore-build:2
```

Once the image is downloaded, you should get a slightly different command prompt. Let's be more ambitious and create a single page app using the React and Redux JavaScript libraries:

```
dotnet new reactredux -o AspNetCoreTwoDocker
```

Next we need to restore the JS packages from npm. Note that we haven't installed npm (or .NET Core); it has come included in the container image:

```
cd AspNetCoreTwoDocker
```

```
npm install
```

Let's run the app in the background again and download the home page. Note that the Kestrel web server is now running on the default HTTP port of 80, so we don't need to specify an alternative non-standard port number:

```
dotnet run &
```

```
wget localhost
```

This is shown in the following screenshot:

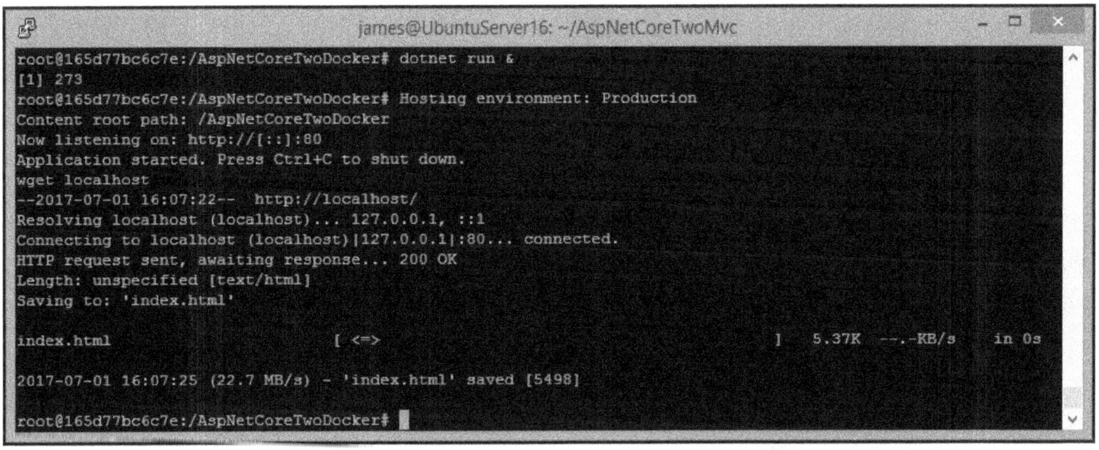

The Docker image doesn't contain a text editor, but we can still view the contents of the file with the `cat` command. We won't get any syntax highlighting, but we can clearly see that this is a React app, as our server rendered the initial state into the page (as `div` with `id` of `react-app`):

```
cat index.html
```

The React app HTML page source, displayed in the terminal using `cat`, is shown in the following screenshot:

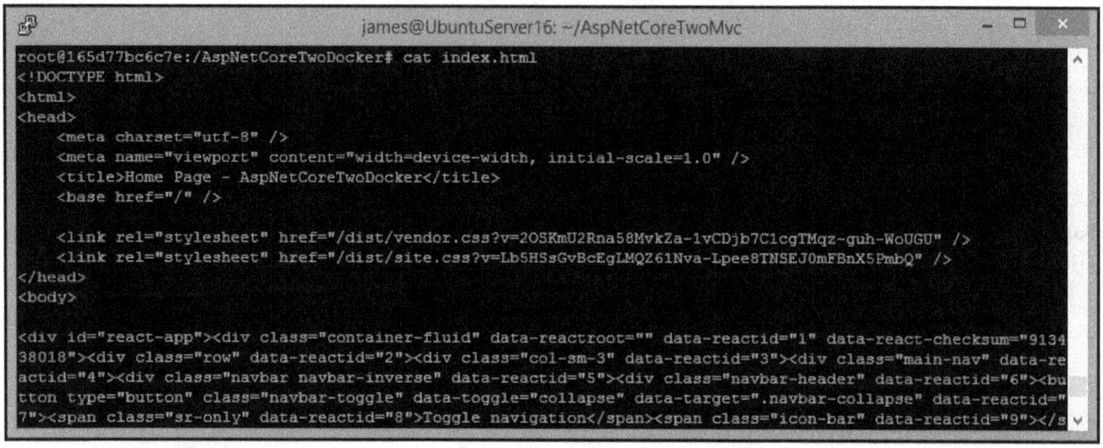

You can again tidy up the `dotnet` process with `kill` and leave the Docker container to return to your host VM with the `exit` command.

Summary

In this chapter, you saw how to get started with the three most popular operating systems that .NET Core 2 supports. You learned about the selection of tools available on each platform and the different ways of using ASP.NET Core 2.

You also discovered the benefits of containers and appreciated how they can be used. You're encouraged to take the examples from this chapter, mix them up, and extend them to the environments that you require. There is a lot of cross-over between platforms and tooling today, so many of these lessons are transferable.

We hope that you will be inspired to try something new by seeing what alternatives are available. Simply spin up a new VM (perhaps in the cloud) and get hacking away!

In the next chapter, we will get into the main focus of this book: performance. We will build on what you have just learned about tooling and show you how to measure your software to see whether it's slow. You will see how to identify what parts of the code need improvement, if indeed it does perform poorly.

4
Measuring Performance Bottlenecks

Measurement is the most crucial aspect of building high-performance systems. You can't change what you don't measure because you won't know what effect your change has had, if any. Without measuring your application, you won't know whether it's performing well.

If you only go by when your software feels slow, then you have left it too late. You are reactively fixing a problem rather than proactively avoiding one. You must measure to achieve good performance, even though it's the feel that matters to a user.

Some books leave measurement, analysis, and profiling until the end. Yet, this is the first thing that should be considered. It's common to fix the wrong problem and optimize areas that do not have performance difficulties.

In this chapter, we will cover the following topics:

- Structured Query Language database profiling
- Web application profiling
- HTTP monitoring
- Network monitoring
- Scientific method and repeatability

This chapter will show you how to check for performance issues and where they are occurring. We will describe the tools that can give you this information and demonstrate how to use them effectively and correctly. We'll also show you how to repeat your experiments consistently so that you can tell whether you have fixed a problem once you've identified it.

We will cover measurement again toward the end of the book, but there, we'll focus on continuous automated monitoring to avoid regressions. This chapter will focus more on manual testing to identify potential performance problems during development and debugging.

Tools

Good debugging tools are essential when you're trying to discover where problems lie. You could write your own crude timing code, and we will show you how to get started with this. However, purpose-built tools are much nicer to work with than simply logging lines of debug information. VS 2017 includes some very useful Application Insights tools that make helpful information easily visible.

Many of the tools discussed in this chapter help you examine areas external to your code. We will cover the profiling of code too, but it's hard to identify problems this way unless the work is purely computational. Slowdowns often happen because of actions your app initiates outside of its immediate stack, and these can be hard to debug by simply stepping through the code. VS 2017 can show you what external actions your app takes, for example, triggering an HTTP API call.

Moving through your program line by line slows down the execution so much that it can make it difficult to identify which lines are fast and which are slow. However, VS does display the time taken since the previous debug step, which can help with this. Nevertheless, the same approach taken for fixing functional bugs cannot always be applied to fix performance issues.

SQL

First off, we will cover SQL-related issues. So, if you're not using a relational database, you can skip this bit; for example, if you use a NoSQL store or a document database instead. Relational databases are a very mature technology and are flexible in their uses. However, it is essential to have a basic knowledge of the SQL syntax and how databases work in order to use them effectively. Even Azure Cosmos DB (previously known as DocumentDB) has an optional SQL API.

It can be tempting when using an O/RM tool, such as **Entity Framework** (**EF**), to ignore SQL and stay in the C# world; however, a competent developer should be able to write a high-performance SQL query. Ignoring the realities of how a database engine works will often lead to performance issues. It's easy to write code with an O/RM tool that's too chatty with the database and issues far too many queries for an operation. Not having the correct indexes on a table will also result in poor performance.

During development, you may not notice these mistakes, unless you use tools to identify the inefficient events that occur. Here, we will show you a couple of ways of doing this.

SQL Server Profiler

SQL Server Profiler is a tool that allows you to inspect what commands are being executed on your SQL Server database. If you have the management tools installed, then you should already have it on your machine. This is how you can access it:

1. If you are using Microsoft SQL Server, then **SQL Server Profiler** can be accessed from the **Tools** menu of **SQL Server Management Studio** (**SSMS**):

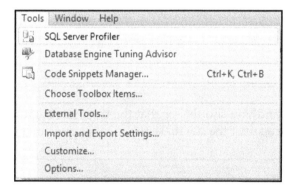

2. Load **SQL Server Profiler** and connect to the database that you are using. Name your trace and select the **Tuning** profile template:

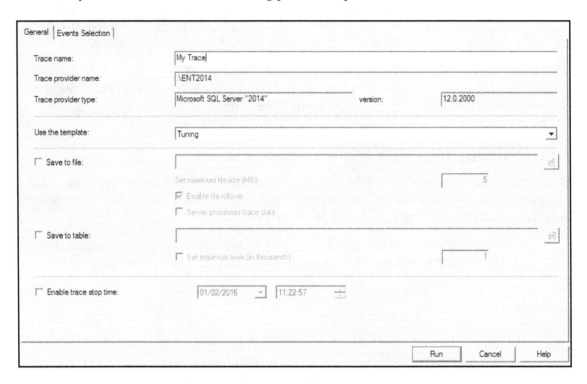

3. Click on **Run** and you should see that the trace has begun. You are now ready to run your code against the database to see what queries it's actually executing:

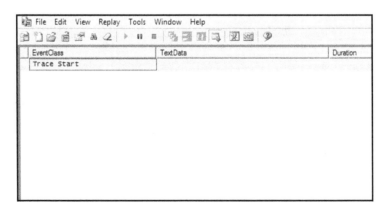

Executing a simple query

As a test, you can execute a simple SELECT query with Management Studio and the profile window should be flooded with entries. Locate the query that you just executed among the noise. This is easier if it starts with a comment, as shown in the following screenshot:

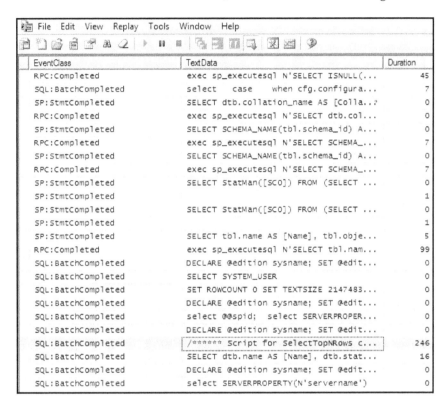

The **Duration** column shows the time taken for the query in **milliseconds** (**ms**). In this example, selecting the top 1,000 rows from a table containing over a million entries took **246 ms**. This would appear very quick, almost instantaneous, to the user. Modifying the query to return all the rows makes it much slower, as shown in the following screenshot:

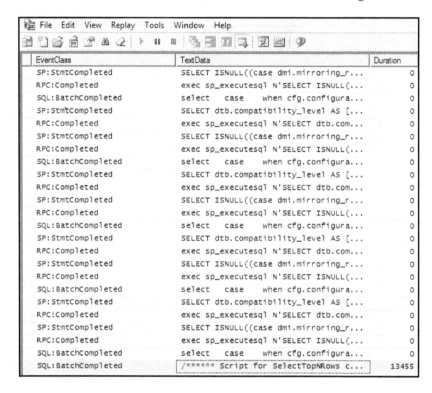

The query has now taken over 13 seconds (**13,455** ms) to complete, which is noticeably slow. This is an extreme example, but it is quite a common mistake to request for more data than needed and filter or sort it in the application code. The database is often much better suited for this task and is usually the correct location to select the data you want.

We will cover specific SQL mistakes and remedies in the following chapters. However, the first step is to know how to detect what is going on with the communication between your application and the database. If you can't detect that your app is making inefficient queries, then it will be difficult to improve performance.

MiniProfiler

MiniProfiler is an excellent open source tool for debugging data queries. It supports SQL databases and some NoSQL databases, such as MongoDB and RavenDB. It came out of Stack Exchange, the people who run the Stack Overflow Q&A website. It embeds a widget into your web pages that shows you how long they take to get their data. It also shows you the SQL queries and warns you about common mistakes. Although MiniProfiler started with .NET, it is also available for Ruby, Go, and Node.js.

The biggest benefit of MiniProfiler over SQL Server Profiler is that it's always there. You don't need to explicitly go looking for SQL problems, so it can highlight issues much earlier. It's even a good idea to run it in production, only visible to logged-in admins, though. This way, every time you work on the website, you will see how data access is performing. Make sure you test the performance impact of this before deploying it, though.

MiniProfiler now supports ASP.NET Core! You can read simple instructions on how to set this up at `http://miniprofiler.com/dotnet/AspDotNetCore`.

Application profiling

Often, you will want a breakdown of where work is being performed within your application and where it is spending most of its time. You may wish to see how computing resources are allocated and how they change. There are various tools available for this, and we will cover a couple of them here.

Application profiling allows you to narrow down the area of your app that is performing poorly. You can start at a higher level, and once you locate the broad area, you can dig down and find the specific issue. Splitting up a large problem into small chunks is a good way to tackle it and make it more manageable.

Glimpse

Glimpse is a fantastic open source add-on for your web application. Like MiniProfiler, it adds a widget to your web pages so that you can see problems as you navigate around and work on your site. It provides information similar to your browser developer tools but also delves inside your server-side application to show you a trace of what actions are taking the most time.

Glimpse is available at `http://getglimpse.com/`, and you can install it with NuGet for the web framework and O/RM you're using. For ASP.NET Core, we will need to use Glimpse version 2. At the time of writing this, this is still a beta prerelease.

Glimpse integrates with Application Insights (via a NuGet package), and you can display information collected by Application Insights in the Glimpse toolbar. There is also a new version of Glimpse that is now available for Node.js, which is available at `http://node.getglimpse.com/`.

Using Glimpse

Installing Glimpse is really simple. There are only three steps:

1. Install with NuGet.
2. Add lines to `Startup.cs`.
3. Build and run the app.

Let's have a look at these steps.

Installing the package

Right-click on your web application project in **Solution Explorer** and select **Manage NuGet Packages...** to open the graphical package manager window. Search for **Glimpse**, select it, and then click on the **Install** button. If you want to install the beta version of Glimpse 2, then make sure the **Include prerelease** checkbox is selected:

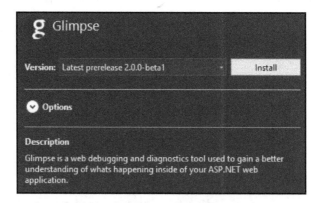

Adding code

You need to add three snippets of code to your `Startup.cs` file. In the `using` directive at the top of the file, add the following:

```
using Glimpse;
```

In the `ConfigureServices` function, add the following:

```
services.AddGlimpse();
```

In the `Configure` function, add the following:

```
app.UseGlimpse();
```

Running your web application

Build and run your web application by pressing *F5*. If you encounter a duplicate type error when running, then simply clean the solution and do a full rebuild. You may need to apply migrations to the database, but this is just a button click in the browser. However, if you add this to an existing project with data, then you should take more care.

When you run the application, you'll find the Glimpse bar at the bottom of the browser window, which looks like the following screenshot. The bar is one long strip, but it has been broken down in this screenshot to display it more clearly:

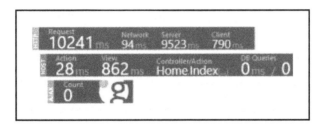

 The first page load may take much longer than subsequent ones, so you should refresh your page for more representative data. However, we won't worry about this for the purposes of this demo.

Mouse over each section in the Glimpse toolbar to expand it for more information. You can minimize and restore each section (HTTP, HOST, or AJAX) by clicking on its title.

If you use the default web application template (and leave the authentication default for all individual user accounts), then you can register a new user to cause the application to perform some database operations. You will then see some values in the **DB Queries** field, as shown in the following screenshot:

Click on the Glimpse logo to see a history of all the page requests. Select one to view the details and expand the SQL queries by clicking on them, which is displayed in the following screenshot:

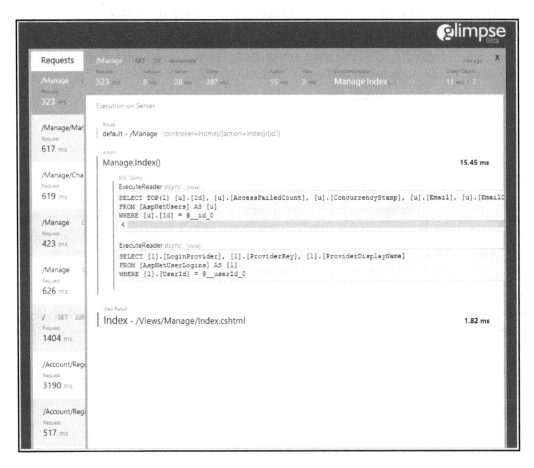

Glimpse shows you how much time is spent in each layer of your application and exactly which SQL queries are being run. In this case, EF Core generates the SQL.

Glimpse is very useful for tracking down where performance problems lie. You can easily see how long each part of the page pipeline takes and identify the slow parts.

IDE

Using the profiling tools that are built into **Visual Studio (VS)** can be very informative to understand the CPU and memory usage of your code. You can also see the time taken for certain operations. These Application Insights tools can be integrated into Azure for when you deploy your app to a cluster of servers; however, you can still use them locally without anything being sent to the cloud. You don't need to add any code to your program as the framework is instrumented automatically.

Application Insights available with VS 2017 can perform something similar to MiniProfiler and Glimpse. It can not only tell you how your servers are performing, but also show you what performance on the client side looks like via some embedded JavaScript added to the web app pages. We will cover Application Insights more in `Chapter 10`, *The Downsides of Performance-Enhancing Tools*; this is just an introduction.

When running your application, open the diagnostic tools window in VS, as shown in the following screenshot:

You can see the CPU and memory profiles, including the automatic garbage collection events that are used to free up memory (the marker prior to memory use decreasing). You will be able to see breakpoint events, and if you have the Enterprise version of VS, then you will be able to see IntelliTrace events as well.

 IntelliTrace is only available in the Enterprise edition of Visual Studio. However, you can still use the performance and diagnostic tools in the free Community edition. You can also access them on Azure via a web interface, but this is optional.

If you have **IntelliTrace**, then you can find it in the VS options, as shown in the following screenshot. However, the diagnostic tools are still useful without this premium feature:

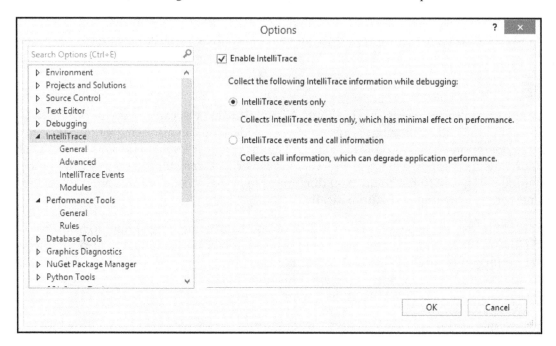

When you put in a breakpoint and your code hits it, then VS will tell you how long it was since the previous event. This is shown in the events list and also overlaid near the breakpoint.

Some alternatives to the VS profiling tools include Redgate ANTS and Telerik JustTrace. JetBrains also has dotTrace and dotMemory. However, all of these tools can be quite expensive, and we won't cover them here.

Monitoring HTTP

When dealing with a web application, you will normally use HTTP as the application protocol. It's very useful to know what requests occur between the browsers and your servers.

Browsers

Most modern browsers have excellent developer tools, which include a **Network** tab to monitor requests to, and responses from, the web server. You can normally access the dev tools by pressing *F12*. These are handy to view web traffic, and you can still see encrypted communications without messing about with certificates.

The dev tools in both Chrome and Firefox are superb. We'll focus on the network and timing component, but we highly recommend that you learn all the features. If you know how to get the best out of them, then web development is much easier.

As an example, Chrome dev tools let you take a screenshot of the entire page when using the device toolbar (for simulating mobile devices), even when the page doesn't all fit on the screen. You can also capture a filmstrip of images, showing how your page progressively loads, using the dev tools.

Chrome

The network dev tools in Chrome are very useful. They provide a good visualization of the request timings, and you can throttle the connection to see how it behaves over various different Internet connections. This is particularly important for mobile devices.

A selection of network requests from the Chrome dev tools are shown in the following screenshot. Additional columns are available if you right-click on the headings bar:

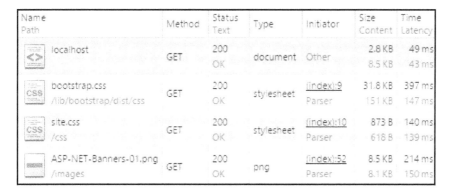

You can disable the cache with a simple checkbox so that the browser will always load assets fresh from your web server. You can also click on a resource for more information, and the **Timing** tab is very useful to provide a breakdown of the connection components, for example, **Time To First Byte** (**TTFB**). Some basic timing details from a local web server are shown in the following screenshot:

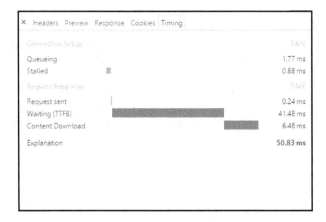

On a local web server, this breakdown won't contain extra information, but, on a remote server, it will display other things, such as the **Domain Name System** (**DNS**) hostname lookup and SSL/TLS handshake. These additional components are shown in the next screenshot:

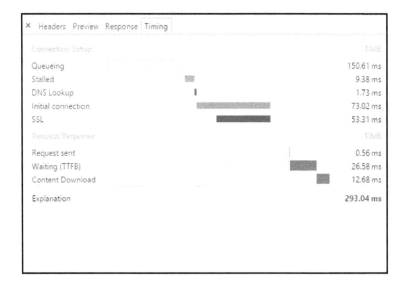

Firefox

Firefox has similar dev tools to Chrome but with some added features. For example, you can edit a request and resend it to the web server. The **Network** tab presents the same sort of information as Chrome does, as shown in the following screenshot:

✓	Method	File	Domain	Type	Transferred	Size
● 200	GET	/	localhost:1353	html	2.78 kB	9.04 kB
● 200	GET	bootstrap.css	localhost:1353	css	31.18 kB	150.62 kB
● 200	GET	site.css	localhost:1353	css	0.44 kB	0.60 kB
● 200	GET	jquery.js	localhost:1353	js	96.58 kB	250.79 kB
● 200	GET	bootstrap.js	localhost:1353	js	20.40 kB	69.58 kB
● 200	GET	site.js?v=EWaMeWsJBYWmL2g_KkgXZQ5n...	localhost:1353	js	0.15 kB	0.03 kB
● 200	GET	hud.js?hash=c127ec0e	localhost:1353	js	31.69 kB	82.18 kB
● 200	GET	agent.js?hash=c127ec0e	localhost:1353	js	2.64 kB	7.55 kB
● 200	GET	ASP-NET-Banners-01.png	localhost:1353	png	8.12 kB	10.83 kB
● 200	GET	Banner-02-VS.png	localhost:1353	png	12.10 kB	16.13 kB
● 200	GET	ASP-NET-Banners-02.png	localhost:1353	png	8.41 kB	11.22 kB
● 200	GET	Banner-01-Azure.png	localhost:1353	png	14.10 kB	18.80 kB
● 200	GET	glyphicons-halflings-regular.woff2	localhost:1353	font-...	17.61 kB	23.48 kB
● 200	GET	/glimpse/context/?contextId=5186459dd77...	localhost:1353	json	7.03 kB	7.03 kB
● 200	GET	glimpse-logo.png	localhost:1353	png	0.79 kB	1.05 kB
● 200	GET	selawk.woff2	localhost:1353	font-...	14.29 kB	19.05 kB
● 202	POST	/glimpse/message-ingress/	localhost:1353	plain	0.04 kB	0.04 kB

The detail view is also very similar, including the **Timings** tab. This tab is shown in the following screenshot:

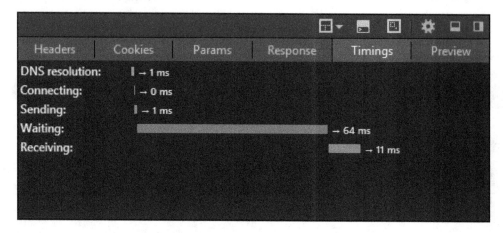

Fiddler

Sometimes, browser tools aren't enough. Say, you are debugging a native application, an HTTP client in your code, or a mobile browser. Fiddler is a free debugging proxy that can capture all of the HTTP traffic between the client and server. With a little bit of work, it can also intercept HTTPS traffic. Fiddler is available to download for free at `http://www.telerik.com/fiddler`.

As this book focuses on web development, we won't go into more detail. The browser dev tools are suitable for most of the work these days. They now fulfill a large part of the role that Fiddler used to play before they acquired the same features (network request capture, throttling, and timing). Fiddler is still there if you need it, and it can be handy if your web server calls an external HTTP API, although this can also often be debugged directly inside VS.

Network

Occasionally, you will need to debug at a lower level than HTTP or SQL. This is where network monitors or packet sniffers come in. Perhaps, you want to debug a **Tabular Data Stream** (**TDS**) message to a SQL Server DB or a TLS handshake to an SSL terminating load balancer. Or, maybe you want to analyze a SOAP web service envelope or **Simple Mail Transfer Protocol** (**SMTP**) email connection, to see why it's not working correctly.

Microsoft Message Analyzer

Microsoft Message Analyzer supersedes Microsoft **Network Monitor** (**Netmon**) and is a tool to capture network traffic on Windows systems. Netmon requires you to log out and then log back in again after the installation, whereas Wireshark doesn't. You can read more about these two Microsoft tools online, but for clarity and brevity, we will focus on Wireshark for low-level network monitoring.

Wireshark

Wireshark (previously called Ethereal) is an open source and cross-platform packet capture and network analysis application. It is probably the most popular tool of its kind and has many uses. You can install Wireshark without needing to restart or log out, which makes it great to debug a live problem that's hard to recreate. You can download Wireshark from `https://www.wireshark.org/`, and it runs on Windows, Mac, and Linux.

Wireshark isn't particularly useful for local development as it only captures traffic going over the network, not to localhost. The only thing you are likely to see if you run it against a local web application is VS reporting analytics of what you do in the IDE back to Microsoft.

You can turn off the **Customer Experience Improvement Program** (**CEIP**) in VS by clicking on the button next to the quick launch box and selecting **Settings....** By default, it is on (it's now opt-out, not opt-in as in the previous products).

Click on the fin icon button at the top-left corner of Wireshark to start a trace. Then, perform some network actions, such as loading a web page from a test server. Once you capture some packets, click on the stop button; you can then examine the collected data at leisure.

Ask your IT administrator before running Wireshark. It can often pick up sensitive information off of the LAN, which may be against your IT acceptable use policy.

The following screenshot shows part of the results from a Wireshark capture:

```
▲ ■ ▮ ◉   ▮ ▣ ▣ ▣   ◌ ⇐ ⇒ 舍 슙 ▮ 三 ▤   ⊕ ⊖ ⊖ ▥

▮ | Apply a display filter ... <Ctrl-/>

No.      Time          Source                Destination            Protocol   Length
    9  5.002002     IntelCor_2a:d1:27      Sagemcom_44:d9:46      ARP           42
   10  31.067962    GreenEne_01:2b:3b      Broadcast              ARP           60
   11  38.449984    IntelCor_2a:d1:27      Broadcast              ARP           42
   12  38.451047    Sagemcom_44:d9:46      IntelCor_2a:d1:27      ARP           42
   13  38.451075    192.168.1.66           192.168.1.254          DNS           85
   14  38.733010    192.168.1.254          192.168.1.66           DNS          211
   15  38.733901    192.168.1.66           191.232.139.254        TCP           66
   16  38.993661    191.232.139.254        192.168.1.66           TCP           66
   17  38.993754    192.168.1.66           191.232.139.254        TCP           54
   18  38.994194    192.168.1.66           191.232.139.254        TLSv1        223
   19  39.030424    191.232.139.254        192.168.1.66           TCP         1502
   20  39.030576    191.232.139.254        192.168.1.66           TCP         1502
   21  39.030616    192.168.1.66           191.232.139.254        TCP           54
   22  39.030837    191.232.139.254        192.168.1.66           TLSv1       1002
   23  39.048837    192.168.1.66           191.232.139.254        TLSv1        220
   24  39.192803    191.232.139.254        192.168.1.66           TLSv1        113
   25  39.195207    192.168.1.66           191.232.139.254        TLSv1        283

        Session ID: e8200000eeaf1732882e61fa0332ea82d845f59a8a2ca9fc...
        Cipher Suite: TLS_ECDHE_RSA_WITH_AES_256_CBC_SHA (0xc014)
        Compression Method: null (0)
        Extensions Length: 9
      ▷ Extension: Extended Master Secret
      ▷ Extension: renegotiation_info
   ◢ Handshake Protocol: Certificate
        Handshake Type: Certificate (11)
        Length: 3383
        Certificates Length: 3380
      ◢ Certificates (3380 bytes)
          Certificate Length: 1865
        ▷ Certificate: 308207453082052da00302010202135a000134a75c1995c6...
```

There can be a lot of noise when using Wireshark. You will see low-level network packets, such as **Address Resolution Protocol** (**ARP**) traffic, which you can filter out or ignore. You may also see data from VoIP phones and other networked devices or data that is intended for other computers on the network.

Select the packet that you are interested in from the top pane. The middle pane will display the contents of the packet. You can normally ignore the lower layers of the network stack, such as Ethernet and TCP/IP (presented at the top of the list).

Dive straight into the application layer that is listed last. If this is a protocol that Wireshark recognizes, then it will break it down into fields that it's made up of.

The bottom pane displays a hex dump of the raw packet. This is not normally as useful as the parsed data in the middle pane.

If you use TLS/SSL (which you really should use), then you won't see the contents of HTTP traffic. You would need a copy of the server's private key to see inside the TLS connection, which wraps and encrypts the HTTP application data. You will only be able to see the domain that was connected to via the DNS lookup and TLS certificate, not the full URL or any payload data.

Using Wireshark is a huge topic, and there are many great resources available to learn about it, both online and offline. We won't go into much more detail here because it's usually not necessary to go down to this low level of network scrutiny. However, this is a good tool to have in your back pocket.

Roll your own

Sometimes, you may want to write your own performance measurement code. Make sure that you have exhausted all other options and investigated the available tools first.

 Perhaps, you want to record the execution time of some process to write to your logs. Maybe you want to send this to a system such as Logstash and then visualize the changes over time with **Kibana**. Both are great open source products from Elastic, and they store data in the Elasticsearch search server. You can read more about both of these tools at `https://www.elastic.co/`.

You can easily record the length of time for a task by storing the current time before it starts and comparing this to the current time after it finishes, but this approach has many limitations. The act of measuring will affect the result to some extent, and the clock is not accurate for short durations. It can be useful for really slow events if you need to share states between processes or multiple runs, but, to benchmark, you should normally use the `Stopwatch` class.

It is usually best to store timestamps in **Coordinated Universal Time (UTC)**, which is otherwise known as **Greenwich Mean Time (GMT)**. You will avoid many issues with time zones and daylight saving if you use `DateTimeOffset.UtcNow` (or at least `DateTime.UtcNow`). Name variables and columns to indicate this, for example, `TimestampUtc`. Use `TimeSpan` for lengths of time, but if you must use primitives (such as integers), then include the units in the variable or column name, for example, `DurationInMilliseconds` or `TimeoutInSeconds`. This will help you avoid confusion when another developer (or your future self) comes to use them. However, to benchmark quick operations, you should use `Stopwatch`. This class is in the `System.Diagnostics` namespace.

If you try to measure a single quick event, then you will not get accurate results. A way around this is to repeat the task many times and then take an average. This is useful to benchmark, but it is not usually applicable to real applications. However, once you identify what works quickest with a test, then you can apply it to your own programs.

Let's illustrate this with a small experiment to time how long it takes to hash a password with the PBKDF2 algorithm (in the `System.Security.Cryptography` namespace). In this case, the operation under test is not important, as we are simply interested in the timing code. A naive approach may look like the following code:

```
var s = Stopwatch.StartNew();
pbkdf2.GetBytes(2048);
s.Stop();
Console.WriteLine($"Test duration = {s.ElapsedMilliseconds} ms");
```

This code will output a different value every time it is run due to the flaws in the measurement process. A better way would be to repeat the test many times and average the output, as in the following code:

```
var s = Stopwatch.StartNew();
for (var ii = 0; ii < tests; ii++)
{
    pbkdf2.GetBytes(2048);
}
s.Stop();
var mean = s.ElapsedMilliseconds / tests;
Console.WriteLine($"{tests} runs mean duration = {mean} ms");
```

This code is still very primitive, but it will output very similar results every time. The higher the value of `tests`, the more accurate it will be, but the longer the test will take.

You could improve the benchmark by warming up the function under test, then running a garbage collection, before starting the timer and entering the loop. You could also store the output in a member variable to prevent clever optimizations by the compiler.

However, at this point, it would be better to just use a full benchmarking tool, such as BenchmarkDotNet. The reason we haven't done so here is simply to make it easier for you to run these samples for yourself.

BenchmarkDotNet is a very helpful tool that has now joined the projects of the .NET Foundation. We will cover it again in Chapter 8, *Understanding Code Execution and Asynchronous Operations*. You can read more about it at https://github.com/dotnet/BenchmarkDotNet.

 In these examples, we are using C# 6 string interpolation, but you can use the traditional overloads to Console.WriteLine if you prefer.

Let's write a quick example application that demonstrates the differences by running these two different versions multiple times. We'll extract the two tests into methods and call them each a few times:

```
var pbkdf2 = new Rfc2898DeriveBytes("password", 64, 256);
SingleTest(pbkdf2);
SingleTest(pbkdf2);
SingleTest(pbkdf2);

Console.WriteLine();
var tests = 1000;
AvgTest(pbkdf2, tests);
AvgTest(pbkdf2, tests);
AvgTest(pbkdf2, tests);

Console.WriteLine();
Console.WriteLine("Press any key...");
Console.ReadKey(true);
```

The output will look something like the following screenshot. You can find the full application listing in the code that accompanies this book if you want to run it for yourself.

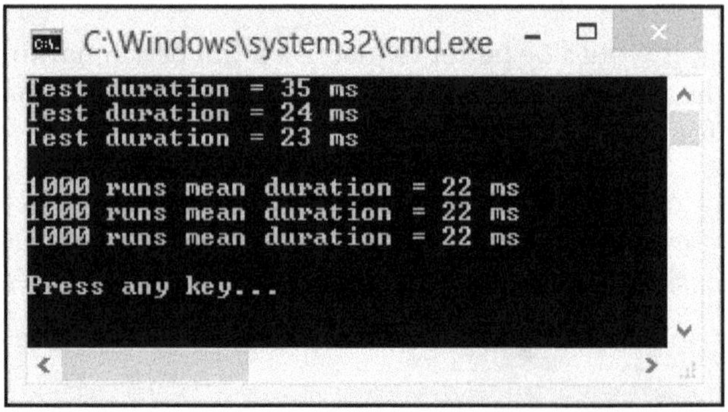

```
C:\Windows\system32\cmd.exe                    –  □  ×
Test duration = 35 ms
Test duration = 24 ms
Test duration = 23 ms

1000 runs mean duration = 22 ms
1000 runs mean duration = 22 ms
1000 runs mean duration = 22 ms

Press any key...

<                                          >
```

You can see that the three individual tests can give wildly different results, yet the averaged tests are identical.

Your results will vary. This is due to the inherent variability in computer systems. Embedded systems that are time-sensitive usually use a real-time OS. Normal software systems typically run on a time-sharing OS, where your instructions can easily get interrupted, and VMs make the problem even worse.

You will get different results, depending on whether you build in debug or release mode and whether you run with or without debugging. Release mode without debugging (*Ctrl + F5*) is the fastest.

The following screenshot shows the same benchmarking demo application running with debugging. You can tell because the `dotnet` executable is shown in the title bar of the Command Prompt. If it ran without debugging, then this would display `cmd.exe` (on Windows), as in the previous screenshot.

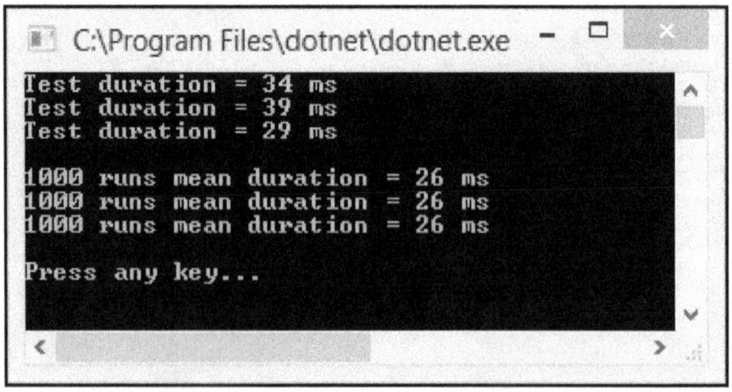

```
C:\Program Files\dotnet\dotnet.exe             –  □  ×
Test duration = 34 ms
Test duration = 39 ms
Test duration = 29 ms

1000 runs mean duration = 26 ms
1000 runs mean duration = 26 ms
1000 runs mean duration = 26 ms

Press any key...

<                                          >
```

Unit testing is very valuable, and you may even practice **test-driven development** (**TDD**), but you should be careful about including performance tests as unit tests. Unit tests must be quick to be valuable, and tests that accurately measure the time taken for operations are often slow. You should set a timeout on your unit tests to make sure that you don't write slow ones with external dependencies. You can still test performance, but you should do it at the integration testing stage along with tests that hit an API, DB, or disk.

Science

We dealt with the computer in computer science by showcasing some hardware access speeds in Chapter 2, *Why Performance Is a Feature*. Now, it's time for the science bit.

It's important to take a scientific approach if you wish to achieve consistently reliable results. Have a methodology or test plan and follow it the same way every time, only changing the thing that you want to measure. Automation can help a lot with this.

It's also important to always measure the use case on your systems with your data. What worked well for someone else may not work out great for you.

We will talk more about science and statistics later in the book. Taking a simple average can be misleading, but it's fine to use it as a gentle introduction. Read Chapter 10, *The Downsides of Performance-Enhancing Tools,* for more on concepts such as medians and percentiles.

Repeatability

Results need to be repeatable. If you get wildly different results every time you test, then they can't be relied upon. You should repeat tests and take the average result to normalize out any variability in the application or hardware under test.

It is also important to clearly record the units of measurement. When you compare a new value to a historic one, you need to know this. NASA famously lost a Mars probe because of unit confusion.

Only change one thing

When testing, you aim to measure the impact of a single change. If you change more than one thing at a time, then you cannot be sure which one has made the difference.

The aim is to minimize the effects of any other changes apart from the one you are interested in. This means keeping external factors as static as possible and performing multiple tests, taking the average result.

Summary

Let's sum up what we covered about measurement in this chapter and what we'll cover in the next chapter. We covered the importance of measurement in solving performance problems. Without measuring, you cannot hope to write high-performance software; you will be coding in the dark.

We highlighted some of the tools that you can use to measure performance. We showed you how to use a selection of these and how to write your own. We also covered the value of taking a scientific approach to measurement. Making sure that your results are repeatable and that you record the correct units of measurement, are important concerns.

In the next chapter, we will learn how to fix common performance problems. You will gain the skills to speed up the low-hanging fruit and make yourself look like a performance wizard to your colleagues. No longer will it be a case of "it worked in test; it's an operations problem now".

5
Fixing Common Performance Problems

This chapter gets into the meat of optimization once you identify and locate the performance problems. It covers a selection of the most common performance issues across a variety of areas and explains simple solutions to some of the mistakes people often make. When using these techniques, you'll look like a wizard to your clients and colleagues by quickly speeding up their software.

Topics covered in this chapter include the following:

- Network latency
- Select N+1 problems
- Disk I/O issues on virtual machines
- Asynchronous operations in a web application
- Performing too many operations in one web request
- Static site generators
- Pragmatic solutions with hardware
- Shrinking overly large images

Most of the problems in this chapter center on what happens when you add latency to common operations or when the throughput is reduced from what it was in development. Things that worked fine in tests, when everything was on one physical machine with minimal data, are now no longer quite as speedy when you have an API on a different continent, a full database on a different machine from your web server, and its virtual disk somewhere else on the network entirely.

You will learn how to identify and fix issues that are not always apparent when everything is running on a single machine. You'll see how to identify when your O/RM or framework behaves badly and is too chatty with the database, which can easily happen if it's not used correctly.

We will see how to ensure that work is performed in the most appropriate place, and we'll look at some ways of keeping your images small using the correct resolution and format. These techniques will ensure that your application is efficient and that data is not sent over the wire unnecessarily.

We'll also discuss how to mitigate performance issues with an alternative approach by improving the underlying hardware to reduce the factors that amplify issues in bad software. This can be a good temporary measure if the software application is already deployed to production and is in use. If you already have live performance problems, then this can buy you some time to engineer a proper fix.

Latency

As covered in the previous chapters, latency is the delay that occurs before an operation can complete, sometimes also known as **lag**. You may not be able to control the latency of the infrastructure that your software application runs on, but you can write your application in such a way that it can cope with this latency in a graceful manner.

The two main types of latency that we will discuss here are **network latency** and **disk latency**. As the names suggest, these are, respectively, the delay in performing an operation over the network and the delay in reading from or writing to a persistent storage medium. You will often deal with both at the same time, for example, a **database (DB)** query to a server on a remote virtual machine will require the following operations:

- A network operation from the web server to the DB server
- A network operation from the DB server to a remote disk on a **Storage Area Network (SAN)**
- A disk operation to look up data on the physical drive

 Although **Solid State Drives (SSDs)** have much lower latency than spinning platter disks, they are still relatively slow. When we talk about disk I/O here, we refer to both types of drive.

You can clearly see that if you issue too many DB operations, the latency present in a typical production infrastructure will compound the problem. You can fix this by minimizing the number of DB operations so that they can't be amplified as much.

Let's illustrate this with an example. Let's suppose you wish to return 200 records from your DB and the round trip latency is 50 **milliseconds (ms)**. If you retrieve all of the records at once, then the total time will be 50 ms plus the time to transfer the records. However, if you first retrieve a list of the record identifiers and then retrieve all of them individually, the total time will be at least *201 * 50 ms = 10.05 seconds!*

Unfortunately, this is a very common mistake. In a system where latency dominates throughput, it is important to keep the requests to a minimum.

Asynchronous operations

Most new .NET Framework APIs that have a significant latency will have **asynchronous (async)** methods. For example, the .NET HTTP client (superseding the web client), SMTP client, and **Entity Framework (EF)** all have async versions of common methods. In fact, the async version is usually the native implementation and the non-async method is simply a blocking wrapper to it. These methods are very beneficial and you should use them. However, they may not have the effect that you imagine when applied to web application programming.

 We will cover async operations and asynchronous architecture later in this book. We'll also go into **Message Queuing (MQ)** and worker services. This chapter is just a quick introduction, and we will simply show you some tools to go after the low-hanging fruit on web applications.

An async API returns control to the calling method before it completes. This can also be awaited so that, on completion, the execution resumes from where the asynchronous call was made. With a native desktop or mobile application, awaiting an async method normally returns control to the **user interface (UI)** thread, which means that the software remains responsive to user input. The app can process user interactions rather than blocking on your method. Traditionally, you may have used a background worker for these tasks.

You should never perform expensive work on the UI thread. Therefore, this technique does increase performance for native applications. However, for a server-side web application, this UI blocking problem does not exist because the browser is the UI. Therefore, this technique will not increase the performance for a single user in isolation.

The JavaScript code that runs in the browser is a different matter, and this can block the UI. We will see how to run this in the background in a non-blocking way (with asynchronous service workers) later in the book.

Awaiting asynchronous API methods in a web application is still good practice, but it only allows the software to scale better and handle more concurrent users. Typically, a web request cannot complete until the async operation also completes. Therefore, although the thread is surrendered back into the thread pool and you can use it for other requests, individual web requests will not complete any quicker.

Simple asynchronous tools

As this book deals with web application programming, we won't go into much more detail on native application UIs in this chapter. Instead, we will showcase some simple tools and techniques that can help with async tasks in web applications.

The tools we are about to cover offer some simple solutions that are only suitable for very small applications. They may not always be reliable, but sometimes they can be good enough. If you are after a more robust solution, then you should read the later chapters on asynchronous programming and distributed architecture.

Background queuing

Background queuing is a useful technique when you have an operation that does not need to occur straightaway, for example, logging stats to a database, sending an email, or processing a payment transaction. If you perform too much work in a single web request, then background queuing may offer a convenient solution, especially if you don't require the operation to always succeed.

If you use ASP.NET 4.7 (or any version from 4.5.2 onward), then you can use `HostingEnvironment.QueueBackgroundWorkItem` to run a method in the background. This is preferable to simply setting a task running because if ASP.NET shuts down, then it will issue a cancellation request and wait for a grace period before killing the item. However, this still does not guarantee completion because the application can die at any point due to an unexpected reboot or hardware failure. If the task needs to complete, then it should be **transactional** and make a record of success upon completion. It can then be retried on failure. Queuing a background work item is okay for fire-and-forget events if you genuinely don't care whether they succeed or not.

Unfortunately, `HostingEnvironment.QueueBackgroundWorkItem` is not part of ASP.NET Core. Therefore, if you want to use this, then you will have to simply queue a job. We will show you how to do this later, but if you use the full version of ASP.NET, then you can do the following to send an email in the background:

```
var client = new SmtpClient();
HostingEnvironment.QueueBackgroundWorkItem(ct =>
    client.SendMailAsync(message));
```

Assuming that you already have your message, this will create an SMTP client and send the email message in the background without blocking further execution. This does not use the `ct` (cancellation token) variable. Keep in mind that the email is not guaranteed to be sent. Therefore, if you need to definitely dispatch it, then consider using another method.

If you use ASP.NET Core, then this functionality is not available. However, you can manually create something similar with `Task.Run` as in the following example. However, this is probably not the best approach for anything nontrivial:

```
Task.Run(() => asyncMethod(cancellationToken));
```

If you can cancel your task, then you can get the `ApplicationStopping` token from an injected instance of the `IApplicationLifetime` interface to pass in as your cancellation token. This will let your task know when the application is about to stop, and you can also block shutdown with it while you gracefully clean up.

You should use this technique with caution, so we won't give you a full example here. Although, you should now have enough pointers to dig deeper and understand the ASP.NET Core application lifecycle if you wish.

Hangfire

Hangfire is an excellent library to run simple background jobs, and it now supports .NET Core. You can more read about Hangfire at `https://www.hangfire.io/`.

You need persistent storage, such as SQL Server, to use Hangfire. This is required so that it can ensure that the tasks are completed. If your tasks are very quick, then this overhead can outweigh the benefits. You can reduce the latency using **message queues** or the in-memory store **Redis**, but these are advanced topics.

If you just want a fire-and-forget event, then using Hangfire can be as easy as the following code:

```
var id = BackgroundJob.Enqueue(() => Console.WriteLine("Hangfire is
awesome!"));
```

There are many more advanced use cases that you may wish to explore, including delayed and recurring jobs. You can even set the jobs to continue with other jobs, so there's no need to write your own batch process handling code.

Select N+1 problems

You may have heard of *select N+1 problems* before. It's the name for a class of performance problems that relate to inefficient querying of a DB. The pathological case is where you query one table for a list of items and then query another table to get the details for each item, one at a time. This is where the name comes from. Instead of the single query required, you perform N queries (one for the details of each item) and one query to get the list to begin with. Perhaps a better name would be *select 1+N*. The example at the end of the *Latency* section (earlier in this chapter) illustrates a *select N+1* problem.

You will hopefully not write such bad-performing queries by hand, but an O/RM can easily output very inefficient SQL if used incorrectly. You might also use some sort of business object abstraction framework, where each object lazily loads itself from the DB. This can become a performance nightmare if you want to put a lot of these objects in a list or calculate some dashboard metrics from a large set.

 We will go into detail about SQL and O/RM optimization in `Chapter 7`, *Optimizing I/O Performance*. This chapter will simply offer some quick fixes to common problems.

If you have a slow application that has performance issues when retrieving data, then *select N+1* may be the problem. Run an SQL profiler tool, as described in the previous chapter, to discover if this is the case. If you see lots of SQL queries for your data instead of just one, then you can move on to the solution stage. For example, if your screen fills with queries on a page load, then you know you have a problem.

In the following example, we will use the micro-O/RM Dapper (made by the team at Stack Overflow) to better illustrate what occurs. However, you are more likely to encounter these problems when using a large lazy loading library or O/RM (such as EF or NHibernate).

Entity Framework Core does not support lazy loading yet, so you are unlikely to encounter *select N+1* problems when using it. The previous full versions of EF do support this and it may be added to EF Core in the future.

Consider a simple blog website. On the home page, we would like a list of the posts along with the number of comments each post has. Our blog post model may look something like the following:

```
namespace SelectNPlusOne.Models
{
    public class BlogPost
    {
        public int BlogPostId { get; set; }
        public string Title { get; set; }
        public string Content { get; set; }
        public int CommentCount { get; set; }
    }
}
```

We also have a model for a comment, which may look like this:

```
namespace SelectNPlusOne.Models
{
    public class BlogPostComment
    {
        public int BlogPostCommentId { get; set; }
        public string CommenterName { get; set; }
        public string Content { get; set; }
    }
}
```

 As this is an example, we kept things simple and only used a single set of models. In a real application, you will typically have separate **view models** and **data access layer models**. The controller will map between these, perhaps assisted by a library such as AutoMapper (http://automapper.org/).

Our view to render this into HTML may look something like the following:

```
@model IEnumerable<SelectNPlusOne.Models.BlogPost>
<table class="table">
    <tr>
        <th>Title</th>
        <th># Comments</th>
    </tr>
    @foreach (var post in Model)
```

```
    {
        <tr>
            <td>@post.Title</td>
            <td>@post.CommentCount</td>
        </tr>
    }
</table>
```

We want to populate these models and view from our database. We have two tables, which look like this:

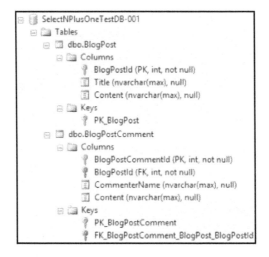

The relationship between the two tables in question looks like the following:

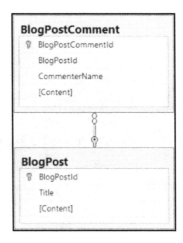

In our controller, we can write code, such as the following, to query the database, populate the model from the database results, and return the view to render it:

```
using (var connection = new SqlConnection(connectionString))
{
    await connection.OpenAsync();
    var blogPosts = await connection.QueryAsync<BlogPost>(@"
        SELECT * FROM BlogPost");
    foreach (var post in blogPosts)
    {
        var comments = await
            connection.QueryAsync<BlogPostComment>(@"
            SELECT * FROM BlogPostComment
            WHERE BlogPostId = @BlogPostId",
            new { BlogPostId = post.BlogPostId });
        post.CommentCount = comments.Count();
    }
    return View(blogPosts);
}
```

We test this and it works! We feel pretty happy with ourselves. It completes quickly on our local test database, which contains a handful of rows. We used the `async` methods everywhere, which must be what makes this so quick. We even only get the comments for each blog in question, not all the comments every time. We also used a parameterized query to avoid **SQL injection**, and everything looks good. Ship it!

 As this is an example, we kept it simple for clarity. In a real application, you will want to use techniques such as Dependency Injection (such as the DI built into ASP.NET Core) to make it more flexible.

Unfortunately, when the data starts to increase (as posts and comments are added), the blog starts to get much slower with pages taking a longer time to load. Our readers get bored waiting and give up. Audience figures drop along with revenue.

Let's profile the database to see what the problem might be. We run SQL Server Profiler filtering on the database in question, and look at the SQL being executed.

The following screenshot shows the filter dialog in SQL Server Profiler:

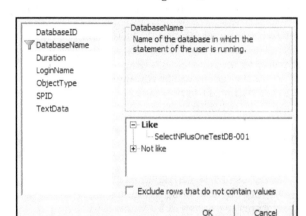

The trace that we capture reveals that lots of queries are being executed, far too many for the data that we need. The problem is that our code is not very efficient, as it uses multiple simple queries rather than one slightly more complicated one.

Our code first gets a list of blog posts and then gets the comments for each post, one post at a time. We also bring back way more data than we need. `Async` does not speed up an individual request because we still need all the data before we can render the page.

The bad coding is obvious in this example because Dapper has the SQL right in your code. However, if you use another O/RM, then you wouldn't typically see the SQL in Visual Studio (or your editor of choice). This is an additional benefit of using Dapper because you see the SQL where it's used, so there are no surprises. However, the main benefit of Dapper is that it's fast, very fast, and much faster than EF. It's a great choice for performance and you can read more about it at `https://github.com/ StackExchange/Dapper`.

We only want a count of the comments for each post, and we can get everything that we need (and only what we need) in one query. Let's alter our previous code to use a slightly more complicated SQL query rather than two simpler queries, one of which was inside a `foreach` loop:

```
using (var connection = new SqlConnection(connectionString))
{
    await connection.OpenAsync();
    var blogPosts = await connection.QueryAsync<BlogPost>(@"
        SELECT
```

```
            bp.BlogPostId,
            bp.Title,
            COUNT(bpc.BlogPostCommentId) 'CommentCount'
        FROM BlogPost bp
        LEFT JOIN BlogPostComment bpc
            ON bpc.BlogPostId = bp.BlogPostId
        GROUP BY bp.BlogPostId, bp.Title");
    return View(blogPosts);
}
```

 An SQL query inside a loop is an obvious **code smell** that indicates things may not be as well thought-out as they can be.

This more efficient code only performs a single query against the database and gets all the information that we need. We join the comments table to the posts in the database and then aggregate by grouping. We only request the columns that we need and add the count of the comments to our selection.

Let's profile the new code to see whether we fixed the problem. The following screenshot shows that we now only have a single query being executed rather than the thousands being executed before:

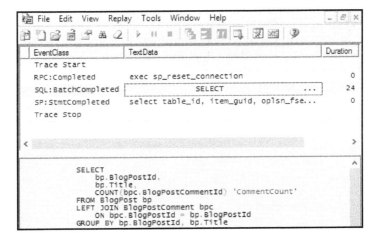

The number of queries has been dramatically reduced. Therefore, the page loads much faster. However, the page is still very big because all the blog posts are listed on it and there are a lot. This slows down rendering and increases the time to deliver the page to a browser.

Efficient paging

In a real application, you want to implement paging so that your list is not too long when a lot of data is in the table. It's a bad idea to list thousands of items on a single page.

You may want to do this with LINQ commands because they are very convenient. However, you need to be careful. If your O/RM is not LINQ-aware, or if you accidentally cast to the wrong type a little too early, then the filtering may occur inside the application when the best place to perform this filtering is actually in the database. Your code may be retrieving all of the data and throwing most of it away without you realizing it.

Perhaps you are tempted to modify the action method `return` statement to look something like the following:

```
return View(blogPosts.OrderByDescending(bp => bp.CommentCount)
                .Skip(pageSize * (pageNumber - 1))
                .Take(pageSize));
```

This works and will speed up your application considerably. However, it may not have the effect that you think it has. The application is quicker because the view rendering is speedier, as a smaller page is being generated. This also reduces the time to send the page to the browser and for the browser to render the HTML.

Yet, the application still gets all of the blog posts from the database and loads them into memory. This can become a problem as the amount of data grows. If you want to use LINQ methods such as this, then you need to check that they are handled all the way to the database. It's a very good idea to read the documentation for your O/RM or framework and double-check the SQL that is generated using a profiler.

Let's have a look at what the SQL should look like. For example, if you use SQL Server starting with the preceding query, you can take only the top ten most-commented posts by altering it as follows:

```
SELECT TOP 10
    bp.BlogPostId,
    bp.Title,
    COUNT(bpc.BlogPostCommentId) 'CommentCount'
FROM BlogPost bp
LEFT JOIN BlogPostComment bpc
    ON bpc.BlogPostId = bp.BlogPostId
GROUP BY bp.BlogPostId, bp.Title
ORDER BY COUNT(bpc.BlogPostCommentId) DESC
```

We order by comment count in descending order. However, you can sort by descending IDs to get a rough reverse chronological order if you like. From this ordered set, we select (or take) only the top ten records.

If you want to skip records for paging, the SELECT TOP clause is not good enough. In SQL Server 2012 and onward, you can use the following instead:

```
SELECT
    bp.BlogPostId,
    bp.Title,
    COUNT(bpc.BlogPostCommentId) 'CommentCount'
FROM BlogPost bp
LEFT JOIN BlogPostComment bpc
    ON bpc.BlogPostId = bp.BlogPostId
GROUP BY bp.BlogPostId, bp.Title
ORDER BY COUNT(bpc.BlogPostCommentId) DESC
OFFSET 0 ROWS
FETCH NEXT 10 ROWS ONLY
```

You can adjust the value for OFFSET to get the correct entries for your page number. The FETCH NEXT value will change the page size (the number of entries on a page). You can pass these values in with a parameterized query, as follows:

```
using (var connection = new SqlConnection(connectionString))
{
    await connection.OpenAsync();
    var blogPosts = await connection.QueryAsync<BlogPost>(@"
        SELECT
            bp.BlogPostId,
            bp.Title,
            COUNT(bpc.BlogPostCommentId) 'CommentCount'
        FROM BlogPost bp
        LEFT JOIN BlogPostComment bpc
            ON bpc.BlogPostId = bp.BlogPostId
        GROUP BY bp.BlogPostId, bp.Title
        ORDER BY COUNT(bpc.BlogPostCommentId) DESC
        OFFSET @OffsetRows ROWS
        FETCH NEXT @LimitRows ROWS ONLY", new
        {
            OffsetRows = pageSize * (pageNumber - 1),
            LimitRows  = pageSize
        }
    );
    return View(blogPosts);
}
```

You can pass in the page size and number as URL parameters if you update your action method signature to the following:

```
public async Task<IActionResult> Index(int pageNumber = 1,
                                       int pageSize  = 10)
```

Here, we have provided default values for both parameters, so they are optional. When no parameters are provided, then the first page of ten results is shown. We need to multiply the page size by the zero-indexed page number to calculate the correct offset. It should be zero for the first page so that no records are skipped.

It would be a very good idea to apply some validation to the paging parameters. Don't allow users to set them to anything outside of a reasonable range. This is left as an exercise to the reader.

If we look in the profiler at the queries being executed on the database server, then we can see what SQL is now being run. We can also see the time taken and compare this with our previous results:

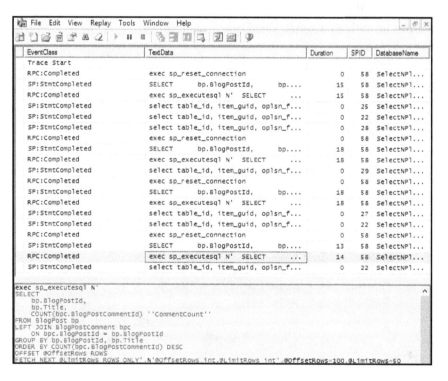

The query in the screenshot gets the data for the third page with the page size set to 50 entries. Therefore, it used an offset of 100 (to skip the first two pages of 50) and fetched the next 50 rows. The URL query string for this can look something like the following:

```
/?pagenumber=3&pagesize=50
```

We can see that the duration of the query has decreased from **24** ms previously to **14** ms now.

> Note how the SQL executes differently when parameters are passed into the query. This is much safer than concatenating user-supplied values directly into an SQL command (so, don't ever do this concatenation). If you build an SQL query with the user input, then you leave your app open to SQL injection attacks. Your entire database could be downloaded via the web using basic point-and-click tools. Your DB could also be altered or deleted and held for ransom, but the attackers won't actually have the backup they claim. Another way your DB could be stolen is if you carelessly put unencrypted backups in a web-accessible location.

If you do not use any parameters, then the default values are used and the home page shows only ten entries, which looks something like the following screenshot, depending on the data in the database:

By default, the home page only displays the top 10 most-commented posts, but you can easily add page navigation with hyperlinks. Simply add the `pagenumber` and `pagesize` query string parameters to the URL.

You can use the example URL query string shown previously on either the home page or the bad paging path, for example, `/Home/BadPaging/?pagenumber=3&pagesize=50`.

The links in the navigation bar load the examples that we just walked through. The best is the same as the home page and is the default. Top 10 and bad paging should be fairly self-explanatory. Bad will take a long time to load, especially if you use the DB creation script included with the project. You can time it with your browser developer tools.

For the previous versions of SQL Server (prior to 2012), there are paging workarounds using `ROW_NUMBER()` or nested `SELECT` statements, which invert the sort order. If you use another database, such as PostgreSQL, MySQL, or SQLite, then you can easily implement paging with the `LIMIT` clause. SQL Server 2017 now has a concatenation aggregator, so this is not correct.

One of the touted benefits of big O/RMs is the layer of abstraction that they offer. This allows you to change the database that you use. However, in practice, it is rare to change something as core as the database. As you can see from the simple paging example, the syntax varies between databases for anything other than simple standard SQL. To get the best performance, you really need to understand the features and custom syntax of the database that you use.

Static site generators

The database is the logical place to perform any work to filter and sort data. Doing this in the application is a waste. However, for a simple blog that is updated infrequently, a database may be unnecessary in the first place. It may even become the bottleneck and slow the whole blog down. This is a typical problem of blog engines, such as **WordPress**. A better approach may be to use a static site generator.

A static site generator prerenders all of the pages and saves the resulting HTML. This can easily be served by a simple web server and scales well. When a change is made and pages need updating, then the site is regenerated and a new version is deployed. This approach doesn't include dynamic features, such as comments, but third-party services are available to provide these added extras.

A popular static site generator is **Jekyll**, which is written in **Ruby**. **GitHub** provides a free static site-hosting service called **GitHub Pages**, which supports Jekyll, and you can read more about it at `https://pages.github.com/`. Another static site generator (written in **Go**) is **Hugo**, which you can read about at `http://gohugo.io/`. These tools are basically a form of extreme caching. We'll cover caching in the next section and later on in this book.

It's often worth taking a step back to see whether the problem that you're trying to solve is even a problem. You may well improve database performance by removing the database.

Pragmatic solutions with hardware

The best approach to take with a poorly performing application is usually to fix the software. However, it is good to be pragmatic and try to look at the bigger picture. Depending on the size and scale of an application, it can be cheaper to throw better hardware at it, at least as a short term measure.

Hardware is much cheaper than a developer's time and is always getting better. Installing some new hardware can work as a quick fix and buy you some time. You can then address the root causes of any performance issues in software as part of the ongoing development. You can add a little time to the schedule to **refactor** and improve an area of the code base as you work on it.

Once you discover that the cause of your performance problem is latency, you have two possible approaches:

- Reduce the number of latency-sensitive operations
- Reduce the latency itself using faster computers or by moving the computers closer together

With the rise of cloud computing, you may not need to buy or install new hardware. You can just pay more for a higher-performing instance class or you can move things around inside your cloud provider's infrastructure to reduce latency.

A desktop example

To borrow an example from native desktop applications, it is quite common to have poorly performing **Line of Business** (**LoB**) applications on corporate desktops. The desktop will probably be old and underpowered. The networking back to the central database may be slow because the connection might be over a remote link to a regional office.

With a badly written application that is too chatty with the DB, it can be better, performance-wise, to run the application on a server close to (or on the same server as) the DB. Perhaps, the application workspace and DB servers can be in the same **server rack** at the **data center** and connected by a Gigabit (or 10 Gigabit) **Ethernet**.

The user can then use a remote desktop connection or **Citrix** session to interact with the application. This will reduce the latency to the DB and can speed things up, even taking into consideration the lag of the remote UI. This effectively turns the desktop PC into a **thin client**, similar to how old mainframes are used.

For example, you can build a high-performance server with RAID SSDs and lots of RAM for much less than the cost of the developer time to fix a large application. Even badly-written software can perform well if you run the application and DB together on the same machine, especially if you run it on **bare metal** with no virtual machines in the way. This tactic would buy you time to fix things properly.

These remote application and virtualization technologies are usually sold as tools to aid deployment and maintenance. However, the potential performance benefits are also worth considering.

Due to the rise of web applications, **thick client** desktop applications are now less common. Architecture seems to oscillate between computation on the server and doing work on the client, as the relative progress of networking speed and processing power race each other.

Web applications

The same relocation approach does not typically work as well for web applications, but it depends on the architecture used. The good news is that for web applications, you usually control the infrastructure. This is not normally the case for native application hardware.

If you use a **three-tier architecture**, then you can move the application servers closer to the DB server. Whether this is effective or not depends on how chatty the web servers are with the application servers. If they issue too many web API requests, then this won't work well.

A **two-tier architecture** (where the web servers talk directly to the database) is more common for typical web applications. There are solutions using **clustered** databases or read-only mirrors to place the data close to the web servers, but these add complexity and cost.

What can make a significant difference are **proxy servers**. A popular open source proxy server is Varnish and you can also use the NGINX web server as a proxy. Proxy servers cache the output of web servers so that a page doesn't have to be regenerated for each user.

This is useful for shared pages but caching is hard; typically, you should not cache personalized pages. You don't want to accidentally serve someone's authenticated private information to another user.

Proxies such as Varnish can also route different parts of your website to different servers. If you have a small area of your site that performs badly due to DB chatter, then you can host that part from web servers on (or very close to, such as on the same VM host) the DB machines and route requests for it to there. The rest of the site could remain on the existing web server farm.

This isn't a long-term solution, but it allows you to split off a poorly performing part of your program so that it doesn't impact the rest of your system. You're then free to fix it, once it's been decoupled or isolated. You can even split off the data required to a separate DB and synchronize it with a background process.

Also, there are **Content Delivery Networks (CDNs)**, such as **Cloudflare**, **Amazon CloudFront**, and **Azure CDN**, which are good to cache static assets. CDNs cache parts of your site in data centers close to your users, reducing the latency. Cloudflare can even add HTTPS to your site for free, including automatically issuing certificates.

However, you need to be careful when trusting a service that proxies and decrypts your traffic. Cloudflare had an embarrassing security incident referred to as Cloudbleed (a play on the Heartbleed vulnerability in OpenSSL), where they were inserting uninitialized memory into web responses. This included the private information of their customers' users, which was then cached by search engines.

Even if you're just using a CDN for static libraries, then you need to trust that the scripts won't change. You can help ensure this by using **Subresource Integrity (SRI)** to pin a script to a specific hash. However, this isn't currently supported by IE or Edge. See `https://caniuse.com/#feat=subresource-integrity` for the latest browser support information. You will also need a local fallback if the hash validation fails or if the CDN goes down, as Cloudflare has done in the past.

ASP.NET Core allows you to very easily add a fallback to your script libraries for when SRI validation fails or a CDN is unavailable. Take a look at `_Layout.cshtml` in the sample web application for this chapter. You will see that for non-development environments, the jQuery and Bootstrap script tags have `asp-fallback-` and `integrity` attributes. The `integrity` attributes contain a SHA-384 hash (a member of the SHA-2 family) of the scripts in Base64 encoded form.

You can read more about the CDN offerings of Cloudflare (including HTTP/2 server push and WebSockets on the free plan) at `https://www.cloudflare.com/`.

We will cover caching in more detail in `Chapter 9`, *Learning Caching and Message Queuing*, so we won't go into more detail here. Caching is a challenging subject and needs to be understood well so that you can use it effectively.

Oversized images

While we're on the subject of static assets, we should briefly mention image optimization. We'll cover this in much more detail in the next chapter, but it's worth highlighting some common problems here. As you have very little control over network conditions between your infrastructure and the user, low throughput may be a problem in addition to high latency.

Web applications use images heavily, especially on landing pages or home pages, where they might form a fullscreen background. It is regrettably common to see a raw photo from a camera simply dropped straight in. Images from cameras are typically many megabytes in size, far too big for a web page.

You can test whether there are problems on a web page using a tool, such as Google's PageSpeed Insights. Visit `https://developers.google.com/speed/pagespeed/insights/`, enter a URL, and click on **ANALYZE** to view the results. Google uses this information as part of their search engine ranking, so you would do well to take its advice up to a point. Slow sites rank lower in search results.

You can also use the browser developer tools to view the size of images. Press *F12* and look at the **Network** tab after a page load to view how much data was transferred and how long it took. You can often miss these performance issues on a local machine or test server because the image will load quickly. After the first load, it will also be stored in the browser's cache, so make sure you do a full hard reload and empty or disable the cache. In Chrome (when the dev tools are open), you can right-click or long-click on the reload button for these extra options. It's also a good idea to use the built-in throttling tools to see how a user will experience the page loading.

The most basic image optimization problems typically fall into two categories:

- Images that are overly large for the display area they are displayed in
- Images that use the wrong compression format for the subject matter

Image resolution

The most common issue is that an image has too high a resolution for the area that displays it. This forces the browser to resize the image to fit the screen or area. If the size of the file is unnecessarily large, then it will take longer to be transferred over an internet connection. The browser will then throw away most of the information. You should resize the image ahead of time before adding it to the site.

There are many image manipulation tools available to resize pictures. If you run Windows, then **Paint.NET** (https://www.getpaint.net/) is an excellent free piece of software. This is much better than the Paint program that comes with Windows (although, this will work if you have no other option).

For other platforms, GIMP (https://www.gimp.org/) is very good. If you prefer using the command line, then you may like ImageMagick (http://imagemagick.org/script/index.php), which can perform lots of image manipulation tasks programmatically or in batches. Also, there are cloud-hosted image management services, such as **Cloudinary** (http://cloudinary.com/).

You should shrink images to the actual size so that they will be displayed on the user's screen. There can be complications when dealing with responsive images, which scale with the size of the user's screen or browser window. Also, keep in mind **high DPI** or Retina displays, which may have more than one physical pixel to every logical pixel. Your images may have to be bigger to not look blurry, but the upper bound is still likely to be lower than the raw size. It is rare to need an image at more than twice the size of the displayed resolution. We will discuss responsive images in more detail later in this book, but it is worth keeping them in mind.

The following image displays the resizing dialog from Paint.NET:

When resizing an image, it is usually important to keep the **aspect ratio** of the image the same. This means changing the horizontal and vertical sizes in proportion to each other.

For example, reducing the **Height** from **600** px to **300** px and reducing the **Width** from **800** px to **400** px (meaning both dimensions are reduced by 50%) keeps the image looking the same, only smaller. Most image-manipulation software will assist with this process. Keeping the aspect ratio the same will avoid images looking stretched. If images need to fit a different shape, then they should be cropped instead.

Image format

The next most common problem is using images in the wrong file format for the content. You should never use raw uncompressed images, such as **bitmap** (**BMP**), on the web.

For natural images such as photos, use the JPEG file format. JPEG is a lossy codec, which means that some information is lost when using it. It is very good for pictures with a lot of gradients in them, such as images of natural scenes or people. JPEG looks poor if there is any text in the image because there will be **compression artifacts** around the edges of the letters. Most mid and low-end cameras natively save images as JPEG, so you do not lose anything by staying with it. However, you should resize the images to make them smaller, as mentioned previously.

For artificial images such as diagrams or icons, use **PNG**. PNG is a lossless codec, which means that no information is discarded. This works best for images with large blocks of solid color, such as diagrams drawn in painting software or screenshots. PNG also supports transparency, so you can have images that don't appear rectangular, or are translucent. You can also have animated PNGs, which are of superior quality than that of **GIFs**, but we won't go into the details of them in this chapter.

You can alter the format of images using the same tools that you use to resize them, as mentioned previously, by simply changing the file format when saving the image. As always, you should test for what works best in your specific use case. You can perform experiments by saving the same image in different formats (and different resolutions), and then observing the sizes of the files on disk.

The following image displays the available image options in Paint.NET. Additional formats are available, and we will go into more detail in `Chapter 6`, *Addressing Network Performance*:

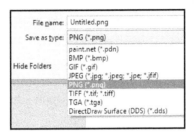

Even when you only choose between **JPEG** and **PNG**, you can still make a significant difference. The following screenshot displays the sizes of files of the same image in two resolutions and two formats:

The following test image is the one used in the experiment. Due to the hard edges, it looks best as a PNG, but the gradient background makes it more difficult to compress:

 The test images used here are available for download with this book, so you can try the experiment for yourself.

In a web context, this particular image may be best served with a transparent background using CSS for the gradient. However, simple shapes such as these can better be represented as **Scalable Vector Graphics (SVG)** or with HTML5 canvas.

Summary

In this chapter, you learned about some common performance problems and how to fix them. We covered asynchronous operations, *select N+1* problems, pragmatic hardware choices, and overly large images.

In the next chapter, we will expand on image optimization and extend this to other forms of compression for different types of resources. We'll look at the process of bundling and minification of static assets in ASP.NET Core using open source tools.

Additionally, we will introduce networking topics such as TCP/IP, HTTP, WebSockets, and encryption. We'll also cover caching, including another look at CDNs.

6
Addressing Network Performance

This chapter builds on a subset of the problems that were discussed in the previous chapter but in more detail. It deals with latency, or lag, which originates at the networking level between the user and the application. This is mostly applicable to web applications where the user interacts with the application via a web browser. You will learn how to optimize your application to cater for bandwidth and latency that is unknown and outside of your control. You'll compress your payloads to be as small as possible, and then you will deliver them to the user as quickly as possible. You will learn about the tools and techniques that can be used to achieve a fast and responsive application. You'll also see the trade-offs involved and be able to calculate whether these methods should be applied to your software.

The topics that we will cover in this chapter include the following:

- TCP/IP
- HTTP and HTTP/2
- HTTPS (TLS/SSL)
- WebSockets and push notifications
- Compression
- Bundling and minification
- Caching and CDNs

This chapter deals with how to speed up the experience for a user of your application. The skills in this chapter are just as applicable to a static site or client-side web app as they are to a dynamic web application.

These topics apply to any web application framework. However, we will focus on how they are implemented with ASP.NET, and in particular with ASP.NET Core. We will also see how Core differs from the full version of ASP.NET in some regards.

Internet protocols

It's important to know about how your HTML and other assets are delivered from the web server to your user's browser. Much of this is abstracted away and transparent to web development, but it's a good idea to have at least a basic understanding in order to achieve high performance.

TCP/IP

Transmission Control Protocol / Internet Protocol (TCP/IP) is the name for a pair of communication protocols that underpin the internet. **IP** is the lower-level protocol of the two, and this deals with routing *packets* to their correct destinations. IP can run on top of many different lower-level protocols (such as Ethernet), and it is where IP addresses come from.

TCP is a layer above IP, and it is concerned with the reliable delivery of packets and *flow control*. TCP is where ports come from, such as port 80 for HTTP, and port 443 for HTTPS. There is also the **User Datagram Protocol (UDP)**, which can be used instead of TCP, but it provides fewer features.

HTTP runs on top of TCP, and it is usually what you will deal with in a web application. You may occasionally need to directly use **Simple Mail Transfer Protocol (SMTP)** to send emails, the **Domain Name System (DNS)** to resolve hostnames to IP addresses, or **File Transfer Protocol (FTP)** to upload and download files.

The basic unencrypted versions of these protocols run directly on TCP, but the secure encrypted versions (HTTPS, SMTPS, and FTPS) have a layer in between. This layer is called **Transport Layer Security (TLS)**, and this is the modern successor to the **Secure Socket Layer (SSL)**. SSL is insecure and deprecated, and it should no longer be used. However, the term SSL is still commonly and confusingly used to describe TLS. All browsers require the use of TLS encryption to support HTTP/2.

You may not often think about the lower-level protocols when you build web applications. Indeed, you may not need to consider even HTTP/HTTPS that much. However, the protocol stack below your application can have significant performance implications.

The following diagram shows how the protocols are typically stacked:

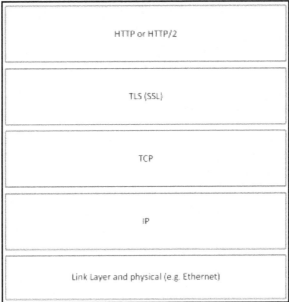

Slow-start

TCP implements an algorithm called *slow-start* for congestion-control purposes. This means that the connection from a browser to a web server is initially slow and ramps up over time to discover the available bandwidth. You can alter the settings for this so that the ramp up is more aggressive and connections get quicker more rapidly. If you increase the initial *congestion window*, then the performance can improve, especially on connections with good bandwidth but high latency, such as mobile **4G** or servers on other continents.

As usual, you should test for your use case perhaps using Wireshark, as described previously in Chapter 4, *Measuring Performance Bottlenecks*. There are downsides to altering this window, and it should be considered carefully. Although this may speed up websites, it can cause buffers in the networking equipment to fill, which can generate latency problems for VoIP applications and games if no **Quality of Service (QoS)** is in use end-to-end.

You can change this value on Windows Server 2008 R2 with a hotfix (KB2472264) and higher. You can also easily adjust this on Linux, and of course, ASP.NET Core enables you to run your .NET web app on Linux (and macOS / OS X) in addition to Windows.

We won't provide detailed instructions here because this should be a cautiously considered decision, and you shouldn't apply advice blindly. You can easily find instructions online for the operating system that you use on your web server.

TCP slow-start is just one example of why you can't ignore the lower levels of internet technology, on the shoulders of which web applications stand. Let's move up the stack a little to the application layer.

HTTP

As a web application developer who wants to deliver high performance, it's important to understand **Hypertext Transfer Protocol** (**HTTP**). You should know what version of HTTP you use, how it works, and how this affects things, such as **request pipelining** and encryption.

HTTP/1.1 is the version that you will probably be most familiar with today, because it has been in use for some time. HTTP/2 is becoming more popular, and it changes the best way to do many things.

Headers

HTTP uses headers to provide metadata about a request along with the main payload in the body of the message, much like emails do. You won't see these headers when you view the source, but you can observe them using the browser developer tools. You can use headers for many things, such as cache control and authentication. Cookies are also sent and received as headers.

Browsers will only open a limited number of HTTP/1.1 connections at one time to a single host. If you require a lot of requests to retrieve all the assets for a page, then they are queued, which increases the total time taken to fully load it. When combined with the TCP slow-start mentioned previously, this effect can be amplified, degrading the performance. This is less of a problem with HTTP/2, which we will cover shortly. You can reduce the impact of this problem by allowing the browser to reuse connections. You can do this by ensuring that your web server doesn't send a `Connection: close` header with HTTP responses.

HTTP methods

There are multiple methods (or verbs) that HTTP uses. The most common are GET and POST, but there are many more. Typically, we use GET requests to retrieve data from a server, and we use POST to submit data and make changes. GET should not be used to alter data.

Other useful verbs are HEAD and OPTIONS. HEAD can check the headers for a GET request without the overhead of downloading the body. This is useful to check caching headers to see whether the resource has changed. OPTIONS is commonly used for **Cross Origin Resource Sharing** (**CORS**) to perform a preflight check to validate a domain.

Other often used verbs are PUT, DELETE, and PATCH. We mainly use these for **Representational State Transfer** (**REST**) APIs because they can mimic operations on resources or files. However, not all software (such as some proxy servers) understands them, so sometimes, we emulate them using POST. You may even have problems with OPTIONS being blocked by proxies and web servers.

Status codes

HTTP uses numeric response codes to indicate a status. You are probably familiar with 200 (OK) and 404 (Not Found), but there are many others. For example, 451 indicates that the content has been blocked by a government-mandated censorship filter.

 The 451 status code is in reference to the book *Fahrenheit 451* (whose title is the purported temperature at which paper burns). You can read the official document (RFC 7725) at http://tools.ietf.org/html/rfc7725. If this code is not used, then it can be tricky to discover if and why a site is unavailable. For example, you can find out whether the UK government is blocking your site at https://www.blocked.org.uk/, but this is just a volunteer effort run by the Open Rights Group, the British version of the **Electronic Frontier Foundation** (**EFF**).

We commonly use 3xx codes for redirection (perhaps to HTTPS). There are various forms of redirection with different performance characteristics (and other effects). You can use a 302 to temporarily redirect a page, but then the browser has to request the original page every time to see whether the redirect has ended. It also has bad implications for **Search Engine Optimization** (**SEO**), but we won't discuss these here.

A better approach is to use a 301 to indicate a permanent redirect. However, you need to be careful, as this can't be undone and clients won't look at the original URL again. If you use redirects to upgrade users from HTTP to HTTPS, then you should also consider using **HTTP Strict Transport Security (HSTS)** headers. Again, do this carefully.

Encryption

HTTP encryption is very important. It not only secures the data in transit to prevent eavesdropping, but it also provides authentication. This ensures that users actually connect to the site that they think they are connecting to, and that the page wasn't tampered with. Otherwise, unscrupulous internet connection providers can inject or replace adverts on your site, or they can block internet access until you have opted out of a parental filter. Or there can be worse things, such as stealing your user's data, which you are usually required by law to protect.

There is really no good reason today to not use encryption everywhere. The overheads are tiny, although we will still consider them and show you how to avoid potential issues. Arguments against using HTTPS are usually hangovers from a long time ago when computation was expensive.

Modern computing hardware is very capable and often has special acceleration for common encryption tasks. There are many studies that show that the processing overheads of encryption are negligible. However, there can be a small delay in initially setting up a secure connection for the first time. In order to understand this, it is useful to illustrate a simple model of how TLS works.

There are two parts to a secure communication: the initial key exchange and the ongoing encryption of the channel. Session ciphers, such as the **Advanced Encryption Standard (AES)**, can be very quick, and they can operate at close to line speed. However, these ciphers are *symmetrical* and both parties need to know the key. This key needs to be distributed securely so that only the two communicating parties possess it. This is called *key exchange*, and it uses asymmetric encryption. This usually also requires a third-party to vouch for the server, so we have a system of certificates. This initial setup is the slow part, although we will show you an alternative for devices that lack the AES acceleration later.

Key exchange

As mentioned previously, key exchange is the process of securely sharing an encryption key between two parties without it being intercepted. There are various methods of doing this, which mostly rely on asymmetric encryption. Unlike symmetric encryption (that we exchange this key for), this can only be performed in one direction with a single key. In other words, the key that is used to encrypt cannot be used to decrypt, and a different key is required. This is not the case for the majority of the data once we have shared a key. The reason that we do this is that symmetric encryption is faster than asymmetric encryption. Therefore, asymmetric encryption is not used for everything and is only needed to encrypt another key.

In addition to exchanging a key, the browser (or other HTTPS client) should check the certificate to ensure that the server belongs to the domain that it claims to. Some programmatic clients fail to do this by default, so this is worth checking out. You can also implement certificate pinning (even in the browser with **HTTP Public Key Pinning**) to improve security, but this is beyond the scope of this book.

We will illustrate two variations of key exchange (by analogy in simplified forms) to show you how the process works. You can look up the technical details if you wish.

RSA is traditionally the most common key-exchange mechanism that is used for TLS. Until recently, we used it on most HTTPS connections.

RSA stands for **Rivest-Shamir-Adleman** after the names of its creators, and it is probably the most popular form of public key cryptography. The British snooping agency, **Government Communications Headquarters (GCHQ)**, supposedly conceived public key cryptography at around the same time, but as it was only made public in 1997, it's impossible to prove this. The invention credit goes to Whitfield Diffie and Martin Hellman, who recently picked up a Turing Award for it. We'll talk more about their work shortly.

 The Turing Award is the Nobel Prize of computing. It's named after Alan Turing, the legendary computing pioneer who helped the allies win WWII while working for the nascent GCHQ, but who was later betrayed by the British government.

RSA uses large prime numbers to generate a public and private key pair. The public key can be used to encrypt information that can only be decrypted with the private key. In addition to this, the private key can be used to sign information (usually a **hash** of it), which can be verified with the public key. RSA is often used to sign TLS certificates even if another algorithm is used as the key exchange mechanism (this is negotiated during the initial TLS handshake).

This hashing and signing of certificates is where you may have heard of **SHA-1** certificates being deprecated by browsers. SHA-1 is no longer considered secure for hashing and, like **MD5** before it, should not be used. Certificate chains must now use at least an **SHA-2** hashing algorithm (such as **SHA-256**) to sign.

An analogy to help explain how RSA works is to think of sending a lock instead of sending a key. You could post an open padlock to someone, retaining the key to it. They can then use your lock to secure a box containing the combination code to a briefcase, and send it back to you. Now, only you can open the box to get the code. Even the person sending you the code can't open the box once they've locked it. Once you both know the code, then you can easily exchange documents using the case.

In reality, this is more complicated. You can't be sure that someone didn't intercept your lock and then use their own lock to get the key and copy it before sending it on to you. Typically, we solve this with **Public Key Infrastructure** (**PKI**). A trusted third party will sign your certificate and verify that it is indeed your public key and that you own the lock. Browsers typically display a warning if a **Certificate Authority** (**CA**) does not countersign the certificate in this way.

Diffie-Hellman (**D-H**) key exchange is another method of gaining a shared key. Invented shortly before RSA, it has only recently become popular on the web. This is partly due to the reduced computational cost of the **elliptic curve** variant. However, another reason is that the ephemeral versions provide a quality called **Perfect Forward Secrecy** (**PFS**). Unlike RSA, the session key for the symmetric encryption never needs to be transmitted. Both parties can calculate the shared key without it needing to be sent on the wire (even in an encrypted state) or permanently stored. This means that an eavesdropped encrypted exchange cannot be decrypted in the future if the keys were recovered. With the RSA key exchange, you can recover a recorded communication in plain text if you obtain the private keys later. PFS is a useful countermeasure against mass surveillance, where all communication is caught in a dragnet and permanently stored.

D-H is better explained with a color mixing analogy, where paints represent numbers. The two parties choose a shared color, and each party chooses a secret color of their own. Both mix the shared color with their secret color and send the result to the other. Each party then mixes the color that they received with their secret color again. Both parties now have the same color without ever having to send this color anywhere where it could be observed.

As this is not a book about security, we won't go into any more detail on encryption algorithms. If you are interested, there is a huge amount of information available that we can't cover here. Encryption is a large subject, but security is an even broader concern.

The point of briefly explaining how TLS key exchange works for various methods is to show that it is complex. Many messages need to be sent back and forth to establish a secure connection, and no matter how fast the connection is, latency slows down every message. All this occurs in the TLS handshake, where the client (usually a web browser) and server negotiate common capabilities and agree on what ciphers they should use. There is also the **Server Name Indication** (**SNI**) to consider, which is similar to the HTTP host header in that it allows multiple sites to use the same IP address. Some older clients don't support SNI.

We can observe the TLS handshake using Wireshark. We won't go into a huge amount of detail, but you can see that at least four messages are exchanged between the client and server. These are *client hello*, *server hello* (including the certificate and server key exchange), *client key exchange*, and *cipher agreement*. The browser may send more messages if we do not optimally configure things, such as requesting an intermediate certificate. It (that is, the browser) may also check a revocation list to see whether the certificate was revoked.

The following screenshot shows a TLS handshake captured with Wireshark:

```
TLSv1     223 Client Hello
TCP      1502 [TCP segment of a reassembled PDU]
TCP      1502 [TCP segment of a reassembled PDU]
TCP        54 2697 → 443 [ACK] Seq=170 Ack=2897 Win=66048 Len=0
TLSv1    1002 Server Hello, Certificate, Server Key Exchange, Server Hello Done
TLSv1     220 Client Key Exchange, Change Cipher Spec, Encrypted Handshake Message
TLSv1     113 Change Cipher Spec, Encrypted Handshake Message
TLSv1     283 Application Data
```

All these network operations happen quickly. However, if the connection has a high latency, then these extra messages can have an amplified effect on performance. The computational delays are typically much smaller than the network delays, so we can discount these, unless you use very old hardware. Fortunately, there are some simple things you can do that will help speed things up and let you enjoy high performance while still being secure.

Delay diagnostics

There are various mechanisms that are built into TLS that you can use to speed it up. However, there are also things that will slow it down if you don't do them correctly. Some great free online tools to assess your TLS configuration are available from Qualys SSL Labs at `https://www.ssllabs.com/`. The server test at `https://www.ssllabs.com/ssltest/` is very useful. You enter a URL, and they give you a grade along with lots of other information.

For example, if we analyze the `https://www.packtpub.com/` site, we can see that on the date of the test it got a **B** grade. This is due to its support for weak Diffie-Hellman parameters and the obsolete and insecure **RC4** cipher. However, it is not always as simple as removing old ciphers. You can have a very secure site, but you might exclude some of your customers, who use older clients that don't support the latest standards. This will, of course, vary depending on the nature of your client base, and you should measure your traffic and consider your options carefully.

The following screenshot shows a part of the report from SSL Labs for `https://www.packtpub.com/`.

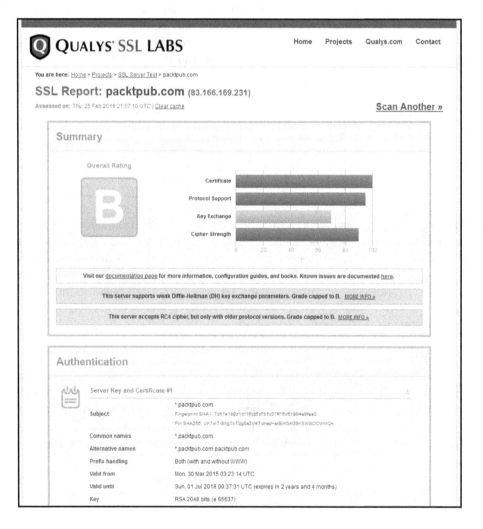

If we have a look at a site with a better configuration (`https://emoncms.org/`), we can see that it gets an **A** grade. You can get an A+ grade by using HSTS headers. Additionally, these headers avoid the overhead of a redirect. You may also be able to get your site embedded in a preloaded list shipped with browsers if you submit the domains to the vendors.

The following screenshot shows some of the report from SSL Labs for `https://emoncms.org/`:

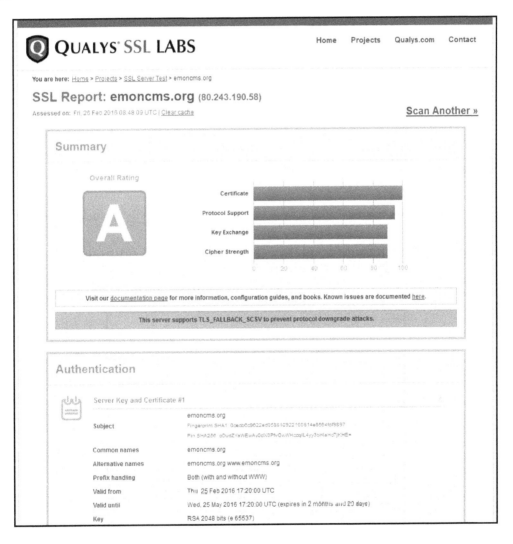

The options chosen by modern browsers would typically be an **Elliptic Curve Diffie-Hellman Ephemeral key exchange** (**ECDHE**) with an RSA SHA-256 signature and AES session cipher. The ephemeral keys provide PFS because they are only held in memory for the session. You can see what connection has been negotiated by looking in your browser.

In Firefox, you can do this by clicking on the lock icon in the URL bar and then clicking on the **More Information** button, as shown in the following image:

In the **Technical Details** section, you will see the cipher suite used. The following image from Firefox shows ECDHE key exchange and RSA certificate signing:

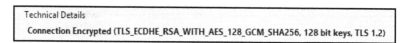

You can also view the certificate details by clicking on the **View Certificate** button. The domain is usually included as the **Common Name** (**CN**) in the **Subject** field. Alternative domains can also be included under the **Certificate Subject Alt Name** extension:

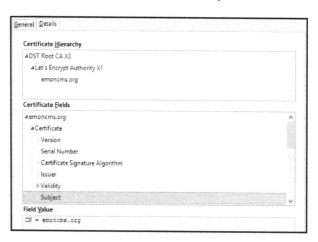

In Chrome, you can look at the TLS connection information in the **Security** tab of the developer tools. For example, the following screenshot displays the security details for `https://huxley.unop.uk/`:

The following screenshot displays the same window for `https://emoncms.org/`:

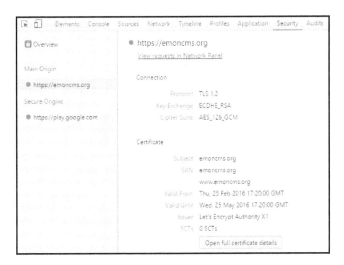

You may need to refresh the page to see TLS information if the site was already loaded when you opened the developer tools. You can access the same tab by clicking on the padlock in the Chrome URL bar and then clicking on the **Details** link.

You can view the certificate (in the native operating system certificate store) by clicking on the **Open full certificate details** button. A link with the same function exists on the equivalent screen of Chrome for Android, although the certificate information is reduced.

Performance tweaks

We already discussed the most important performance tweak for TLS because it is not about TLS. You should ensure that your HTTP connections are reusable, because if this is not the case, then you will incur the added penalty of the TLS negotiation along with the TCP overhead. Caching is also very important, and we will talk more about this later.

 TLS and HTTP both support compression, but these have security implications. Therefore, consider them carefully. They can leak information, and a determined adversary can use an analysis of them to recover encrypted data. TLS compression is deprecated, and it will be removed in TLS 1.3. Therefore, do not use it. We will discuss HTTP compression later on in this chapter.

With regards to specific advice for TLS, there are a few things that you can do to improve performance. The main technique is to ensure that you use **session resumption**. This is different from reusing HTTP connections, and this means that clients can reuse an existing TLS connection without having to go through the whole key exchange.

 You can implement sessions with IDs on the server or with encrypted tickets (in a similar manner to ASP.NET cookies that are encrypted with the machine key). There was a bug in the Microsoft client implementation around ticket encryption key rotation, but the **KB3109853** patch fixed it. Make sure that you install this update, especially if you see exceptions thrown when connecting to secure endpoints from your .NET code.

It is important to not overdo things and bigger is not always better, especially when it comes to key size. It is a trade-off between performance and security, and this will depend on your specific situation. In general, a good balance is not using 256 bit AES keys when 128 bit will do.

A 2048 bit RSA key is big enough; lower is insecure and larger is too slow. You can use the **Elliptic Curve Digital Signature Algorithm** (**ECDSA**) to sign instead of RSA, as it is much quicker. However, support is limited, so you would need to deploy RSA in parallel.

If you use ECDSA, then a 256-bit key is sufficient. For ECDHE, 256 bit is also fine, and for the slower version without elliptic curves (DHE), 2048 bit is sufficient. If you use ECDSA, then you will see this listed instead of the RSA signing in the connection details. For example, when visiting `https://huxley.unop.uk/`, the details in the following screenshots are displayed in Firefox. This difference is also displayed in the previous Chrome screenshots:

Technical Details

Connection Encrypted (TLS_ECDHE_ECDSA_WITH_AES_128_GCM_SHA256, 128 bit keys, TLS 1.2)

Additionally, it is important to include the full certificate chain with your certificate. If you fail to include all the intermediate certificates, then the browser will need to download them until it finds one in its trusted root store. You can also use a technique called **Online Certificate Status Protocol** (**OCSP**) stapling, by embedding revocation data, so browsers don't need to check a certificate revocation list.

Both of these certificate techniques may increase the size of payloads, which can be an issue if bandwidth is a concern. However, they will reduce the number of messages, which will increase performance if latency is the main problem, which is usually the case. Keeping key sizes small also helps a little with bandwidth. It is hard to recommend one generic approach. Therefore, as always, test for your unique situation.

There is also an alternative stream cipher called **ChaCha/Poly**, which is especially useful for mobile devices. This uses the **ChaCha20** stream cipher and the **Poly1305 Message Authentication Code** (**MAC**) algorithm to create a secure alternative to RC4. AES is a block cipher and is fast with hardware support, but many mobile devices and some older computers don't have this acceleration. ChaCha/Poly is faster when just using software. Therefore, this is better for the battery life. This is supported in Chrome, including Chrome for Android, and in Firefox. You can see the latest browser support at `https://caniuse.com/#feat=chacha20-poly1305`.

As all algorithms are different, you can't directly compare key sizes as a measure of how secure they are. For example, a 256-bit ECDHE key is equivalent to a 3072-bit RSA key. AES is very secure with relatively small keys, but you cannot use it for key exchange. ChaCha/Poly is more comparable to the security of AES 256 than AES 128.

In the following screenshot of Chrome on Android, you can see that when connecting to `https://huxley.unop.uk/`, Chrome uses **CHACHA20_POLY1305** as the stream cipher, ECDHE for the key exchange, and ECDSA for the signature:

 The new version of TLS (1.3) is currently a draft, but it is still supported in many places. It will only allow **Authenticated Encryption with Additional Data (AEAD)** ciphers. AES-GCM and ChaCha/Poly are the only two ciphers that currently meet these criteria. It will also remove some other obsolete features, such as TLS compression. The good news is that TLS 1.3 not only improves security but also delivers higher performance. It is already supported by the stable versions of Firefox and Chrome. You can check support at `https://caniuse.com/#feat=tls1-3`.

It may sometimes sound like using TLS is not always worth it, but it is an excellent idea to use HTTPS on your entire site, including any third-party resources that you load in. By doing this, you will be able to take advantage of the performance-enhancing features of HTTP/2, which include techniques that mean that it is no longer crucial to serve resources (such as JavaScript libraries) from multiple domains. You can securely host everything yourself and avoid the DNS, TCP, and TLS overhead of additional requests.

All of this can be free, because *Let's Encrypt* and *Cloudflare* provide certificates at zero cost. *Cloudflare* also has a TLS 1.3 beta but there can be security implications when using them. *Let's Encrypt* allows you to generate certificates for use on your own servers and from 2018, it will offer wildcard certificates too. Let's look at HTTP/2 in detail now.

HTTP/2

As the name suggests, HTTP/2 is the new version of HTTP. It contains some significant performance improvements for the modern web. It was predated by **SPDY**, which has since been deprecated in favor of HTTP/2.

As mentioned previously, the first step toward using HTTP/2 is to use HTTPS on your entire site. Although not technically required, most clients (all the major browsers) mandate the use of TLS to enable HTTP/2. This is mainly due to the **Application-Layer Protocol Negotiation** (**ALPN**) that TLS provides, which allows easy support for HTTP/2. It also stops proxy servers from messing up the data, which many ISPs use to reduce their costs and record what their customers do online.

HTTP/2 improves performance in a number of ways. It uses compression, even for the headers, and multiplexing, which allows multiple requests to share the same connection. It also allows the server to push resources that it knows the client will need before the client has realized it needs them. Although, this requires some configuration to set the correct headers and it can waste bandwidth if it is overused.

Multiplexing has implications for bundling and image concatenation (**sprites**), which we will talk about in the *Compression* section later on in this chapter. This also means that you don't need to split assets over multiple domains (**shards**), where the extra overheads may even slow things down. However, you may still wish to use a cookie-free subdomain to serve static assets without cookies, even though the new header compression means that the bandwidth savings will be smaller. If you use a naked domain (without a www), then you may need a new domain name for cookie-less use.

You can identify what version of HTTP is used to deliver your assets using the browser developer tools. In Firefox, you can see this on the details panel of the **Network** tab. You will see the version listed as HTTP/1.1 when the old protocol is in use.

The following screenshot shows that `https://www.packtpub.com/` uses **HTTP/1.1**:

In Chrome, you can right-click on the column headers in the network inspector and add a **Protocol** column. You can also see more detailed network information by entering `chrome://net-internals` into the address bar. This displays things, such as sessions for HTTP/2 and **Quick UDP Internet Connections** (**QUIC**), an experimental multiplexed stream transport.

The following screenshot shows that `https://emoncms.org/` also uses **HTTP/1.1**, even though TLS is configured differently. The encrypted transport layer is transparent to HTTP:

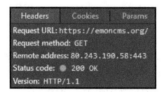

When HTTP/2 is used, you will see the version listed as **HTTP/2.0**. The following screenshot displays this for `https://huxley.unop.uk/`, and it also displays CORS, caching, and content compression headers:

WebSockets

The WebSocket protocol (also colloquially referred to as WebSockets) is a different protocol from HTTP. However, HTTP initiates it and it uses the same ports so we'll discuss it briefly here. This HTML5 feature is useful for **push notifications** and **Real Time Communication** (**RTC**) applications. WebSockets use the `ws://` and `wss://` protocol prefixes instead of `http://` and `https://`. Once established by an existing HTTP connection, the protocol is full-duplex and binary, in contrast to HTTP/1.

Before WebSockets, if your web server wanted to notify a client of a change, then you would have to use a technique such as long polling.

This is where a web request is held open by the server in case it wants to send something. When the request gets a response or it times out, it is reestablished. Needless to say, polling is never very efficient.

Push notifications can improve performance from a user's point of view because they receive updates as soon as they occur. Users don't need to refresh anything or keep checking. You can immediately respond to the user when a long running process starts, run it asynchronously, and notify them immediately upon its completion.

Socket.IO is a popular WebSocket library for Node.js. To see it in action, you can look in the browser developer tools on a site that uses it. For example, if you open the dev tools and go to `https://www.opentraintimes.com/maps/signalling/staines`, you will see the connection being upgraded from HTTPS to WSS (or from HTTP to WS if you use the insecure version).

WebSockets predate HTTP/2, but they are still relevant despite the new server push technology. These two features appear similar, but they serve different purposes. WebSockets are for real-time and two-way data transfers, and server push is currently just to preload.

In addition to HTTP/2 server push preloading, there is a new browser feature that is currently supported in Android, Chrome, and Opera, which allows you to declare resource preloading in markup by using `rel="preload"` on a `link` tag. You can read the spec at `https://w3c.github.io/preload/` and check the current state of browser support at `http://caniuse.com/#feat=link-rel-preload`.

In Chrome, the protocol switch will look something like the following screenshot. You can't see the contents of a WebSocket connection, so you won't be able to view the data being transferred from within the dev tools:

```
▼ General
    Request URL: wss://data.opentraintimes.com/socket.io/?EIO=3&transport=websocket
    Request Method: GET
    Status Code: ● 101 Switching Protocols
▼ Response Headers    view source
    Connection: upgrade
    Date: Sat, 27 Feb 2016 16:19:09 GMT
    Sec-WebSocket-Accept: dfOqW7FtWTX9yf1qYhgJ1z2VJ8g=
    Sec-WebSocket-Extensions: permessage-deflate
    Server: nginx/1.8.1
    Upgrade: websocket
▼ Request Headers    view source
    Accept-Encoding: gzip, deflate, sdch
    Accept-Language: en-US,en;q=0.8,en-GB;q=0.6
    Cache-Control: no-cache
    Connection: Upgrade
```

There is a Microsoft library for ASP.NET, which is called SignalR. This library allows you to perform push notifications with WebSockets. It also falls back to long polling if the client or server does not support them. You will need a fairly recent version of Windows Server (2012 or later) and IIS (8.0 and above) to use WebSockets.

Unfortunately, the latest stable version (SignalR 2) does not officially support .NET Core 2.0. A new version is being written and will ship after ASP.NET Core 2.0.

You may also wish to look at `StackExchange.NetGain` as a WebSocket server.

Compression

Data compression is a broad topic, and we can't hope to cover it all. Here, we will learn about lossless compression and how to use it in HTTP. We will also cover lossy image compression of pictures later in the chapter. Compression is important because if we can make files smaller, we can shorten the time that it takes to transfer them over a network.

Lossless compression algorithms

You may have noticed HTTP headers from some of the previous screenshots were related to encoding. The most common compression algorithms for HTTP are GZIP and **DEFLATE**, which are very similar. These are both related to the algorithm used in ZIP files. If you do not already use HTTP compression, then this is a quick win, and it will improve the performance of your site if you enable it.

There are many other more advanced compression algorithms, such as **xz**, which is similar to the **7-Zip (7z)** format and uses the **Lempel-Ziv-Markov chain algorithm (LZMA/LZMA2)**. However, there are currently only two additional algorithms in common use in major browsers. These are **Brotli** and **Shared Dictionary Compression for HTTP (SDCH)**. Both are from Google, but only Chrome supports SDCH, and it requires a large dictionary.

Brotli is more interesting as most modern browsers now support it. Many browsers require the use of HTTPS to support Brotli (yet another good reason to use TLS), and the encoding token used in the headers is `br`. Brotli has significant performance improvements, especially for mobile devices on slow connections. You can see the latest support data at `https://caniuse.com/#search=brotli`.

If you access a site over HTTP, you will see the following request headers in the Chrome dev tools network inspector, in the details of a request:

```
Accept-Encoding: gzip, deflate
```

However, if you use HTTPS then you will see this instead:

```
Accept-Encoding: gzip, deflate, br
```

The server can then respond with Brotli-encoded content using this response header:

```
Content-Encoding: br
```

For example, if you visit https://www.bayden.com/test/brotliimg.aspx in a supported browser, then Brotli will deliver the content (an image of a star). Here is a subset (for clarity and brevity) of the request headers from Chrome:

```
GET /test/brotliimg.aspx HTTP/1.1
Host: www.bayden.com
Connection: keep-alive
Accept-Encoding: gzip, deflate, sdch, br
```

This is a subset of the corresponding response headers:

```
HTTP/1.1 200 OK
Content-Type: image/png
Content-Encoding: br
Server: Microsoft-IIS/7.5
X-AspNet-Version: 4.0.30319
YourAcceptEncoding: gzip, deflate, sdch, br
```

Fiddler (the awesome HTTP debugging proxy by Eric Lawrence that we mentioned previously) also supports Brotli with a simple add-on (drop https://bayden.com/dl/ Brotli.exe into fiddler2\tools and restart it). You can use this to easily test the impact on your site without deploying anything to your web servers.

 You can try out Brotli compression in .NET with the System.IO.Compression.Brotli package. You could use this in combination with the ASP.NET Core response compression middleware (https://docs.microsoft.com/en-us/aspnet/core/performance/ response-compression?tabs=aspnetcore2x). Hopefully Brotli will be included in future versions of the core .NET Framework and then the response compression middleware can support it by default.

Bundling and minification

When developing a web application, you will usually end up with lots of static files that need to be delivered to the browser. These files include style sheets, scripts, and images. It's easier to work on many small files than one large one (particularly when part of a team), but this is not always the best approach for performance.

Bundling and minification are two techniques that speed up the delivery of these static assets. They are usually used for text files, such as JavaScript and CSS content. However, you can also shrink images and we will cover this later.

Bundling

Bundling is the technique of combining or concatenating multiple files together so that they can be delivered as one. This is a good idea when using HTTP/1.1 because the number of concurrent connections is limited. However, bundling is less necessary with HTTP/2, and in fact, it can reduce performance. The new multiplexing in HTTP/2 means that there is no longer a large penalty when you request many files instead of one, which contain all of the same content. You can take advantage of this by only delivering what is needed for a page rather than the entire client side code base for every page. Even if you selectively bundle per page, this could be inefficient.

For example, you may include a validation library for use with forms. However, because this is bundled, it will be sent to all pages, including the ones with no forms to validate. If you have a separate bundle for validated pages, then there may be duplication in the common core code, which is also sent. By keeping things separated, the client can cache them individually and reuse the components. This also means that if you change something, you only need to invalidate the cache of this one part. The client can keep using the other unmodified parts and not have to download them again.

As always, you should measure for your particular use case. You may find that bundling still reduces the total file size. The overheads for HTTP/2 are much lower but still not zero, and compression can work better on larger files. However, keep in mind the implications for caching and reusability.

Minification

Minification is the process of reducing the file size of a textual static asset. We do this by various means, including stripping out comments, removing whitespace, and shortening variable names. It can also be useful to *obfuscate* code to make it harder to reverse engineer.

Minification is still useful when you use HTTP/2, but you should be careful when testing to compare pre-minified and post-minified file sizes, after the lossless compression has also been applied.

As discussed previously, you should use HTTP content compression with at least the GZIP or DEFLATE algorithms, and preferably with Brotli. These algorithms are pretty efficient at shrinking your files. You may find that when compressed, your minified file is not much smaller than the compressed raw source file.

Changes in ASP.NET Core

In the full .NET Framework and previous versions of MVC, there was an integrated bundling and minification system built in to the platform, which worked dynamically at runtime. This changed for ASP.NET Core, and there are new tools to perform this work.

The default option now is the `BuildBundlerMinifier` NuGet package. However, you can use other tools, including the task runners, Gulp and Grunt, if you prefer to. There are also package managers such as **Bower** and **npm**, which are similar to NuGet but are for frontend libraries. For example, NuGet no longer delivers jQuery and Twitter Bootstrap, and they use Bower instead by default.

Most of these tools are written in JavaScript, and they run on Node.js. The package manager for Node.js is npm. These tools are popular in other open source web frameworks, and they are well established. They're not new to the scene, only new to .NET.

Minification of your static assets is now done at build time, as opposed to request time, which was previously the case. It works much more like a static site generator than a dynamic web application. A configuration file (`bundleconfig.json`) in the root of your project defines the bundling and minification behavior with JSON.

The new tooling is not only restricted to ASP.NET Core, and you can use these features with traditional ASP.NET applications in Visual Studio. This is a good example of the cross-pollination and benefits that the new frameworks can provide to the existing ones.

Image optimization

Digital media compression is much more complicated than the lossless file compression that we talked about previously even if we just stick to images. We briefly mentioned when to use PNG and when to use JPEG in the previous chapter. Here, we'll go into much more detail and explore some other exotic options.

We covered the rule of thumb, which says that PNG is the best image format for icons and JPEG is better for photos. These two formats are the most common for lossless and lossy image compression, respectively.

We will talk more about other image formats later, but you are usually constrained to the popular formats by what browsers support. So, how can you get more out of the common choices?

PNG

Portable Network Graphics (**PNG**) is a lossless image compression format that internally works similarly to a ZIP file (using the DEFLATE algorithm). It's a good choice for images that contain solid blocks of color, and it has a higher image quality (with more colors) than the old **Graphics Interchange Format** (**GIF**).

PNG supports transparency in all modern browsers, so you should use it instead of GIF for static images. This is not a problem unless you need to support Internet Explorer 6, in which case, this is probably the least of your troubles. PNG also supports animation with **Animated Portable Network Graphics** (**APNG**) files. These are like animated GIFs but of a much higher quality. Unfortunately, only Firefox and Safari support APNGs.

 A great site to look up the browsers that support a particular feature is `http://caniuse.com/`. You can search for feature support and then check this against the user agent analytics of your site. For example, you could search for PNG-alpha, Brotli, or APNG.

Some ZIP algorithm implementations are better than others, and they produce smaller files that can still be decoded by everyone. For example, 7-Zip is much more efficient than most other ZIP compression software on Windows, even when using the ZIP format, not its native `7z` format. Likewise, you can compress a PNG more compactly without losing any data and still have it work in all browsers. This usually comes with a higher upfront computational cost. However, if you compress static assets, which rarely change, then it can be well worth the effort.

You may already use the PNGOUT tool to losslessly reduce the size of your PNG images. If you're not, then you probably should. You can read more about it and download it at `http://advsys.net/ken/utils.htm`.

However, there is a new algorithm called Zopfli that offers better compression, but it is very slow to compress. Decompression is just as quick, so it's only a single optimization cost for precompiled resources. Zopfli is a precursor to Brotli, but it's compatible with DEFLATE and GZIP, as it's not a new format.

You can get Zopfli from `https://github.com/google/zopfli`, but you should always test with your images and verify that there is indeed a file size reduction. You may find that these tools can help you deliver your assets quicker and achieve higher performance.

You may also use the practice of combining many sprites into one image. As with bundling, this is less necessary when using HTTP/2. However, the same caveats apply as with compression, and you should always test for your set of images.

JPEG

JPEG is a lossy image compression format, which means that it usually discards data from the picture to make it smaller. It is best suited to natural gradients and continuous tones, such as those found in photographs. JPEG does not support transparency like PNG does, so if you want to use one on different backgrounds, then you will need to prerender them.

 It's a good space-saving idea to remove the **Exchangeable image file format** (**Exif**) metadata from your JPEG files for the web. This contains information about the camera used and geographic data of where the photo was taken.

JPEG has a quality setting, which affects the image file size and the level of detail. The lower the quality, the smaller the file, but the worse it will look. You can perform tests on your images to see what settings provide an acceptable trade-off. Crucially, the best value for this quality setting will vary per image, depending on the content. There are tools that allow you to automatically detect the optimal quality level, such as Google's butteraugli.

There is an interesting project from Mozilla (the makers of the Firefox browser) called **mozjpeg**. This aims to better compress JPEG images and is similar to what PNGOUT and Zopfli do for PNG images. You can use mozjpeg to compress your JPEG images to a smaller size than normal, without affecting decompression or quality. It is available at `https://github.com/mozilla/mozjpeg`, but you will need to compile it yourself. As always, results may vary, so test it for the photos on your site.

JPEG Archive (`https://github.com/danielgtaylor/jpeg-archive`) is a handy tool that uses mozjpeg to compress JPEG images, using various comparison metrics. Another similar tool is **imgmin** (`http://github.com/rflynn/imgmin`), which is slightly older.

Other image formats

Many other image formats are available, but you are usually limited on the web by what browsers support.

As discussed in the previous chapter, you shouldn't scale images in the browser, or you will get poor performance. This usually means having to save multiple separate copies of smaller images, for example, when displaying thumbnails. Clearly, this results in duplication, which is inefficient. Some of these new image formats have clever solutions to the problem of responsive and scalable images.

BPG is an image format by the talented Fabrice Bellard, and you can read more about it at `http://bellard.org/bpg`. It has a JavaScript polyfill to support browsers before native support is added to any of them.

WebP is an image format from Google, and only Chrome, Android, and Opera support it. It has impressive space savings over JPEG, and it will be a good choice if it becomes more widely supported, so check `http://caniuse.com/` for the latest adoption stats.

JPEG 2000 is an improved version of JPEG, although it may be encumbered by software patents, so it hasn't seen widespread adoption outside of medical imaging. Only Safari supports JPEG 2000, and there is also JPEG XR, which is only supported in IE.

Whereas JPEG uses a **Discrete Cosine Transform (DCT)**, JPEG 2000 is based on a Wavelet Transform. One of the properties this provides is a *progressive* download. This means that the image is stored in such a way that if you download a small part from the beginning of the file, then you have a smaller and lower quality version of the full image. This has obvious applications for responsive and scalable images. The browser would only need to download enough of the image to fill the area it is rendering to, and the file need only be stored once. No resizing and no duplication for thumbnails would be required. This technique is also used in the **Free Lossless Image Format (FLIF)**.

FLIF is one of the more exciting upcoming image formats, as it is progressive and responsive, but free and not patented. FLIF is still in development, but it promises to be very useful if browsers support it. You can read more about it at `http://flif.info/`.

 JPEG and PNG can support progressive download, but this isn't normally useful for responsive images. Progressive JPEG subjectively loads more gracefully and can even make files smaller, but interlaced PNG usually makes files bigger.

The problem is that most of these progressive image formats are not yet ready for the mainstream because all of the major browsers do not support them. It's a good idea to keep an eye on the future, but for now, we need to resize images for high performance.

Resizing images

Until new image formats gain widespread adoption, resizing is still required, and you may need to do this dynamically for different devices. Perhaps, you also have user-submitted image content, although you need to be very careful with this from a security point of view. Some image libraries are not safe, and a specially-crafted image can exploit your system. In fact, many image-processing libraries have issues when they are used in a web context.

If you are not extremely diligent and careful, then you can easily end up with memory leaks, which can take down your web server. It is always a good idea to separate and sandbox a process that deals with large media files.

Coming from a .NET standpoint, it can be tempting to use WinForms `System.Drawing` or its WPF successor (`System.Windows.Media`). However, these were designed for desktop software, and Microsoft strongly recommends against using them in a service or web application. Microsoft recommends the **Windows Imaging Component** (**WIC**), but this is a **Component Object Model** (**COM**) API that is meant for use from C or C++ apps. In addition to this, none of these imaging libraries are cross-platform, so they are not suitable for use in .NET Core.

If you use Windows, then you could try using ImageResizer by Imazen (`http://www.imazen.io/`), from `http://imageresizing.net/`. While it still uses the **GDI+** `System.Drawing`, it is pretty battle hardened, so most of the bugs should have been worked out. There's also **DynamicImage**, which wraps the newer WPF image functions and uses shaders. You can read more about it at `http://dynamicimage.apphb.com/`, although it hasn't been updated in a while and doesn't support .NET Core.

A popular option in open source circles is ImageMagick, which we've mentioned previously, and a fork called **GraphicsMagick**, which claims to be more efficient. Another popular image library is **LibGD**, and it's suitable for server use. You can read more at `http://libgd.github.io/`. Although it's written in C, there are wrappers for other programming languages, for example, **DotnetGD** targeting .NET Core.

One of the features that .NET Core lacks is that there is not yet a compelling option for image processing. ImageResizer 5 and Imageflow (`https://www.imageflow.io/`) may help with this when complete. There is also a new cross-platform version of the open source **ImageProcessor** libraries (`http://imageprocessor.org/`), called ImageSharp (`http://imagesharp.net/`), but this is still a work in progress. If you want to try it out, then you can get the pre-release packages from MyGet or build it from source.

Platform support and compatibility changes rapidly, so check `https://github.com/jpsingleton/ANCLAFS` for the latest information. Feel free to contribute to this list or to the projects.

For now, it may be easier to install an open source service, such as Thumbor, or use a cloud-based imaging service, such as ImageEngine (`http://wurfl.io/`) or Cloudinary, which we've already mentioned. Image manipulation is a common task, and it is effectively a solved problem. It may be better to use an existing solution and not reinvent the wheel, unless it's part of your core business or you have very unusual requirements.

Once you have your resized images, you can load them responsively with the `picture` and `source` tags using the `srcset` and `sizes` attributes. You can also use this technique to provide newer image formats (such as WebP), with a fallback for browsers that don't yet support them. Or you can use **Client Hints** (refer to `http://httpwg.org/http-extensions/client-hints.html` and `http://caniuse.com/#feat=client-hints-dpr-width-viewport`).

Caching

It is often said (originally by Phil Karlton) that caching is one of the hardest problems in computer science, along with naming things. This may well be an exaggeration, but caching is certainly difficult. It can also be very frustrating to debug if you are not methodical and precise in your approach.

Caching can apply at various different levels from the browser to the server using many diverse technologies. You rarely use just a single cache even if you don't realize it. Multiple caches don't always work well together, and it's vexing if you can't clear one.

We briefly touched upon caching in the previous chapter, and we'll go into much more detail in `Chapter 9`, *Learning Caching and Message Queuing*. However, as caching has an impact on network performance, we'll cover it here as well.

Browser

A lot of caching happens in the web browser, which is inconvenient because you don't have direct control over it (unless it's your browser). Asking users to clear their cache is unsatisfactory and confusing to many. Yet, you can exert influence on how browsers cache resources by carefully controlling the HTTP headers that you set and the URLs that you use.

If you fail to declare what resources are cacheable and for how long, then many browsers will just guess this. The heuristics for this can be wildly different between implementations. Therefore, this will result in sub-optimal performance. You should be explicit and always declare cache information even (and especially) for assets that shouldn't be cached by marking them as non-cacheable.

> You need to be vigilant with what you advertise as cacheable because if you are careless, then you can get yourself into a situation where you're unable to update a resource. You should have a cache-busting strategy in place, and tested, before using caching.

There are various technologies that are used to cache in browsers. Many different HTTP headers can be set, such as `Age`, `Cache-Control`, `ETag` (Entity tag), `Expires`, and `Last-Modified`. These come from a few different standards, and the interactions can be complex, or they vary between browsers. We will explain these in more detail in `Chapter 9`, *Learning Caching and Message Queuing*.

Another technique is to use a unique URL for content. If a URL changes, then a browser will treat it as a different resource, but if it is the same, then it may load it from its local cache. Some frameworks calculate a hash of the file contents, and then they use this as a query string parameter. This way, when the contents of the file changes, so does the URL.

There are other and more modern features that you can use to cache, such as the **HTML5 Application Cache** (or **AppCache**). This was designed for offline web applications and wasn't very flexible. Busting the cache was complicated to put it mildly. AppCache is already deprecated, and you should use **Service Workers** instead. These provide much more flexibility, although support is pretty recent.

There are many improvements coming, in the latest browsers that give you more control, and we'll also show you how to use them in `Chapter 9`, *Learning Caching and Message Queuing*.

Server

The web server is a great place to cache because it is usually under your complete control. However, it's not really part of network performance, apart from generating the correct headers. There can be other great performance benefits with server-side caching in terms of improving the speed to generate pages, but we will cover these in later chapters.

If you use the traditional .NET Framework on Microsoft's **Internet Information Services (IIS)** web server, then you can use **output caching** from within your application. This will take care of setting the correct headers and sending 304 (Not Modified) responses to browser requests. It will also cache the output on the server in memory, on disk or using Memcached/Redis. You can add attributes to your controller action methods to control the caching options, but other ways of doing this are available, for example, in the configuration files.

Output caching is now available in ASP.NET Core, so you can store copies of your output within your infrastructure if you choose. As this section is about networking, we'll only cover the ResponseCache attribute here, which is a subset of output caching. Visit the author's website at https://unop.uk/ for more on other topics.

If you want to disable caching on an ASP.NET Core page, then add this annotation to your controller action:

```
[ResponseCache(NoStore = true, Duration = 0)]
```

This will set the following header on the HTTP response and ensure that it is not cached:

```
Cache-Control: no-store
```

To cache a page for an hour, add the following instead, Duration is in seconds:

```
[ResponseCache(Duration = 3600, VaryByHeader = "Accept")]
```

The cache control header will then look like the following:

```
Cache-Control: public,max-age=3600
```

There's plenty more to say about other caching configuration options and profiles. Therefore, if you're interested, then read the later chapters. It's a complex topic, and we've only scratched the surface here.

You can read the documentation about response caching in ASP.NET Core at `https://docs.microsoft.com/en-gb/aspnet/core/performance/caching/response`.

These caching directives not only instruct the browser, but they also instruct any proxies on the way. Some of these may be in your infrastructure if you have a caching proxy, such as Squid, Varnish, or HAProxy. Or perhaps, you have a TLS-terminating load balancer (such as **Azure Application Gateway**) to reduce the load on your web servers that also caches. You can forcibly flush the caches of servers that you control, but there may be other caches in between you and your users where you can't do this.

Proxy servers between you and your users

There can be many proxy servers between you and your users over which you have no direct control. They may ignore your caching requests, block parts of your site, or even modify your content. The way to solve these problems is to use TLS, as we have already discussed. TLS creates a secure tunnel so that the connection between your infrastructure and the browser can't easily be tampered with.

Corporate proxies, commonly **Man in the Middle (MitM)**, attack your connection to the user so that they can spy on what employees are doing online. This involves installing a custom trusted root certificate on users' workstations so that your certificate can be faked. Unfortunately, there isn't much you can do about this apart from educating users. **Certificate pinning** is effective in native apps, but it's not so useful for web applications. **HTTP Public Key Pinning (HPKP)** is available but, as it is a **Trust on First Use (TOFU)** technique, the initial connection could be intercepted. Client certificates are another option, but they can be difficult to distribute, and they aren't commonly used.

If you use HSTS and get your domain pre-installed in browsers then this can help avoid interception, but your site might simply be blocked. For example, Firefox ships with its own certificate store and doesn't use the OS-provided one like Chrome does. You can't add security exceptions for sites that have HSTS enabled and Firefox knows this before connecting, for HSTS sites that are included in the browser installation.

MitM can be useful if you trust the third party and remain in control. This is used by some **Content Delivery Networks (CDNs)** to speed up your site. However, you need to carefully assess the risk impact of this. Read about the Cloudbleed incident, mentioned in the previous chapter, for a poignant example of this.

CDNs

CDNs can improve the performance of your site by storing copies of your content at locations closer to your users. Services, such as the ones provided by Cloudflare, perform a MitM on your connection and save copies at data centers around the world. The difference from an unauthorized proxy is that you control the configuration, and you can purge the cache whenever you like.

You should be careful because if you don't use the caching features, then this can reduce the responsiveness of your site due to the extra hops involved. Make sure that you monitor the response times with and without a CDN, and you need a fallback plan in case they go down.

Another common use case for CDNs is to distribute popular libraries, for example, the jQuery JavaScript library. There are free CDNs from jQuery (MaxCDN), Google, Microsoft, and cdnjs (Cloudflare) that do this. The hypothesis is that a user may already have the library from one of these in their cache. However, you should be extremely careful that you trust the provider and connection. When you load a third-party script into your site, you are effectively giving them full control over it or at least relying on them to always be available.

If you choose to use a CDN, then ensure that it uses HTTPS to avoid tampering with scripts. You should use explicit `https://` URLs on your secure pages or at least protocol agnostic URLs (`//`), and never `http://`. Otherwise, you will get mixed content warnings, which some browsers display as totally unencrypted or even block.

SRI can help avoid scripts being tampered with in some browsers. Don't worry about any potential performance overhead of hashing the scripts. The SHA-2 algorithms used are very fast, which is why they shouldn't be used for hashing passwords or key stretching. See the previous chapter for more on this script integrity checking feature.

You will need a fallback that is hosted on your own servers anyway in case the CDN goes down. If you use HTTP/2, then you may find that there is no advantage to using a CDN. Obviously, always test for your situation.

There are some useful features in ASP.NET Core views to easily enable local fallback for CDN resources. We'll show you how to use them in later chapters.

Summary

In this chapter, you learned how to improve performance at the network level between the edge of your infrastructure and your users. You now know more about the internet protocols under your application and how to optimize your use of them for the best effect.

We covered many layers of the networking stack at a high level, from IP and TCP to HTTP and HTTP/2. We also showed how TLS is used to protect communications and how key exchange works. We highlighted the different cipher algorithms that can be used and touched upon alternative protocols, such as WebSockets.

You learned how to take advantage of compression to shrink text and image files. This will reduce bandwidth and speed up delivery of assets. We also highlighted caching, and you should now see how important it is. We'll cover caching more in Chapter 9, *Learning Caching and Message Queuing*.

In the next chapter, you will learn how to optimize the performance inside your infrastructure. You will see how to deal with I/O latency, and how to write high-performance SQL.

7
Optimizing I/O Performance

This chapter addresses issues that often occur when you take your functionally tested application and split it up into parts for deployment. Your web servers host the frontend code, your database is somewhere else in the data center, you may have a **Storage Area Network (SAN)** for centralized files, an app server for APIs, and the virtual disks are all on different machines as well.

These changes add significant latency to many common operations and your application now becomes super slow, probably because it's too chatty over the network. In this chapter, you will learn how to fix these issues by batching queries together, and performing work on the best server for the job. Even if everything runs on one machine, the skills that you'll learn here will help to improve performance by increasing efficiency.

The topics covered in this chapter include the following:

- Input/output
- Network diagnostics
- Batching API requests
- Efficient DB operations
- Simulation and testing

You will learn about various operations that you shouldn't use synchronously, and about returning only the data that you need from a DB in an efficient manner. You'll also see how to tame your O/RM, and learn to write high-performance SQL with **Dapper**.

We briefly covered some of these topics in Chapter 5, *Fixing Common Performance Problems*, but here we'll delve into greater detail. The first half of this chapter will focus on background knowledge and using diagnostic tools, while the second half will show you solutions to issues you may come across. You'll also learn about some more unusual problems, and how to fix or alleviate them.

We'll initially focus on understanding the issues, because if you don't appreciate the root cause of a problem, then it can be difficult to fix. You shouldn't blindly apply advice that you read, and expect it to work successfully. Diagnosing a problem is normally the hard part, and once this is achieved, it is usually easy to fix it.

Input/output

I/O is a general name for any operation in which your code interacts with the outside world. There are many things that count as I/O, and there can be plenty of I/O that is internal to your software, especially if your application has a distributed architecture.

The increasing use by tech companies of the `.io` **Top Level Domain** (**TLD**), for example `http://github.io`, can be partly attributed to it standing for I/O, but that is not its real meaning. As is the case for some other TLDs, it is actually a country code. Other examples include `.ly` for Libya and `.tv` for Tuvalu (which, like the neighboring Kiribati, may soon be submerged beneath the Pacific Ocean due to climate change). The TLD `.io` is intended for the **British Indian Ocean Territory** (**BIOT**), a collection of tiny but strategic islands with a shameful history. The `.io` TLD is therefore controlled by a UK-based registry even though the BIOT is nothing more than a US military base.

In this chapter, we will focus on improving the speed of I/O, not on avoiding it. Therefore, we won't cover caching here. Both I/O optimizing and caching are powerful techniques on their own, and when they're combined, you can achieve impressive performance. See `Chapter 9`, *Learning Caching and Message Queuing*, for more on caching.

Categories of I/O

The first challenge is to identify the operations that trigger I/O. A general rule of thumb in .NET is that, if a method has an asynchronous API (`MethodAsync()` variants), then it is declaring that it can be slow, and may be doing I/O work. Let's take a closer look at some of the different kinds of I/O.

Disks

The first type of I/O we will cover is reading from, and writing to, persistent storage. This will usually be some sort of a disk drive such as a spinning platter **Hard Disk Drive** (**HDD**), or, as is more common these days, a flash memory-based **Solid State Drive** (**SSD**).

HDDs are slower than SSDs for random reads and writes, but are competitive for large block transfers. The reason for this is that the arm on the HDD has to physically move the head to the correct location on the magnetic platter before it can begin the read or write operations. If the disk is powered down, then it can take even longer, as the platters will have to spin up from a stationary position to the correct **revolutions per minute** (**rpm**) beforehand.

You may have heard the term *spin up* in reference to provisioning a generic resource. This historically comes from the time taken to spin the platters on a rotating disk up to the operational speed. The term is still commonly used, even though these days there may not be any mechanical components present. Terminology like this often has a historical explanation. As another example, a floppy disk icon is normally used to represent the save function. Yet floppy disks are no longer in use, and many younger users may never have encountered one.

Knowing what type of drive your code is running on is important. HDDs perform badly if you make lots of small reads and writes. They prefer to have batched operations, so writing one large file is better than many smaller ones.

The performance of disks is similar to that of a network, in that there is both latency and throughput, often called bandwidth in networking parlance. The latency of an HDD is high, as it takes a relatively long time to get started, but once started the throughput can be respectable. You can read data rapidly if it's all in one place on the disk, but it will be slower if it is spread all over, even if the total data is less. For example, copying a single large file disk-to-disk is quick, but trying to launch many programs simultaneously is slow.

SSDs experience fewer of these problems as they have lower latency, but it is still beneficial to keep random writes to a minimum. SSDs are based on **flash memory** (similar to the chips used in memory cards for phones and cameras), and they can only be written to a fixed number of times. The controller on the SSD manages this for you, but the SSD's performance degrades over time. Aggressive writing will accelerate this degradation.

Multiple disks can be combined to improve their performance and reliability characteristics. This is commonly done using a technology called **Redundant Array of Independent Disks** (**RAID**). Data is split across multiple disks to make it quicker to access, and more tolerant to hardware failures. RAID is common in server hardware, but can increase the startup time, as spin up is sometimes staggered to reduce the peak power draw.

HDDs offer much larger capacity than SSDs, and so are a good choice for storage of infrequently used files. You can get hybrid drives, which combine an HDD with an SSD.

These claim to offer the best of both worlds, and are cheaper than SSDs of an equivalent size. However, if you can afford it, and if you can fit all of your data on an SSD, then you should use one. You will also decrease your power and cooling requirements, and you can always add an additional HDD for mass storage or backups.

Virtual filesystems

File access can be slow at the best of times due to the physical nature of the disks storing the data, as mentioned previously. This problem can be compounded in a virtualized environment such as a cloud-hosted infrastructure. The storage disks are usually not on the same host server as the virtual machine, and will generally be implemented as network shares even if they appear to be mounted locally. In any case, there is always an additional problem, which is present whether the disk is on the VM host or somewhere else on the network, and that is contention.

On a virtualized infrastructure, such as those provided by AWS and Azure, you share the hardware with other users, but a physical disk can only service a single request at a time. If multiple tenants want to access the same disk simultaneously, then their operations will need to be queued and timeshared. Unfortunately, this abstraction has much the same detrimental effect on performance as reading lots of random files. Users are likely to have their data on disk stored in locations different from those of other customers. This will cause the arm on the drive to frequently move to different sectors, reducing throughput and increasing latency for everyone on the system.

All this means that on shared virtual hosting, using an SSD can have a bigger positive performance impact than normal. Even better is to have a local SSD, which is directly attached to the VM host, and not to another machine on the network. If disks must be networked, then the storage machine should be as close as possible to the VM using it.

You can pay extra for a dedicated VM host where you are the only tenant. However, you may as well then be running on bare metal, and reaping the benefits of reduced costs and higher performance. If you don't require the easy provisioning and maintenance of VMs, then a bare-metal dedicated server may be a good option.

Many cloud hosting providers now offer SSDs, but most only offer ephemeral local disks. This means that the local disk only exists while your VM is running, and vanishes when it is shut down, making it unsuitable for storing the OS if you want to bring a VM back up in the same state.

You have to write your application in a different way to take advantage of an ephemeral local drive, as it could disappear at any time, and so can only be used for temporary working storage. This is known as an **immutable server**, which means it doesn't change and is disposable. This normally works better when the OS is Linux, as it can be tricky to bootstrap new instances when running Windows.

Databases

Databases can be slow, because they rely on disks for the storage of their data, but there are other overheads as well. However, DBs are usually a better way of storing significant data than flat files on disk. Arbitrary data can be retrieved quickly if it is indexed, much quicker than scanning a file by brute force.

Relational databases are a mature and very impressive technology. However, they only shine when used correctly, and how you go about querying them makes a massive difference to performance. DBs are so convenient that they're often overused, and are typically the bottleneck for a web application.

An unfortunately common *anti-pattern* is requiring a database call in order to render the homepage of a website. An example is when you try to visit a website mentioned on live TV, only to discover that it has crashed due to the MySQL DB being overloaded. This sort of a website would be better architected as a static site with the client-side code hitting cached and queued web APIs.

The pathological case for a slow DB is where the web server is in one data center, the database server is in another, and the disks for the DB are in a third. Also, all the servers may be shared with other users. Obviously, it's best not to end up in this situation, and to architect your infrastructure in a sane way, but you will always have some latency.

There are application programming techniques that allow you to keep your network and DB chatter to a minimum. These help you to improve the performance and responsiveness of your software, especially if it is hosted in a high-latency virtualized environment. We will demonstrate some of these skills later on in this chapter.

APIs

Modern web application programming generally involves using third-party services and their associated APIs. It's beneficial to know where these APIs are located, and what the latency is. Are they in the same data center, or are they on the other side of the planet? Unless you've discovered some exciting new physics, then light only travels so fast.

Today, almost all intercontinental data travels by fiber optic cables. Satellites are rarely used anymore, as the latency is high, especially for geostationary orbits. Many of these cables are under the oceans, and are hard to fix. If you rely on an API on a different continent, not only can it slow you down, but it also exposes you to additional risk. You probably shouldn't build an important workflow that can be disrupted by a fisherman trawling in the wrong place. You also need to further secure your data, as some countries (such as the UK) are known to tap cables and store the communications, if they cross their borders.

One of the issues with APIs is that latency can compound. You may need to call many APIs, or maybe an API calls another API internally. These situations are not normally designed this way, but can grow organically as new features are added, especially if no refactoring is performed periodically to tidy up any mess.

One common form of latency is startup time. Websites can go to sleep if not used, especially if using the default **Internet Information Services** (**IIS**) settings. If a website takes a non-negligible amount of time to wake up, and all the required APIs also need to wake up, then the delays can quickly add up to a significant lag for the first request. It may even time-out.

There are a couple of solutions to this initial lag problem. If you use IIS, then you can configure the application pool to not go to sleep. The defaults in IIS are optimized for shared hosting, so they will need tweaking for a dedicated server. The second option is to keep the site alive by regularly polling it with a health check or uptime monitoring tool. You should be doing this anyway so that you know when your site goes down, but you should also ensure that you are exercising all the required dependencies (such as APIs and DBs). If you are simply retrieving a static page or just checking for a 200 status code, then services may go down without you realizing.

Similarly, scaling can have a lag. If you need to scale up, then you should preheat your load balancers and web servers. This is especially important if using an AWS **Elastic Load Balancing** (**ELB**). If you're expecting a big peak in traffic, then you can ask AWS to have your ELBs pre-warmed. An alternative would be using **Azure Load Balancer**, **Azure Application Gateway**, or running HAProxy yourself so that you have more control. You should also be running load tests, which we'll cover in Chapter 11, *Monitoring Performance Regressions*.

Network diagnostics tools

As we discovered earlier, practically all I/O operations in a virtualized or cloud-hosting infrastructure are now network operations. Disks and databases are rarely local, as this would prevent scaling out horizontally. There are various command-line tools that can help you discover where the API, DB, or any other server you're using is located, and how much latency is present on the connection.

While all of these commands can be run from your workstation, they are most useful when run from a server via a **Secure Shell** (**SSH**) or **Remote Desktop Protocol** (**RDP**) connection. This way, you can check where your databases, APIs, and storage servers are, in relation to your web servers. Unfortunately, it is common for hosting providers to geographically separate your servers, and put them in different data centers.

For example, if using AWS, then you would want to configure your servers to be in at least the same region, and preferably in the same **Availability Zone** (**AZ**), which usually means the same data center. You can replicate (cluster) your DB or file server across AZs (or even across regions) so that your web servers are always talking to a server on their local network. This also adds redundancy, so in addition to increasing performance, it will make your application more resilient to hardware faults or power supply failures.

Ping

Ping is a simple networking diagnostics tool, available on almost all operating systems. It operates at the IP level and sends an **Internet Control Message Protocol** (**ICMP**) echo message to the host specified.

Not all machines will respond to pings, or requests may be blocked by firewalls. However, it's good netiquette to allow servers to respond for debugging purposes, and most will oblige. For example, open a Command Prompt or terminal, and type the following:

```
ping ec2.eu-central-1.amazonaws.com
```

This will ping an **Amazon Web Services** (**AWS**) data center in Germany. In the response, you will see the time in milliseconds. From the UK, this **round-trip time** (**RTT**) may be something like 33ms, but your results will vary.

 On Windows, by default, ping performs four attempts, then exits. On a Unix-like OS (such as macOS, BSD, or Linux), by default it continues indefinitely. Press *Ctrl + C* to stop and quit.

Try this command next, which will do the same but for an AWS data center in Australia:

```
ping ec2.ap-southeast-2.amazonaws.com
```

From the UK, the latency now goes up, by almost an order of magnitude, to around 300 ms. To ping a UK hosting provider, enter the following:

```
ping bytemark.co.uk
```

The latency now decreases to an average of 23ms, as our connection has (probably) not left the country. Obviously, your results will vary depending on where you are. Next we'll see how to discover what route our data is taking, as it's not always only distance that's important. The number of hops can likewise be significant.

The following screenshot shows the output of the three `ping` operations that we have just performed to Germany, Australia, and the UK. Note the difference in the timings; however, your results will be different, so try this for yourself.

```
C:\Users\James>ping ec2.eu-central-1.amazonaws.com

Pinging ec2.eu-central-1.amazonaws.com [54.239.54.36] with 32 bytes of data:
Reply from 54.239.54.36: bytes=32 time=33ms TTL=241
Reply from 54.239.54.36: bytes=32 time=33ms TTL=241
Reply from 54.239.54.36: bytes=32 time=33ms TTL=241
Reply from 54.239.54.36: bytes=32 time=33ms TTL=241

Ping statistics for 54.239.54.36:
    Packets: Sent = 4, Received = 4, Lost = 0 (0% loss),
Approximate round trip times in milli-seconds:
    Minimum = 33ms, Maximum = 33ms, Average = 33ms

C:\Users\James>ping ec2.ap-southeast-2.amazonaws.com

Pinging ec2.ap-southeast-2.amazonaws.com [54.240.195.29] with 32 bytes of data:
Reply from 54.240.195.29: bytes=32 time=297ms TTL=237
Reply from 54.240.195.29: bytes=32 time=298ms TTL=237
Reply from 54.240.195.29: bytes=32 time=297ms TTL=237
Reply from 54.240.195.29: bytes=32 time=297ms TTL=237

Ping statistics for 54.240.195.29:
    Packets: Sent = 4, Received = 4, Lost = 0 (0% loss),
Approximate round trip times in milli-seconds:
    Minimum = 297ms, Maximum = 298ms, Average = 297ms

C:\Users\James>ping bytemark.co.uk

Pinging bytemark.co.uk [80.68.81.80] with 32 bytes of data:
Reply from 80.68.81.80: bytes=32 time=22ms TTL=53
Reply from 80.68.81.80: bytes=32 time=22ms TTL=53
Reply from 80.68.81.80: bytes=32 time=27ms TTL=53
Reply from 80.68.81.80: bytes=32 time=22ms TTL=53

Ping statistics for 80.68.81.80:
    Packets: Sent = 4, Received = 4, Lost = 0 (0% loss),
Approximate round trip times in milli-seconds:
    Minimum = 22ms, Maximum = 27ms, Average = 23ms
```

IPv4 addresses starting with 54 (the ones in the form 54.x.x.x) are a clue that the server may be running on an AWS **Elastic Compute Cloud** (EC2) virtual server. Perform a reverse DNS lookup with nslookup or ping (covered later in this chapter) to confirm if this is the case. AWS provides IP address ranges at the following link:

http://docs.aws.amazon.com/general/latest/gr/aws-ip-ranges.html

Tracert

Tracert (or traceroute on a Unix-like OS) is a tool that, as the name suggests, traces the route to a destination host. Enter the following command:

```
tracert www.google.com
```

You should be able to see the connection leaving the network of your **Internet Service Provider** (ISP), and entering the domain 1e100.net, which is Google's domain. *1.0 x 10^100* is a **googol**, which is their namesake. The following screenshot shows the output that you might see for this trace:

```
C:\Users\James>tracert www.google.com

Tracing route to www.google.com [173.194.112.180]
over a maximum of 30 hops:

  1     1 ms     1 ms     1 ms  BThomehub.home [192.168.1.254]
  2     *        *        *     Request timed out.
  3    16 ms    18 ms    15 ms  31.55.186.181
  4    16 ms    16 ms    17 ms  31.55.186.180
  5    17 ms    16 ms    16 ms  core4-hu0-6-0-3.faraday.ukcore.bt.net [195.99.127.202]
  6    19 ms    17 ms    17 ms  peer1-xe0-1-0.faraday.ukcore.bt.net [213.121.193.173]
  7    17 ms    16 ms    16 ms  109.159.253.67
  8    16 ms    16 ms    16 ms  209.85.244.182
  9    17 ms    17 ms    17 ms  209.85.250.184
 10    22 ms    23 ms    23 ms  209.85.253.108
 11    26 ms    27 ms    28 ms  74.125.37.102
 12    75 ms    74 ms    73 ms  66.249.95.38
 13   231 ms    29 ms    28 ms  216.239.57.148
 14    37 ms    28 ms    38 ms  72.14.238.57
 15    68 ms    71 ms    70 ms  fra07s32-in-f20.1e100.net [173.194.112.180]

Trace complete.
```

Next, let's trace a route to Australia by running the following command with the same AWS host name as our earlier example, as follows:

```
tracert ec2.ap-southeast-2.amazonaws.com
```

This may take some time to run, especially if some hosts don't respond to pings and traceroute has to time-out. If you get asterisks (* * *), then this could indicate the presence of a firewall.

Your results may look something like the following screenshot:

```
C:\Users\James>tracert ec2.ap-southeast-2.amazonaws.com

Tracing route to ec2.ap-southeast-2.amazonaws.com [54.240.195.144]
over a maximum of 30 hops:

  1     1 ms     3 ms     3 ms  BThomehub.home [192.168.1.254]
  2     *        *        *     Request timed out.
  3     *        *        *     Request timed out.
  4    16 ms    16 ms    16 ms  31.55.186.180
  5    16 ms    16 ms    16 ms  195.99.127.42
  6    26 ms   235 ms    17 ms  peer2-et-9-3-0.faraday.ukcore.bt.net [62.6.201.195]
  7   198 ms    19 ms    15 ms  213.137.183.98
  8    16 ms    16 ms    16 ms  82.112.115.185
  9   175 ms   174 ms   174 ms  ae-1.r03.londen05.uk.bb.gin.ntt.net [129.250.6.230]
 10   173 ms   173 ms   171 ms  ae-15.r03.amstn102.nl.bb.gin.ntt.net [129.250.6.25]
 11    22 ms    23 ms    23 ms  ae-4.r25.amstn102.nl.bb.gin.ntt.net [129.250.2.146]
 12   100 ms   100 ms   101 ms  ae-5.r23.asbnva02.us.bb.gin.ntt.net [129.250.6.162]
 13   101 ms   101 ms   102 ms  ae-0.r22.asbnva02.us.bb.gin.ntt.net [129.250.3.84]
 14   167 ms   166 ms   166 ms  ae-5.r23.lsanca07.us.bb.gin.ntt.net [129.250.3.189]
 15   176 ms   175 ms   176 ms  ae-2.r00.lsanca07.us.bb.gin.ntt.net [129.250.3.238]
 16   167 ms   168 ms   168 ms  ae-1.amazon.lsanca07.us.bb.gin.ntt.net [129.250.198.98]
 17     *        *        *     Request timed out.
 18     *        *        *     Request timed out.
 19     *        *        *     Request timed out.
 20   305 ms   305 ms   304 ms  54.240.203.85
 21   305 ms   305 ms   305 ms  54.240.192.115
 22   305 ms   305 ms   305 ms  54.240.192.181
 23   305 ms   305 ms   305 ms  54.240.195.144

Trace complete.
```

In the preceding example, we can see the connection leaving the **British Telecom** (**BT**) network, and entering the **Nippon Telegraph and Telecom** (**NTT**) Global IP Network. We can even see the route taken from London to Sydney, via Amsterdam, Ashburn (east US, in Virginia), and Los Angeles. The hostnames suggest that the connection has gone via the Faraday telephone exchange building, near St. Paul's Cathedral in London (named after electrical pioneer Michael Faraday), and entered Amazon's network in LA.

 This isn't the whole story as it only shows the IP level. At the physical level, the fiber likely comes back to the UK from the Netherlands (possibly via Porthcurno, Goonhilly Satellite Earth Station, or more likely Bude, where GCHQ conveniently has a base). Between LA and Australia, there will also probably be a stopover in Hawaii (where the NSA base that Edward Snowden worked at is located). There are maps of the connections available at http://submarinecablemap.com/ and http://www.us.ntt.net/about/network-map.cfm. It's good idea to have at least a basic understanding of how the internet is physically structured, in order to achieve high performance.

If we now trace the routes to the AWS data centers in Korea and Japan, we can see that, initially, they both take the same route as each other. They go from London to New York and then to Seattle, before reaching Osaka in Japan. The Korean trace then carries on for another eleven hops, but the Japanese trace is done in six, which makes logical sense.

The following screenshot shows the typical results of a trace to Korea first, then the results of a second trace to Japan:

```
C:\Users\James>tracert ec2.ap-northeast-2.amazonaws.com

Tracing route to ec2.ap-northeast-2.amazonaws.com [52.95.192.85]
over a maximum of 30 hops:

  1     1 ms     1 ms     1 ms  BThomehub.home [192.168.1.254]
  2     *        *        *     Request timed out.
  3     *        *        *     Request timed out.
  4    36 ms    16 ms    16 ms  31.55.186.188
  5    16 ms    16 ms    15 ms  core4-hu0-6-0-1.faraday.ukcore.bt.net [195.99.127.200]
  6    25 ms    15 ms    15 ms  peer2-et-10-3-0.faraday.ukcore.bt.net [62.6.201.199]
  7    19 ms    15 ms    15 ms  213.137.183.100
  8    17 ms    17 ms    16 ms  82.112.115.185
  9   273 ms   274 ms   273 ms  ae-13.r02.londen03.uk.bb.gin.ntt.net [129.250.2.118]
 10    17 ms    16 ms    16 ms  ae-4.r22.londen03.uk.bb.gin.ntt.net [129.250.5.24]
 11    87 ms    87 ms    88 ms  ae-5.r24.nycmny01.us.bb.gin.ntt.net [129.250.2.18]
 12   172 ms   179 ms   157 ms  ae-1.r21.sttlwa01.us.bb.gin.ntt.net [129.250.4.13]
 13   250 ms   250 ms   250 ms  ae-2.r20.osakjp02.jp.bb.gin.ntt.net [129.250.3.86]
 14   252 ms   248 ms   311 ms  ae-4.r22.osakjp02.jp.bb.gin.ntt.net [129.250.6.188]
 15   280 ms   275 ms   274 ms  ae-1.r00.osakjp02.jp.bb.gin.ntt.net [129.250.2.253]
 16   255 ms   256 ms   254 ms  ae-0.amazon.osakjp02.jp.bb.gin.ntt.net [61.200.82.122]
 17   261 ms   261 ms   261 ms  54.239.52.142
 18   286 ms   286 ms   286 ms  54.239.52.149
 19     *        *        *     Request timed out.
 20   294 ms   291 ms   298 ms  54.239.122.238
 21   322 ms   289 ms   295 ms  54.239.122.245
 22   422 ms   335 ms   295 ms  54.239.122.38
 23     *        *        *     Request timed out.
 24     *        *        *     Request timed out.
 25     *        *        *     Request timed out.
 26     *        *        *     Request timed out.
 27   292 ms   296 ms   295 ms  52.95.192.85

Trace complete.

C:\Users\James>tracert ec2.ap-northeast-1.amazonaws.com

Tracing route to ec2.ap-northeast-1.amazonaws.com [27.0.1.195]
over a maximum of 30 hops:

  1     2 ms     1 ms     1 ms  BThomehub.home [192.168.1.254]
  2     *        *        *     Request timed out.
  3     *        *        *     Request timed out.
  4    16 ms    16 ms    16 ms  31.55.186.180
  5    16 ms    16 ms    16 ms  core3-hu0-6-0-1.faraday.ukcore.bt.net [195.99.127.192]
  6    15 ms    16 ms    16 ms  peer2-et-9-3-0.faraday.ukcore.bt.net [62.6.201.195]
  7    15 ms    15 ms    16 ms  213.137.183.96
  8    16 ms    16 ms    16 ms  82.112.115.185
  9   273 ms   274 ms   274 ms  ae-13.r02.londen03.uk.bb.gin.ntt.net [129.250.2.118]
 10    16 ms    17 ms    17 ms  ae-4.r22.londen03.uk.bb.gin.ntt.net [129.250.5.24]
 11    82 ms    83 ms    83 ms  ae-5.r24.nycmny01.us.bb.gin.ntt.net [129.250.2.18]
 12   153 ms   153 ms   152 ms  ae-1.r21.sttlwa01.us.bb.gin.ntt.net [129.250.4.13]
 13   242 ms   243 ms   242 ms  ae-2.r20.osakjp02.jp.bb.gin.ntt.net [129.250.3.86]
 14   294 ms   309 ms   283 ms  ae-4.r23.osakjp02.jp.bb.gin.ntt.net [129.250.6.90]
 15   273 ms   273 ms   273 ms  ae-2.r00.osakjp02.jp.bb.gin.ntt.net [129.250.3.197]
 16   247 ms   246 ms   246 ms  ae-0.amazon.osakjp02.jp.bb.gin.ntt.net [61.200.82.122]
 17   259 ms   259 ms   259 ms  27.0.0.250
 18   255 ms   412 ms   306 ms  54.239.52.135
 19   261 ms   262 ms   260 ms  27.0.0.67
 20   254 ms   254 ms   254 ms  27.0.0.155
 21   255 ms   255 ms   255 ms  27.0.0.175
 22   255 ms   255 ms   255 ms  27.0.1.195

Trace complete.
```

You can use the difference in time between hops to work out the approximate geographic distance. However, there are occasionally anomalies if some systems respond quicker than others.

If you're on a flight with free Wi-Fi, then a traceroute is an interesting exercise to perform. The internet connection is likely going via satellite, and you'll be able to tell the orbit altitude from the latency. For example, a geostationary orbit will have a large latency of around 1,000 ms, but a **Low Earth Orbit (LEO)** will be much smaller. You should also be able to work out where the ground station is located.

Nslookup

Nslookup is a tool for directly querying a DNS server. **Dig** is another similar tool, but we won't cover it here. Both `ping` and traceroute have performed DNS lookups, but you can do this directly with `nslookup`, which can be very useful. You can call `nslookup` with command-line parameters, but you can also use it interactively. To do this, simply type the name of the tool into a console or a Command Prompt, as follows:

```
nslookup
```

You will now get a slightly different Command Prompt from within the program. By default, the DNS name servers of the computer you're on are used, and this bypasses any entries in your local *hosts file*.

A hosts file can be very useful for testing changes prior to adding them to DNS. It can also be used as a crude blocker for adverts and trackers by setting their addresses to `0.0.0.0`. There are local DNS servers you can run to do this for your whole network. One such project is `http://pi-hole.net/`, which is based on **dnsmasq** simplifies setting it up and updating the hosts on a **Raspberry Pi**.

Enter the hostname of a server to resolve its IP address; for example, type the following:

```
polling.bbc.co.uk
```

The results show that this hostname is a CNAME (an alias for the real Canonical Name) of `polling.bbc.co.uk.edgekey.net`, which resolves to `e3891.g.akamaiedge.net`, and this currently has an IP address of `23.67.87.132`. We can perform a reverse DNS lookup on the IP address by entering it:

```
23.67.87.132
```

We then get the hostname of that machine, conveniently containing the IP address, which is `a23-67-87-132.deploy.static.akamaitechnologies.com`. The domain name is owned by Akamai, which is a **Content Delivery Network** (**CDN**) used to distribute load.

If you are using a DNS server on your local network, possibly with your router running dnsmasq, then it may cache results, and give you stale data. You can see more up-to-date information by changing the server to a core one that propagates changes quicker. For example, to use one of Google's public DNS servers, enter the following (but be aware that Google will log all the internet sites you visit if you use this normally):

```
server 8.8.8.8
```

Then run the same query again. Notice how the hostname now resolves to a different IP address. This is a common behavior for CDNs, and the record will change over time, even on the same DNS server. It is often used as a technique to balance network load. Changing DNS servers can also sometimes be used to get around naive content filters or location restrictions.

To exit the `nslookup` interactive mode, type `exit` and press *return*. The following screenshot shows the output for the previous commands:

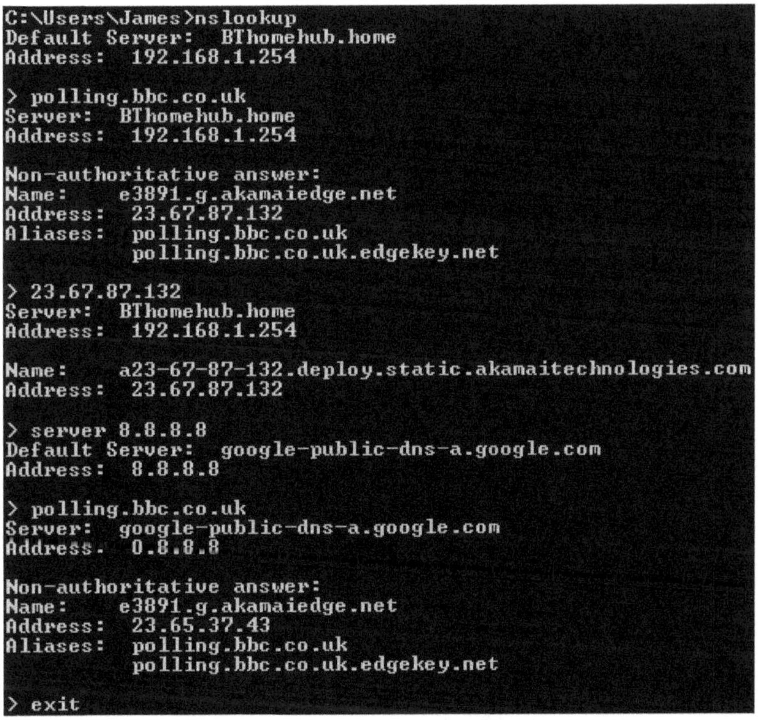

```
C:\Users\James>nslookup
Default Server:  BThomehub.home
Address:  192.168.1.254

> polling.bbc.co.uk
Server:  BThomehub.home
Address:  192.168.1.254

Non-authoritative answer:
Name:     e3891.g.akamaiedge.net
Address:  23.67.87.132
Aliases:  polling.bbc.co.uk
          polling.bbc.co.uk.edgekey.net

> 23.67.87.132
Server:  BThomehub.home
Address:  192.168.1.254

Name:     a23-67-87-132.deploy.static.akamaitechnologies.com
Address:  23.67.87.132

> server 8.8.8.8
Default Server:  google-public-dns-a.google.com
Address:  8.8.8.8

> polling.bbc.co.uk
Server:  google-public-dns-a.google.com
Address.  0.8.8.8

Non-authoritative answer:
Name:     e3891.g.akamaiedge.net
Address:  23.65.37.43
Aliases:  polling.bbc.co.uk
          polling.bbc.co.uk.edgekey.net

> exit
```

IPv4 is the version of IP that you will probably be most familiar with. It uses 32-bit addresses that are usually represented as four dotted decimal octets, such as 192.168.0.1. However, we have run out of IPv4 addresses, and the world is (slowly) moving to the new version of IP, called **IPv6**. The address length has increased fourfold, to 128-bit, and is usually represented in hexadecimal such as 2001:0db8:0000:0000:0000:ee00:0032:154d. Leading zeros can be omitted, such as 2001:db8::ee00:32:154d, to make them easier to write. Localhost loopback (127.0.0.1) is now simply ::1 in IPv6.

On Windows, you can use ping -a x.x.x.x to do a reverse DNS lookup, and resolve IP addresses to hostnames. On Linux (and on other Unix-like systems such as OS X), this feature is not available, and the -a flag serves a different purpose. You will have to use nslookup, or dig for reverse DNS on these OSes.

Build your own

You can build your own tools (such as console applications) using C#, and the functions you need are provided by .NET. The underlying implementations are platform-specific, but the framework will take care of calling the native code on the OS you're using.

You won't normally need to programmatically resolve a hostname, as most networking commands will do this automatically. However, it can occasionally be useful, especially if you want to perform a reverse DNS lookup and find the hostname for an IP address.

The .NET Dns class differs from nslookup, as it includes entries from the local hosts file rather than just querying a DNS server. It is, therefore, more representative of the IP addresses that other processes are resolving.

To programmatically perform a DNS lookup, follow these steps:

1. Add the `System.Net` namespace.

   ```
   using System.Net;
   ```

2. To resolve a hostname to an IP address, use the following static method. This will return an array of IP addresses, although there will usually only be one.

   ```
   var results = await Dns.GetHostAddressesAsync(host);
   ```

3. To resolve an IP address to a hostname, use the following method instead:

   ```
   var revDns = await Dns.GetHostEntryAsync(result);
   ```

4. If successful, then the hostname will be available as `revDns.HostName`.

To programmatically ping a host, follow these steps:

1. Add the `System.Net.NetworkInformation` namespace.

   ```
   using System.Net.NetworkInformation;
   ```

2. You can then instantiate a new `Ping` object.

   ```
   var ping = new Ping();
   ```

3. With this object, you can now ping an IP address or hostname (that will perform a DNS lookup internally) by using the following method:

   ```
   var result = await ping.SendPingAsync(host);
   ```

4. You can get the status of the ping with `result.Status` and, if successful, then you can get the RTT in milliseconds with `result.RoundtripTime`.

The source code for our console application, illustrating how to use the .NET Core `Dns` and `Ping` classes, is available for download along with this book.

A reverse DNS lookup can usually reveal the hosting company being used by a website. Usually, there is only one IP address per hostname, as shown in the following screenshot of our .NET Core console app output:

```
Enter a hostname or IP address:
emonCMS.org

Performing DNS lookup of emonCMS.org
Complete, emonCMS.org = 80.243.190.58
Performing reverse DNS lookup of 80.243.190.58
Complete, 80.243.190.58 = redstation.com

Pinging emonCMS.org 4 times
Ping attempt #1 of 4
Success
20 ms
Ping attempt #2 of 4
Success
20 ms
Ping attempt #3 of 4
Success
20 ms
Ping attempt #4 of 4
Success
20 ms

Press any key to exit...
```

In the preceding screenshot, we can see that `https://emoncms.org/` is using `http://redstation.com/` as a host. The low latency suggests that the server is located in the same country as our computer.

DNS is often used for load balancing. In this case, you will see many IP addresses returned for a single domain name, as shown in the following screenshot:

```
Enter a hostname or IP address:
DuckDuckGo.com

Performing DNS lookup of DuckDuckGo.com
Complete, DuckDuckGo.com = 54.229.105.92
Performing reverse DNS lookup of 54.229.105.92
Complete, 54.229.105.92 = ec2-54-229-105-92.eu-west-1.compute.amazonaws.com

Complete, DuckDuckGo.com = 54.229.105.203
Performing reverse DNS lookup of 54.229.105.203
Complete, 54.229.105.203 = ec2-54-229-105-203.eu-west-1.compute.amazonaws.com

Complete, DuckDuckGo.com = 176.34.131.233
Performing reverse DNS lookup of 176.34.131.233
Complete, 176.34.131.233 = ec2-176-34-131-233.eu-west-1.compute.amazonaws.com

Complete, DuckDuckGo.com = 176.34.155.20
Performing reverse DNS lookup of 176.34.155.20
Complete, 176.34.155.20 = ec2-176-34-155-20.eu-west-1.compute.amazonaws.com

Complete, DuckDuckGo.com = 46.51.197.89
Performing reverse DNS lookup of 46.51.197.89
Complete, 46.51.197.89 = ec2-46-51-197-89.eu-west-1.compute.amazonaws.com

Complete, DuckDuckGo.com = 176.34.135.167
Performing reverse DNS lookup of 176.34.135.167
Complete, 176.34.135.167 = ec2-176-34-135-167.eu-west-1.compute.amazonaws.com

Pinging DuckDuckGo.com 4 times
Ping attempt #1 of 4
Success
27 ms
Ping attempt #2 of 4
Success
27 ms
Ping attempt #3 of 4
Success
27 ms
Ping attempt #4 of 4
Success
27 ms

Press any key to exit...
```

We can see in the preceding screenshot that the privacy-focused search engine
DuckDuckGo (which doesn't track its users like Google does) is using AWS. DNS is being
used to balance the load across various instances; in this case they're all in the Dublin data
center, because that's the closest one. Notice how the ping times are now slightly higher
than the UK-based host in the previous example.

It's likely that they're using the AWS DNS service **Route 53** (so named because DNS uses port 53). This can balance the load across regions, whereas an ELB (which DuckDuckGo doesn't appear to be using) can only balance inside a region (but both inside and across AZs). Azure offers a similar service called **Traffic Manager** for DNS load balancing.

Solutions

Now that you understand a bit more about the causes of latency-based problems, and how to analyze them, we can demonstrate some potential solutions. The measurements that you have taken using the previously illustrated tools will help you quantify the scale of the problems, and choose the appropriate fixes to be applied.

Batching API requests

Rendering a typical web page may require calls to many different APIs (or DB tables) to gather the data required for it. Due to the style of object-oriented programming encouraged by C# (and many other languages), these API calls are often performed in series. However, if the result of one call does not affect another, then this is suboptimal, and the calls could be performed in parallel. We'll cover DB tables later in this chapter, as there are better approaches for them.

Concurrent calls can be more pertinent if you implement a **microservices** architecture (as opposed to the traditional monolith, or big ball of mud), and have lots of different distributed endpoints. Message queues are sometimes a better choice than HTTP APIs in many cases, perhaps using a publish and subscribe pattern. However, maybe you're not responsible for the API, and are instead integrating with a third-party. Indeed, if the API is yours, then you could alter it to provide all the data that you need in one shot anyway.

Consider the example of calling two isolated APIs that have no dependencies on each other. The sequence diagram for this may look something like the following:

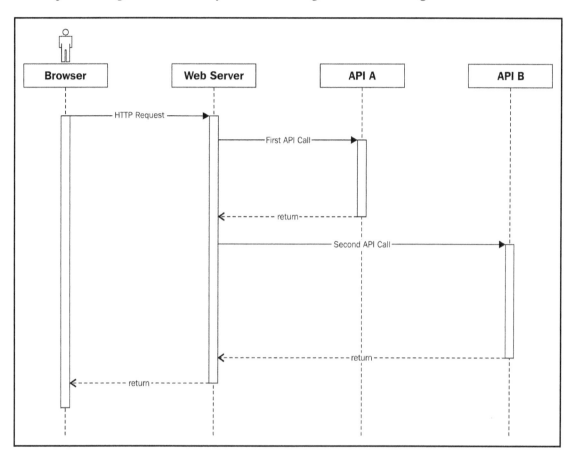

This linear process of calling **A**, and then calling **B** when **A** is done, is simple, as it requires no complex orchestration to wrangle the results of the API calls, but it is slower than necessary. By calling both APIs synchronously and in sequence, we waste time waiting for them to return. A better way of doing this, if we don't require the result of the first API for the request to the second, may be to call them together asynchronously.

The sequence diagram for this new flow may look something like the following:

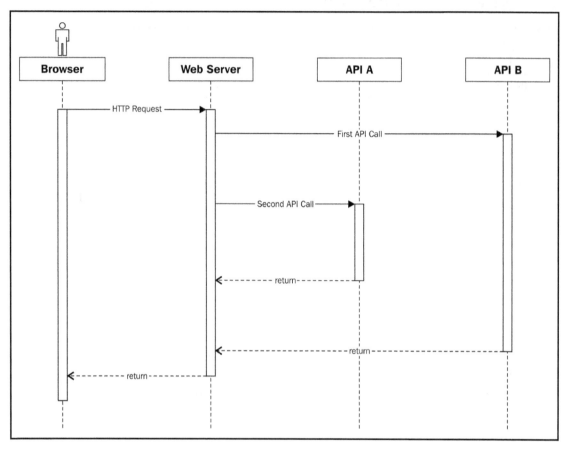

There are two changes in this new sequence, one obvious and the other subtle. We call both APIs asynchronously and in parallel so that they are simultaneously in flight. This first change will have the greatest impact, but there is a smaller tweak that can also help, which is calling the slowest API first.

In the original sequence diagram, we call **API A** and then **API B**, but **B** is slower. Calling **A** and **B** at the same time will have a big impact, but calling **B** and then **A** is slightly better. **B** dominates the timeline, and we will be killing a (relatively) large amount of time waiting for it.

We can use this downtime to call **A**, as there will be some small fixed overhead in any API method call. Both of these changes combined mean that we are now only waiting for **B**, and effectively get the call to **A** for free, in terms of time.

We can illustrate this principle with a simple console application. There are two methods that simulate the APIs, and both are similar. **API A** has the following code:

```
private static async Task CallApiA()
{
    Thread.Sleep(10);
    await Task.Delay(100);
}
```

Thread.Sleep simulates the fixed overhead, and Task.Delay simulates waiting for the API call to return. **API B** takes twice as long to return as **API A**, but the fixed overhead is the same, and it has the following code:

```
private static async Task CallApiB()
{
    Thread.Sleep(10);
    await Task.Delay(200);
}
```

Now, if we synchronously call the methods in sequence, we discover that all of the delays add up, as expected.

```
CallApiA().Wait();
CallApiB().Wait();
```

These operations take a total of around 332 ms on average, as there is about 10 ms of additional intrinsic overhead in the method invocation. If we call both methods simultaneously, the time reduces significantly.

```
Task.WaitAll(CallApiA(), CallApiB());
```

The operations now take an average total of 233 ms. This is good, but we can do better if we swap the order of the methods.

```
Task.WaitAll(CallApiB(), CallApiA());
```

This now takes, on average, a total of 218 ms, because we have swallowed the fixed overheads of **API A** into the time we are waiting for **API B**.

 The full console application that benchmarks these three variants is available for download with this book. It uses the Stopwatch class to time the operations, and averages the results over many runs.

The results of these three different approaches are shown in the following screenshot:

```
Benchmarking over an average of 20 runs
A then B mean elapsed time: 332 ms
A and B mean elapsed time: 233 ms
B and A mean elapsed time: 218 ms
Press any key to exit...
```

As is always the case, measure your results to make sure there really is an improvement. You may find that if you are making many calls to one API, or reusing the same API client, then your requests are processed sequentially, regardless.

This parallelizing of tasks not only works for I/O, but can also be used for computation, as we will discover in the next chapter. For now, we will move on and take a deeper look at database query optimization.

Efficient DB operations

Although this isn't a book aimed at **Database Administrators** (**DBAs**), it's advantageous for you to appreciate the underlying technology that you're using. As is the case with networking, if you understand the strengths and weaknesses, then you can achieve high performance more easily.

This is additionally relevant for the trend of developers doing more work outside of their specialization, particularly in small organizations or startups. You may have heard the related buzzwords **full-stack** developer or **DevOps**. These similar concepts refer to roles that blur the traditional technical boundaries, and merge development (both frontend and backend), quality assurance, networking, infrastructure, operations, and database administration into one job. Being a developer today is no longer a case of just programming or shipping code. It helps to know something about the other areas too.

Previously, in Chapter 5, *Fixing Common Performance Problems*, we covered using the micro O/RM Dapper, and how to fix *select N+1* problems. Now, we'll build on that knowledge, and highlight a few more ways that you can consolidate queries and improve the performance of your DB operations.

As detailed in Chapter 4, *Measuring Performance Bottlenecks*, the first step is to profile your application and discover where the issues lie. Only then should you move on to applying solutions to the problem areas.

Database tuning

We're going to focus more on improving poorly performing queries, so we won't go into DB tuning too much. This is a complex topic, and there is a lot you can learn about indexes and how data is stored.

However, if you haven't run the **Database Engine Tuning Advisor** (**DETA**), then this is an easy step to identify if you have any missing indexes. Yet you should be careful when applying the recommended changes, as there are always downsides and tradeoffs to consider. For example, indexes make retrieving data quicker, but also make it slower to add and update records. They also take up additional space, so it is best not to overdo it. Whether you wish to optimize upfront, or take the hit later on retrieval, will depend on your particular business use case.

The first step is to capture a trace with SQL Server Profiler and save the resulting file. See `Chapter 4`, *Measuring Performance Bottlenecks* for how to do this. The tuning profile is a good choice for capturing a trace and to get good results you should make sure that what you capture is representative of genuine DB use. You can launch the DETA from the same menu as the SQL Server Profiler in SSMS, as shown in the following screenshot:

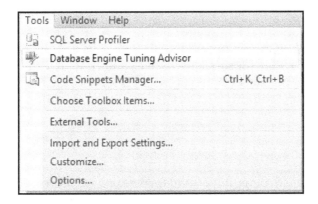

You can then load in your trace as a workload, and after processing it will give you some recommendations. We won't cover the details of how to do this here for space reasons, and it is pretty self-explanatory. There are many good guides available online, if required. You can also see suggested missing indexes if you enable the actual query plan when running a query in SSMS.

Reporting

A common use case, that can often bring a database to its knees, is reporting. Reports usually run on large amounts of data, and can take considerable time if poorly written.

If you already have a method for retrieving a single item from a DB, then it can be tempting to reuse this for reporting purposes and for calculating metrics inside the application. However, this is best avoided and reports should generally have their own dedicated queries.

Even better is to have another database, dedicated to reporting, which is populated from the main DB or from backups. This way, intensive reports won't affect the performance of the main application at the expense of not including real-time data. This is sometimes known as a **data warehouse** or **data mart**, and the data is occasionally denormalized for simplicity or performance reasons. Populating another DB can also be a convenient way to test your backups, as database backups should always be tested to ensure that they can be restored correctly and that they contain all of the required data.

 In the ensuing examples, we will focus on **Microsoft SQL Server (MS SQL)** and the **Transact-SQL (T-SQL)** dialect of SQL. Other databases, such as PostgreSQL, are available as well. PostgreSQL has its own dialect called **Procedural Language / PostgreSQL (PL/pgSQL)**, which is similar to **Oracle PL/SQL**. These dialects all support basic SQL commands, but use different syntax for some operations, and contain different or additional features. The latest version of MS SQL Server, SQL Server 2017, supports running on Linux and in Docker containers, in addition to running on Windows.

Aggregates

Aggregate functions are an incredibly useful feature of a RDBMS. You can compute values that summarize many records in the database and only return the result, keeping the source data rows in the DB.

You will be familiar with the COUNT aggregate function from earlier in the book, if not before. This gives you the total number of records returned by your query, but without returning them. You may have read that COUNT(1) performs better than COUNT(*), but this is no longer the case, as SQL Server now optimizes the latter to perform the same as the former.

By default, SQL Server will return a message detailing the count of the records returned, along with the result of every query. You can turn this off by prefixing your query with the SET NOCOUNT ON command, which will save a few bytes in the **Tabular Data Stream** (**TDS**) connection, and increase performance slightly. This is significant only if a **cursor** is being used, which is bad practice anyway for locking reasons. It's good practice to re-enable row count after the query, even though it will be reset outside the local scope anyway.

In Chapter 5, *Fixing Common Performance Problems*, we solved our *select N+1* problem by joining tables in the DB, and using COUNT instead of performing these calculations in our application code. There are many other aggregate functions available that can be useful in improving performance, especially for reporting purposes.

Going back to our earlier example, suppose we now want to find out the total number of blog posts. We also want to find the total number of comments, the average comment count, the lowest number of comments for a single post, and the highest number of comments for a single post.

The first part is easy, just apply COUNT to the posts instead of the comments, but the second part is harder. As we already have our list of posts with a comment count for each, it may be tempting to reuse that, and simply work everything out in our C# code.

This would be a bad idea, and the query would perform poorly, especially if the number of posts is high. A better solution would be to use a query such as the following:

```
;WITH PostCommentCount AS(
SELECT
    bp.BlogPostId,
    COUNT(bpc.BlogPostCommentId) 'CommentCount'
FROM BlogPost bp
LEFT JOIN BlogPostComment bpc
    ON bpc.BlogPostId = bp.BlogPostId
GROUP BY bp.BlogPostId
) SELECT
    COUNT(BlogPostId) 'TotalPosts',
    SUM(CommentCount) 'TotalComments',
    AVG(CommentCount) 'AverageComments',
    MIN(CommentCount) 'MinimumComments',
    MAX(CommentCount) 'MaximumComments'
FROM PostCommentCount
```

This query uses a **Common Table Expression** (CTE), but you could also use a nested SELECT to embed the first query into the FROM clause of the second. It illustrates a selection of the aggregate functions available, and the results on the test database from before look like the following:

	TotalPosts	TotalComments	AverageComments	MinimumComments	MaximumComments
1	3000	44748	14	0	141

The semicolon at the start is simply a good practice to avoid errors and remove ambiguity. It ensures that any previous command has been terminated, as WITH can be used in other contexts. It isn't required for the preceding example, but might be if it were part of a larger query. CTEs can be very useful tools, especially if you require recursion. However, they are evaluated every time, so you may find that temporary tables perform much better for you, especially if querying one repeatedly in a nested SELECT.

Now suppose that we wish to perform the same query, but only include posts that have at least one comment. In this case, we could use a query such as the following:

```
;WITH PostCommentCount AS (
SELECT
    bp.BlogPostId,
    COUNT(bpc.BlogPostCommentId) 'CommentCount'
FROM BlogPost bp
LEFT JOIN BlogPostComment bpc
    ON bpc.BlogPostId = bp.BlogPostId
GROUP BY bp.BlogPostId
HAVING COUNT(bpc.BlogPostCommentId) > 0
) SELECT
    COUNT(BlogPostId) 'TotalPosts',
    SUM(CommentCount) 'TotalComments',
    AVG(CommentCount) 'AverageComments',
    MIN(CommentCount) 'MinimumComments',
    MAX(CommentCount) 'MaximumComments'
FROM PostCommentCount
```

We have added a HAVING clause to ensure that we only count posts with more than zero comments. This is similar to a WHERE clause, but for use with a GROUP BY. The query results now look something like the following:

	TotalPosts	TotalComments	AverageComments	MinimumComments	MaximumComments
1	1361	44748	32	1	141

Sampling

Sometimes, you don't need to use all of the data, and can sample it. This technique is particularly applicable to any time-series information that you may wish to graph. In SQL Server, the traditional way to perform random sampling was using the NEWID() method, but this can be slow. For example, consider the following query:

```
SELECT TOP 1 PERCENT *
FROM [dbo].[TrainStatus]
ORDER BY NEWID()
```

This query returns exactly 1% of the rows with a random distribution. When run against a table with 1,205,855 entries, it returned 12,059 results in about four seconds, which is slow. A better way may be to use TABLESAMPLE, which is available in any reasonably recent version of SQL Server (2005 onwards), as follows:

```
SELECT *
FROM [dbo].[TrainStatus]
TABLESAMPLE (1 PERCENT)
```

This preceding query is much quicker, and when run against the same data as the previous example, it completes almost instantly. The downside is that it's cruder than the earlier method, and it won't return exactly 1% of the results. It will return roughly 1%, but the value will change every time it is run. For example, running against the same test database, it returned 11,504, 13,441, and 11,427 rows when executing the query three times in a row.

Inserting data

Querying databases may be the most common use case, but you will usually need to put some data in there in the first place. One of the most commonly used features when inserting records into a relational DB is the identity column. This is an auto-incrementing ID that is generated by the database, and doesn't need to be supplied when adding data.

For example, in our `BlogPost` table from earlier, the `BlogPostId` column is created as `INTIDENTITY(1,1)`. This means that it's an integer value starting at one and increasing by one for every new row. You `INSERT` into this table, without specifying `BlogPostId`, like so:

```
INSERT INTO BlogPost (Title, Content)
VALUES ('My Awesome Post', 'Write something witty here...')
```

Identities can be very useful, but you will usually want to know the ID of your newly created record. It is typical to want to store a row, then immediately retrieve it so that the ID can be used for future editing operations. You can do this in one shot with the `OUTPUT` clause, like so;

```
INSERT INTO BlogPost (Title, Content)
OUTPUT INSERTED.BlogPostId
VALUES ('My Awesome Post', 'Write something witty here...')
```

In addition to inserting the row, the ID will be returned.

 You may see `SCOPE_IDENTITY()` (or even `@@IDENTITY`) advocated as a way of retrieving the identity, but these are outdated. The recommended way of doing this, on modern versions of SQL Server, is to use `OUTPUT`.

`OUTPUT` works on the `INSERT`, `UPDATE`, `DELETE`, and `MERGE` commands. It even works when operating on multiple rows at a time, as in this example of bulk-inserting two blog posts:

```
INSERT INTO BlogPost (Title, Content)
OUTPUT INSERTED.BlogPostId
VALUES ('My Awesome Post', 'Write something witty here...'),
       ('My Second Awesome Post', 'Try harder this time...')
```

The preceding query will return a result set of two identities, for example, 3003 and 3004. In order to execute these inserts with Dapper, you can use the following method for a single record. First, let us create a blog post object, which we'll hardcode here but would normally come from user input:

```
var post = new BlogPost
{
    Title = "My Awesome Post",
    Content = "Write something witty here..."
};
```

To insert this one post, and set the ID, you can use the following code. This will execute the INSERT statement, and return a single integer value.

```
post.BlogPostId = await connection.ExecuteScalarAsync<int>(@"
    INSERT INTO BlogPost (Title, Content)
    OUTPUT INSERTED.BlogPostId
    VALUES (@Title, @Content)",
    post);
```

You can then assign the returned ID to the post, and return that object to the user for editing. There is no need to select the record again, assuming the insert succeeds and no exceptions are thrown.

You can insert multiple records at once with the same SQL by using the execute method. However, the SQL will be executed multiple times, which may be inefficient, and you only get back the number of inserted rows, not their IDs. The following code supplies an array of posts to the same SQL used in the previous example:

```
var numberOfRows = await connection.ExecuteAsync(@"
    INSERT INTO BlogPost (Title, Content)
    OUTPUT INSERTED.BlogPostId
    VALUES (@Title, @Content)",
    new[] { post, post, post });
```

If you want multiple IDs returned, then you will need to use the query method to return a collection of values, as we have done previously. However, it is difficult to make this work for a variable number of records, without dynamically building SQL. The following code performs a bulk insert, using multiple separate parameters for the query:

```
var ids = await connection.QueryAsync<int>(@"
    INSERT INTO BlogPost (Title, Content)
    OUTPUT INSERTED.BlogPostId
    VALUES (@Title1, @Content1),
           (@Title2, @Content2)", new
    {
        Title1 = post.Title,
        Content1 = post.Content,
        Title2 = post.Title,
        Content2 = post.Content
    });
```

This will perform all the work in a single command, and return an enumerable collection of the identities. However, this code is not very scalable (or even elegant) and you can only insert up to 1,000 records this way.

There are many helper methods in the `Dapper.Contrib` package that can assist you with inserting records and other operations. However, they suffer from the same limitations as the examples here, and you can only return a single identity or the number of rows inserted.

GUIDs

Integer identities can be useful to a database internally, but perhaps you shouldn't be using an identifying key externally, especially if you have multiple web servers or expose the IDs to users. An alternative is to use a **Globally Unique Identifier** (**GUID**), referred to as `UNIQUEIDENTIFIER` in SQL Server. We have already touched on these, as they are generated by the `NEWID()` function used in the suboptimal sampling example.

GUIDs are used ubiquitously and are 16 bytes long, four times bigger than an integer. The size of GUIDs means that you are unlikely to get a **unique constraint** conflict when inserting a random GUID into an already populated table.

People sometimes worry about GUID collisions, but the numbers involved are so staggeringly huge that collisions are incredibly unlikely. The GUIDs generated by .NET (using a `COM` function on Windows) are, specifically, **Universally Unique Identifiers** (**UUIDs**) version 4. These have 122 bits of randomness, so you would need to generate nearly three quintillion GUIDs before having even half a chance of a collision. At one new record per second, that would take over 90 billion years. Even at two million GUIDs per second (what an average computer today could produce), it would still take over 45 thousand years (more time than human civilization has been around). If you think that this will be an issue for your software, then you should probably be future-proofing it by using five-digit years, such as 02017, to avoid the *Y10K* (or *YAK* in hexadecimal) problem.

This uniqueness property allows you to generate a GUID in your application code and store it in a distributed database, without worrying about merging data later. It also allows you to expose IDs to users, without caring if someone will enumerate them or try and guess a value. Integer IDs often expose how many records there are in a table, which could be sensitive information depending on your use case.

One thing you have to watch out for with random GUIDs is using them as keys, as opposed to IDs. The difference between these two terms is subtle, and they are often one and the same. The key (**primary** or **clustered**) is what the DB uses to address a record, whereas the ID is what you would use to retrieve one. These can be the same value but they don't have to be. Using a random GUID as a key can cause performance issues with indexing. The randomness may cause fragmentation, which will slow down queries.

You can use sequential GUIDs, for example `NEWSEQUENTIALID()` can be the `DEFAULT` value for a column, but then you lose most of the beneficial qualities of GUIDs that mainly come from the randomness. You now effectively just have a really big integer, and if you're only concerned with the maximum number of rows in a table, and require more than two billion, then a `big int` (twice an `int`, but half a GUID) should suffice.

A good compromise is to have an `int` identity as the primary key, but to use a GUID as the ID (and enforce this with a unique constraint on the column). It's best if you generate the GUID in application code with `Guid.NewGuid()`, as using a default column value in the DB means you have to retrieve the ID after an insert, as shown previously.

A table using this strategy may partially look something like the following screenshot. This is a screen capture of part of a table from the **MembershipReboot** user management and authentication library:

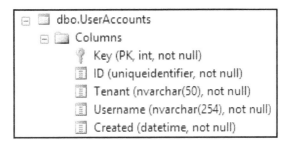

Advanced DB topics

There are many other database performance enhancing techniques that we could cover here, but don't have space for. We'll briefly mention some additional topics in case you want to look into them further. Visit the author's website at `https://unop.uk/` for more information on other topics.

A common requirement when saving data is to insert a record if it doesn't yet exist, or to update an existing record if there is already a row containing that ID. This is sometimes referred to as an **upsert**, which is a portmanteau word combining update and insert.

You can use the MERGE command to do this in one operation and not worry about choosing between UPDATE or INSERT (wrapped in a **transaction** inside a **stored procedure**). However, MERGE does not perform as well as UPDATE or INSERT, so always test the effects for your use case, and use it sparingly.

Stored procedures, transactions, and **locking** are all big subjects on their own. They are important to understand, and not only from a performance perspective.

We can't fit all of these in here, but we will touch upon maintaining stored procedures later in the book.

Some other techniques you could look into are **cross-database joins**, which can save you from querying multiple DBs. There is also the practice of **denormalizing** your data, which involves flattening your relational records ahead of time to provide a single row rather than needing to join across many tables for a query. We briefly mentioned this in relation to data warehouses earlier.

 You can find lots of useful SQL documentation and information on MSDN (http://msdn.microsoft.com/) and TechNet (http://technet. microsoft.com/). Additionally, there are many good books on advanced SQL techniques.

Finally, a note on housekeeping. It's important to have a plan for managing the size of a database. You can't simply keep inserting data into a table, and hope it will continue to perform well forever. At some point, it will get so large that even deleting records from it will cause your DB to grind to a crawl (even if you use TRUNCATE, which performs better than a simple DELETE). You should know ahead of time how you will remove or archive rows, and it is better to do this regularly in small batches.

Simulation and testing

To wrap up this chapter, let's reiterate the importance of being able to test your application on realistic infrastructure. Your test environments should be as live-like as possible. If you don't test on equivalent DBs and networks, then you may get a nasty surprise come deployment time.

When using a cloud hosting provider (and if you automate your server builds), then this is easy. You can simply spin up a staging system that matches production. You don't have to provision it to the exact same scale as long as all the parts are there and in the same place. To reduce costs further, you only need to keep it around for as long as your test.

Alternatively, you could create a new live environment, deploy and test it, then switch over, and destroy or reuse the old live environment. This swapping technique is known as **blue-green deployment**. Another option is to deploy new code behind a **feature switch**, which allows you to toggle the feature at runtime, and only for some users. Not only does this allow you to functionally verify features with test users, you can also gradually roll out a new feature, and monitor the performance impact as you do so. We cover both of these techniques in `Chapter 11`, *Monitoring Performance Regressions*.

Summary

We've covered a lot in this chapter, and it should hopefully be clear that being a high-performance developer requires more than simply being a capable programmer. There are many externalities to consider around your code.

You now understand the basics of I/O, and the physical causes of the intrinsic limitations present. You can analyze and diagnose how a network logically fits together. We have covered how to make better use of the network to reduce overall latency, which is important as more I/O operations now happen over a network. You have also seen how to make better use of a database, and how to do more with fewer operations.

In the next chapter, we will dig into code execution in detail, and show you how to speed up your C#. We'll see how .NET Core and ASP.NET Core perform so much better than the previous versions, and how you can take advantage of these improvements.

8
Understanding Code Execution and Asynchronous Operations

This chapter covers solving performance problems in the execution of your code, which is not normally the first location where speed issues occur, but can be a good additional optimization. We'll discuss the areas where performance is needed, and where it is okay (or even required) to be slow. The merits of various data structures will be compared, from the standard built-in generic collections to the more exotic. We will demonstrate how to compute operations in parallel, and how to take advantage of extra instruction sets that your CPU may provide. We'll dive into the internals of ASP.NET Core and .NET Core to highlight the improvements that you should be aware of.

The topics covered in this chapter include the following:

- .NET Core and the standard library
- **Common Language Runtime (CLR)** services
- ASP.NET Core and the Kestrel web server
- Generic collections and Bloom filters
- Serialization and data representation formats
- Relative performance of hashing functions
- Parallelization (SIMD, TPL, and PLINQ)
- Multithreading, concurrency, and locking
- Poorly performing practices to avoid

You will learn how to compute results in parallel and combine the outputs at the end. This includes how to avoid incorrect ways of doing this, which can make things worse. You'll also learn how to reduce server utilization, and to choose the most appropriate data structures in order to process information efficiently for your specific situation.

Getting started with the core projects

There are many benefits to using .NET Core and ASP.NET Core over the old full versions of the frameworks. The main enhancements are open source development and cross-platform support, but there are also significant performance improvements. Open development is important and not only is the source code is available, but also the development work happens in the open on GitHub. The community is encouraged to make contributions and these may be merged-in upstream if they pass a code review; the flow isn't just one way. This has led to increased performance and additional platform support coming from outside Microsoft. If you find a bug in a framework, you can now fix it rather than work around the problem and hope for a patch.

The multiple projects that make up frameworks are split across two organizations on GitHub. One of the driving principles has been to split the frameworks up into modules, so you can just take what you need rather than the whole monolithic installation. The lower-level framework, .NET Core, can be found, along with other projects, under `https://github.com/dotnet`. The higher-level web application framework, ASP.NET Core, can be found under `https://github.com/aspnet`.

Let's have a quick look at some of the various .NET Core repositories and how they fit together.

.NET Core

There are a couple of projects that form the main parts of .NET Core and these are CoreCLR and **CoreFX**. CoreCLR contains the .NET Core CLR and the base core library, `mscorlib`. The CLR is the virtual machine that runs your .NET code. CoreCLR contains a **just-in-time (JIT) compiler** (**RyuJIT**), **Garbage Collector** (**GC**), and also base types and classes in mscorlib. CoreFX includes the foundational libraries and sits on top of CoreCLR. This includes most built-in components that aren't simple types. There is also the Roslyn compiler, which turns your C# (or other .NET language code) into **Common Intermediate Language** (**CIL**) bytecode. RyuJIT then turns this into native machine code at runtime.

You may have heard of the upcoming native tool chain. This promises even more performance improvements, as the compilation does not have to happen quickly, in real time, and can be further optimized. For example, a build can be tuned for execution speed at the expense of compilation speed. It's conceptually similar to the **Native Image Generator** (**NGen**) tool, which has been in the full .NET Framework since its inception. Unfortunately, .NET native for Core projects has been delayed and pushed back until after the release of .NET Core 2. Currently it is only available for UWP Windows Store apps but when expanded it will be worth considering.

Although .NET Core generally performs better than the previous .NET Framework, some performance settings are configured differently. For example, you may be familiar with the `<gcServer>` element, used to set a GC mode, that performs better on machines with more than two processors. In .NET Core you can set `ServerGarbageCollection` to `true` in your `.csproj` file like so:

```
<PropertyGroup>
    <ServerGarbageCollection>true</ServerGarbageCollection>
</PropertyGroup>
```

ASP.NET Core

ASP.NET Core runs on top of .NET Core, although it can also run on the full .NET Framework. We will only cover running on .NET Core, as this performs better and ensures enhanced platform support. There are many projects that make up ASP.NET Core and it's worth briefly mentioning some of them.

It's useful to not include any framework references to .NET 4 in your project, so that you can be sure you're only using .NET Core and don't accidentally reference any dependencies that are not yet supported. This is less of a problem with .NET Standard 2.0, so if you stick to the supported APIs then your project should work on all frameworks that implement them.

ASP.NET Core includes **Model-View-Controller** (**MVC**), **Web API,** and **Razor Pages** (a way to make simple pages with the **Razor** view engine, similar to PHP, and the spiritual successor to classic ASP). These features are all merged together, so you don't need to think of MVC and Web API as separate frameworks anymore. There are many other projects and repositories, including **EF Core**, but the one we will highlight here is the Kestrel HTTP server.

Kestrel

Kestrel is a new web server for ASP.NET Core and it performs brilliantly. It's based on **libuv**, which is an asynchronous I/O abstraction and support library that also runs below Node.js. Kestrel is blazingly fast, and the benchmarks are very impressive. However, it is pretty basic, and for production hosting, you should put it behind a reverse proxy, so that you can use caching and other features to service a greater number of users. You can use many HTTP or proxy servers for this purpose such as IIS, nginx, Apache, or HAProxy.

 You should be careful with your configuration if using nginx as a reverse proxy, as by default it will retry POST requests if the response from your web server times out. This could result in duplicate operations being performed, especially if used as a load balancer across multiple backend HTTP servers.

Data structures

Data structures are objects that you can use to store the information you're working on. Choosing the best implementation for how your data is used can have dramatic effects on the speed of execution. Here, we'll discuss some common and some more interesting data structures that you might like to make use of.

As this is a book about web application programming and not one on complex algorithm implementation or micro-optimization, we won't be going into a huge amount of detail on data structures and algorithms. As briefly mentioned in the introduction, other factors can dwarf execution speed in a web context, and we assume you're not writing a game engine. However, good algorithms can help speed up applications, so, if you are working in an area where execution performance is important, you should read more about them.

We're more interested in the performance of the system as a whole, not necessarily the speed the code runs at. It is often more important to consider what your code expresses (and how this affects other systems) than how it executes. Nevertheless, it is still important to choose the right tool for the job, and you don't want to have unnecessarily slow code. Just be careful of over-optimizing when it already executes fast enough, and above all, try to keep it readable.

Lists

A .NET `List<T>` is a staple of programming in C#. It's type-safe, so you don't have to bother with casting or boxing. You specify your generic type and can be sure that only objects of that primitive or class (or ones that inherit from them) can be in your list. Lists implement the standard list and enumerable interfaces (`IList` and `IEnumerable`), although you get more methods on the concrete list implementation, for example, adding a range. You can also use **Language-Integrated Query** (**LINQ**) expressions to easily query them, which is trivial when using **fluent lambda functions**. However, although LINQ is often an elegant solution to a problem, it can lead to performance issues, as it is not always optimized.

A list is really just an enhanced, one-dimensional, array. In fact, it uses an array internally to store the data. In some cases, it may be better to directly use an array for performance. Arrays can occasionally be a better choice, if you know exactly how much data there will be, and you need to iterate through it inside a tight loop. They can also be useful if you need more dimensions, or plan to consume all of the data in the array.

You should be careful with arrays; use them sparingly and only if benchmarking shows a performance problem when iterating over a list. Although they can be faster, they also make parallel programming and distributed architecture more difficult, which is where significant performance improvements can be made.

Modern high performance means scaling out to many cores and multiple machines. This is easier with an **immutable** state that doesn't change, which is easier to enforce with higher level abstractions than with arrays. For example, you can help enforce a read-only list with an interface.

If you are inserting or removing a lot of items in the middle of a large list, then it may be better to use the `LinkedList<T>` class. This has different performance characteristics from a list, as it isn't really a list, it's more of a chain. It may perform better than a list for some specialized cases, but, in most common cases, it will be slower. For example, access by index is quick with a list (as it is array-backed), but slow with a linked list (as you will have to walk the chain).

It is normally best to initially focus on the what and why of your code rather than the how. LINQ is very good for this, as you simply declare your intentions, and don't need to worry about the implementation details and loops. It is a bad idea to optimize prematurely, so do this only if testing shows a performance problem. In most common cases, a list is the correct choice unless you need to select only a few values from a large set, in which case, dictionaries can perform better.

Dictionaries

Dictionaries are similar to lists, but excel at quickly retrieving a specific value with a key. Internally, they are implemented with a hash table. There's the legacy `Hashtable` class (in the `System.Collections.NonGeneric` package) but this is not type safe, whereas `Dictionary<T>` is a generic type, so you probably shouldn't use `Hashtable` unless you're porting old code to .NET Core. The same applies to `ArrayList`, which is the legacy, non-generic version of `List`.

A dictionary can look up a value with a key very quickly, whereas a list will need to go through all the values until the key is found. You can, however, still enumerate a dictionary as it is ordered, although this isn't really how it is intended to be used. If you don't need ordering, then you can use a `HashSet`. There are sorted versions of all of these data structures, and you can again use read-only interfaces to make them difficult to mutate.

Collection benchmarks

Accurate benchmarking is hard and there are lots of things that can skew your results. Compilers are very clever and will optimize, which can make trivial benchmarks less valuable. The compiler may output very similar code for different implementations.

What you put in your data structures will also have a large effect on their performance. It's usually best to test or profile your actual application and not optimize prematurely. Readability of code is very valuable and shouldn't be sacrificed for runtime efficiency unless there is a significant performance problem (or if it's already unreadable).

There are benchmarking frameworks that you can use to help with your testing, such as BenchmarkDotNet, which is available at `https://github.com/dotnet/BenchmarkDotNet`. However, these can be an overkill, and are sometimes tricky to set up. Other options include **Simple Speed Tester** (which you can read more about at `http://theburningmonk.github.io/SimpleSpeedTester/`) and **MiniBench** (available from `https://github.com/minibench`).

> You can read more about the benchmarks of the ASP.NET Core framework at `https://github.com/aspnet/benchmarks`.

We'll perform some simple benchmarks to show how you might go about this. However, don't assume that the conclusions drawn here will always hold true, so test for your situation. The examples here have been kept deliberately simple so that you can run them easily, although we do try to avoid some obvious errors.

First, we will define a simple function to run our tests:

```
private static long RunTest(Func<double> func, int runs = 1000)
{
    var s = Stopwatch.StartNew();
    for (int j = 0; j < runs; j++)
    {
        func();
    }
    s.Stop();
    return s.ElapsedMilliseconds;
}
```

We use `Stopwatch` here as using `DateTime` can cause problems, even when using UTC, as the time could change during the test and the resolution isn't high enough. We also need to perform many runs to get an accurate result. We'll then define our data structures to test and prepopulate them with random data:

```
var rng = new Random();
var elements = 100000;
var randomDic = new Dictionary<int, double>();
for (int i = 0; i < elements; i++)
{
    randomDic.Add(i, rng.NextDouble());
}
var randomList = randomDic.ToList();
var randomArray = randomList.ToArray();
```

We now have an array, list, and a dictionary containing the same set of 100,000 key/value pairs. Next, we can perform some tests on them to see what structure performs best in various situations:

```
var afems = RunTest(() =>
{
    var sum = 0d;
    foreach (var element in randomArray)
    {
        sum += element.Value;
    }
    return sum;
}, runs);
```

The preceding code times how long it takes to iterate over an array in a `foreach` loop and sums up the double precision floating point values. We can then compare this to other structures and the different ways of accessing them. For example, iterating a dictionary in a `for` loop is done as follows:

```
var dfms = RunTest (() =>
{
    var sum = 0d;
    for (int i = 0; i < randomDic.Count; i++)
    {
        sum += randomDic[i];
    }
    return sum;
}, runs);
```

This performs very badly, as it is not how dictionaries are supposed to be used. Dictionaries excel at extracting a record by its key very quickly. So quickly in fact that you will need to run the test many more times to get a realistic value:

```
var lastKey = randomList.Last().Key;
var dsms = RunTest (() =>
{
    double result;
    if (randomDic.TryGetValue(lastKey, out result))
    {
        return result;
    }
    return 0d;
}, runs * 10000);
Console.WriteLine($"Dict select {(double)dsms / 10000} ms");
```

Getting a value from a dictionary with `TryGetValue` is extremely quick. You need to pass the variable to be set into the method as an `out` parameter. You can see if this was successful and if the item was in the dictionary by testing the Boolean value returned by the method.

Conversely, adding items to a dictionary one by one can be slow, so it all depends on what you're optimizing for.

The following screenshot shows the output of a very simple console application that tests various combinatorial permutations of data structures and their uses:

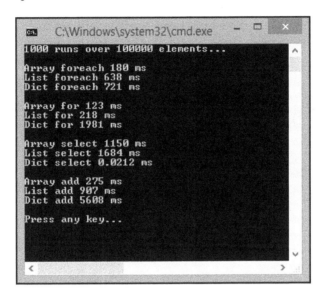

These results, shown in the preceding image, are informative, but you should be skeptical, as many things can skew the output, for example, the ordering of the tests. If the gap is small, then there is probably not much to choose between the two variants, but you can clearly see large differences.

To get more realistic results, be sure to compile in release mode and run without debugging. The absolute results will depend on your machine and architecture but the relative measures should be useful for comparisons, if the differences are large.

The main lesson here is to measure for your specific application and choose the most appropriate data structure for the work that you are performing. The collections in the standard library should serve you well for most purposes; others that are not covered here can sometimes be useful, such as a `Queue` or `Stack`.

You can find more information about built-in collections and data structures on MSDN (`http://msdn.microsoft.com/en-us/library/system.collections.generic`). You can also read about them on the .NET Core documentation site on the GitHub pages (`https://docs.microsoft.com/en-us/dotnet/standard/collections/`).

However, there are some rarer data structures, not in the standard collection, that you may occasionally wish to use. We'll show an example of one of these now.

Bloom filters

Bloom filters are an interesting data structure that can increase performance for certain use cases. They use multiple overlaid hashing functions and can quickly tell you if an item definitely does not exist in a set. However, they can't say with certainty if an item exists, only that it is likely to. They are useful as a pre-filter, so that you can avoid performing a lookup, because you know for sure that the item won't be there.

The following diagram shows how a Bloom filter works. **A**, **B**, and **C** have been hashed and inserted into the filter. **D** is hashed to check if it is in the filter but, as it maps to a zero bit, we know that it is not in there:

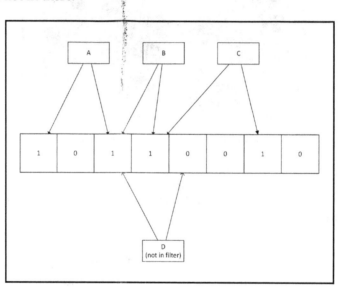

Bloom filters are much smaller than holding all the data or even a list of hashes for each item in the set. They can also be much quicker, as the lookup time is constant for any size of set. This constant time can be lower than the time to look up an item in a large list or dictionary, especially if it is on the filesystem or in a remote database.

An example application for a Bloom filter could be a local DNS server, which has a list of domains to override, but forwards most requests to an upstream server. If the list of custom domains is large, then it may be advantageous to create a Bloom filter from the entries and hold this in memory.

When a request comes in, it is checked against the filter, and if it doesn't exist, then the request is forwarded to the upstream server. If the entry does exist in the filter, then the local hosts file is consulted; if the entry is there, its value is used. There is a small chance that the entry will not be in the list, even if the filter thinks it is. In this case, when it isn't found, the request is forwarded, but this approach still avoids the need to consult the list for every request.

Another example of using a Bloom filter is in a caching node, perhaps as part of a proxy or CDN. You wouldn't want to cache resources that are only requested once, but how can you tell when the second request occurs if you haven't cached it? If you add the request to a Bloom filter, you can easily tell when the second request occurs and then cache the resource.

Bloom filters are also used in some databases to avoid expensive disk operations and in **Cache Digests**, which allow an agent to declare the contents of its cache. HTTP/2 may support Cache Digests in the future, but this will probably use **Golomb-coded sets** (**GCS**), which are similar to Bloom filters but smaller, at the expense of slower queries.

There is an open source implementation of a Bloom filter in .NET available at `http://bloomfilter.codeplex.com/` among others. You should test the performance for yourself to make sure it offers an improvement.

Hashing and checksums

Hashing is an important concept that is often used to ensure data integrity or lookup values quickly and so it is optimized to be fast. This is why general hashing functions should not be used on their own to securely store passwords. If the algorithm is quick, then the password can be guessed in a reasonably short amount of time. Hashing algorithms vary in their complexity, speed of execution, output length, and collision rate.

A very basic error detection algorithm is called a **parity check**. This adds a single bit to a block of data and is rarely used directly in programming. It is, however, extensively used at the hardware level, as it is very quick. Yet, it may miss many errors where there are an even number of corruptions.

A **Cyclic Redundancy Check** (**CRC**) is a slightly more complex error detecting algorithm. The **CRC-32** (also written **CRC32**) version is commonly used in software, particularly in compression formats, as a **checksum**.

You may be familiar with the built-in support for hash codes in .NET (with the `GetHashCode` method on all objects), but you should be very careful with this. The only function of this method is to assist with picking buckets in data structures that use hash tables internally, such as a dictionary, and also in some LINQ operations. It is not suitable as a checksum or key, because it is not cryptographically secure and it varies across frameworks, processes, and time.

You may have used the **Message Digest 5** (**MD5**) algorithm in the past, but today its use is strongly discouraged. The security of MD5 is heavily compromised and collisions can be produced easily. Since it is very quick, it may have some non-secure uses, such as non-malicious error checking, but there are better algorithms that are fast enough.

If you need a strong but quick hashing function, then the **Secure Hash Algorithm** (**SHA**) family is a good choice. However, **SHA-1** is not considered future-proof, so for new code **SHA-256** is generally a better choice.

When signing messages, you should use a dedicated **Message Authentication Code** (**MAC**), such as a **Hash-based MAC** (**HMAC**), which avoids vulnerabilities in a single pass of the hashing function. A good option is the `HMACSHA256` class built into .NET. Various APIs, such as some AWS REST APIs, use **HMAC-SHA256** to authenticate requests. This ensures that, even if the request is performed over an unencrypted HTTP channel, the API key can't be intercepted and recovered.

As briefly mentioned in Chapter 2, *Why Performance Is a Feature*, password hashing is a special case and general-purpose hashing algorithms are not suitable for it as they are too fast. A good choice is **Password-Based Key Derivation Function 2** (**PBKDF2**), which we used as an example in Chapter 4, *Measuring Performance Bottlenecks*. PBKDF2 is a particularly popular choice for .NET, as it is built into the framework, and so the implementation is more likely to be correct. It has been built against an RFC and reviewed by Microsoft, which you can't say for any random piece of code found online. For example, you could download an implementation of **bcrypt** for .NET, but you have to trust that it was coded correctly or verify it yourself.

Hashing benchmarks

Let's do some simple benchmarking of various hash functions to see how they compare performance-wise. In the following code snippet, we define a method for running our tests, similar to the one for the previous collection benchmarks:

```
private static long RunTest(Action func, int runs = 1000)
{
    var s = Stopwatch.StartNew();
    for (int j = 0; j < runs; j++)
    {
        func();
    }
    s.Stop();
    return s.ElapsedMilliseconds;
}
```

We include the following using statement:

```
using System.Security.Cryptography;
```

Next, we define a short private constant string (hashingData) to hash in the class and get the bytes for it in an 8-bit Unicode (UTF8) format:

```
var smallBytes = Encoding.UTF8.GetBytes(hashingData);
```

We also want to get a larger block of bytes to hash to see how it compares performance-wise. For this, we use a cryptographically secure random number generator:

```
var largeBytes = new byte[smallBytes.Length * 100];
var rng = RandomNumberGenerator.Create();
rng.GetBytes(largeBytes);
```

We need a key for some of our functions, so we use the same technique to generate this:

```
var key = new byte[256];
var rng = RandomNumberGenerator.Create();
rng.GetBytes(key);
```

Next, we create a sorted list of the algorithms to test and execute the tests for each one:

```
var algos = new SortedList<string, HashAlgorithm>
{
    {"1.            MD5", MD5.Create()},
    {"2.          SHA-1", SHA1.Create()},
    {"3.        SHA-256", SHA256.Create()},
    {"4.     HMAC SHA-1", new HMACSHA1(key)},
    {"5. HMAC SHA-256", new HMACSHA256(key)},
};
foreach (var algo in algos)
{
    HashAlgorithmTest(algo);
}
```

Our test method runs the following tests on each algorithm. They all inherit from `HashAlgorithm`, so we can run the `ComputeHash` method on each of them for small and large byte arrays:

```
var smallTimeMs = RunTest(() =>
{
    algo.Value.ComputeHash(smallBytes);
}, runs);
var largeTimeMs = RunTest(() =>
{
    algo.Value.ComputeHash(largeBytes);
}, runs);
```

We then calculate the average (mean) time for both sizes. We cast the long integer to a double precision floating point number so that we can represent small values between one and zero:

```
var avgSmallTimeMs = (double)smallTimeMs / runs;
var avgLargeTimeMS = (double)largeTimeMs / runs;
```

The preceding method then outputs these mean times to the console. We need to test PBKDF2 separately, as it doesn't inherit from `HashAlgorithm`:

```
var slowRuns = 10;
var pbkdf2 = new Rfc2898DeriveBytes(hashingData, key, 10000);
var pbkdf2Ms = RunTest(() =>
{
    pbkdf2.GetBytes(256);
}, slowRuns);
```

PBKDF2 is so slow that it would take a considerable amount of time to perform 100,000 runs (this is the point of using it). Internally, this RFC2898 implementation of the key-stretching algorithm runs HMAC SHA-1 10,000 times. The default is 1,000 but, due to the computing power available today, it is recommended to set this to at least an order of magnitude higher. For example, **Wi-Fi Protected Access II (WPA2)** uses 4,096 rounds of iterations to produce a 256-bit key with the **Service Set Identifier (SSID)** as the **salt**.

The output will look something like the following:

```
Over 100000 runs:
1.          MD5 average time 42B 0.00072 ms 4200B 0.01245 ms
2.        SHA-1 average time 42B 0.00080 ms 4200B 0.01310 ms
3.      SHA-256 average time 42B 0.00096 ms 4200B 0.03125 ms
4.   HMAC SHA-1 average time 42B 0.00096 ms 4200B 0.01339 ms
5. HMAC SHA-256 average time 42B 0.00162 ms 4200B 0.03201 ms
6.       PBKDF2 average time 125 ms (over 10 runs)

Press any key...
```

From the preceding output, you can see that the time taken for one hash varies from about 720 nanoseconds for a small MD5 to 32 microseconds for a large HMAC SHA-256 and **125** milliseconds for a small PBKDF2 with typical parameters.

Benchmarking results can vary dramatically, so you shouldn't read too much into absolute values. For example, the output from the BenchmarkDotNet tool comparing MD5 and SHA-256 on the same machine looks like this:

```
// ***** BenchmarkRunner: Finish *****

// * Export *
  Algo_Md5VsSha256-report.csv
  Algo_Md5VsSha256-report-stackoverflow.md
  Algo_Md5VsSha256-report-default.md
  Algo_Md5VsSha256-report-github.md
  Algo_Md5VsSha256-report.txt
  Algo_Md5VsSha256-measurements.csv
  BuildPlots.R
  Algo_Md5VsSha256-report.html

// * Detailed results *
Algo_Md5VsSha256_Md5
Mean = 31.2803 us, StdError = 0.0880 us (0.28%); N = 20, StdDev = 0.3936 us
Min = 30.5574 us, Q1 = 31.0145 us, Median = 31.2130 us, Q3 = 31.6598 us, Max = 31.9157 us
IQR = 0.6453 us, LowerFence = 30.0466 us, UpperFence = 32.6277 us
ConfidenceInterval = [31.1078 us; 31.4528 us] (CI 95%)


Algo_Md5VsSha256_Sha256
Mean = 201.0418 us, StdError = 1.5320 us (0.76%); N = 33, StdDev = 8.8008 us
Min = 186.5222 us, Q1 = 193.0558 us, Median = 199.2981 us, Q3 = 208.7261 us, Max = 221.1175 us
IQR = 15.6703 us, LowerFence = 169.5503 us, UpperFence = 232.2315 us
ConfidenceInterval = [198.0391 us; 204.0446 us] (CI 95%)


Total time: 00:00:31 (31.33 sec)

// * Summary *
BenchmarkDotNet-Dev=v0.9.3.0+
OS=Microsoft Windows NT 6.2.9200.0
Processor=Intel(R) Core(TM) i5-3317U CPU @ 1.70GHz, ProcessorCount=4
Frequency=1656392 ticks, Resolution=603.7218 ns
HostCLR=MS.NET 4.0.30319.42000, Arch=64-bit DEBUG

Type=Algo_Md5VsSha256  Mode=Throughput

 Method |   Median   |  StdDev  |
--------|------------|----------|
    Md5 | 31.2130 us | 0.3936 us |
 Sha256 | 199.2981 us | 8.8008 us |

// * Warnings *
Benchmark was built in DEBUG configuration. Please, build it in RELEASE.

// ***** BenchmarkRunner: End *****

Global total time: 00:00:32 (32 sec)
```

You can see in the preceding screenshot that the results are different from our homemade benchmark. However, this uses the full .NET Framework, calculates the median rather than mean for the average time, and runs in debug mode (which it helpfully warns us of), among other things.

A faster machine will have a higher throughput (as can be seen in the BenchmarkDotNet README.md on GitHub). Dedicated hardware such as **Graphics Processing Units (GPUs)**, **Field-Programmable Gate Arrays (FPGAs)**, and **Application-Specific Integrated Circuits (ASICs)** can be much faster. These tend to be used in the mining of bitcoin (and other crypto currencies), as these are based on hashing as a proof-of-work. Bitcoin uses SHA-256, but other currencies use different hashing algorithms.

The same algorithms form the basis of TLS, so faster hardware can handle a greater number of secure connections. As another example, Google built a custom ASIC called a **Tensor Processing Unit** (**TPU**) to accelerate their machine learning cloud services.

Other benchmarking samples are available in BenchmarkDotNet, and when you first run it, you will be presented with the following menu:

```
Available Benchmarks:
  #0   Algo_BitCount
  #1   Algo_Md5VsSha256
  #2   Algo_MostSignificantBit
  #3   Cpu_Atomics
  #4   Cpu_BranchPerdictor
  #5   Cpu_Ilp_Inc
  #6   Cpu_Ilp_Max
  #7   Cpu_Ilp_RyuJit
  #8   Cpu_Ilp_VsBce
  #9   Cpu_MatrixMultiplication
 #10   Framework_DateTime
 #11   Framework_DictionaryVsIDictionary
 #12   Framework_SelectVsConvertAll
 #13   Framework_StackFrameVsStackTrace
 #14   Framework_Stopwatch
 #15   Framework_StringConcatVsStringBuilder
 #16   IL_Loops
 #17   IL_ReadonlyFields
 #18   IL_Switch
 #19   IntroBaseline
 #20   IntroBasic
 #21   IntroColumns
 #22   IntroCommandStyle
 #23   IntroConfigSource
 #24   IntroConfigUnion
 #25   IntroDefaultToolchain
 #26   IntroJobsFull
 #27   IntroMultipleRuntimes
 #28   IntroParams
 #29   IntroTags
 #30   Jit_ArraySumLoopUnrolling
 #31   Jit_AsVsCast
 #32   Jit_Bce
 #33   Jit_BoolToInt
 #34   Jit_GenericsMethod
 #35   Jit_Inlining
 #36   Jit_InterfaceMethod
 #37   Jit_LoopUnrolling
 #38   Jit_RegistersVsStack
 #39   Jit_RotateBits
 #40   Array_AccessNormalRefUnsafe
 #41   Array_HeapAllocVsStackAlloc
 #42   Math_DoubleSqrt
 #43   Math_DoubleSqrtAvx
 #44   Os_Sleep
```

The previous benchmark was the second option, (number **#1 Algo_Md5VsSha256**).

Benchmarking is hard, so it's a good idea to use a library such as BenchmarkDotNet if you can. The only conclusion we can draw from our benchmarks is that SHA-256 is slower than MD5. However, SHA-256 should be fast enough for most applications and it's more secure for integrity checking. However, it is still not suitable for password storage.

SHA-256 can be used to provide signatures for verifying downloaded files, which must be retrieved over HTTPS to be safe, and for signing certificates. When used as part of an HMAC, it can also be used to securely authenticate messages, such as API requests. You will only connect successfully if you know the correct API key to hash with.

Serialization

Serialization is the process of turning objects into data suitable for transmission over a network or for storage. We also include deserialization, which is the reverse, under this umbrella. Serialization can have significant performance implications, not only on the network transmission speed but also on computation, as it can make up most of the expensive processing on a web server. You can read more about serialization at `https://docs.microsoft.com/en-us/dotnet/csharp/programming-guide/concepts/serialization/index`.

Serialization formats can be text-based or binary. Some popular text-based formats are **Extensible Markup Language** (**XML**) and **JavaScript Object Notation** (**JSON**). A popular binary format is **protocol buffers**, which was developed at Google. There's a .NET binary serialization format (`BinaryFormatter`), which is now supported in .NET Core 2.

XML has fallen out of fashion with developers, and JSON is now generally preferred. This is partly due to the smaller size of equivalent JSON payloads, but it may also be due to the use of XML in the originally named **Simple Object Access Protocol** (**SOAP**). This is used in **Windows Communication Foundation** (**WCF**), but SOAP is no longer an acronym, as developers discovered it is far from simple.

JSON is popular due to it being compact and human-readable, and because it can easily be consumed by JavaScript, particularly in web browsers. There are many different JSON serializers for .NET, with different performance characteristics. However, because JSON is not as rigidly defined as XML, there can be differences in implementations that make them incompatible, especially when dealing with complex types such as dates. For example, the very popular **Json.NET** represents dates in the **International Organization for Standardization** (**ISO**) format, whereas the JSON serializer used in old versions of ASP.NET MVC represented dates as the number of milliseconds since the Unix **epoch**, wrapped in a JavaScript date constructor.

The .NET developer community has converged on Json.NET, and compatibility is always preferable to performance. ASP.NET Web API has used Json.NET as the default for a while now, and ASP.NET Core also uses Json.NET. There is a serializer that's part of the **ServiceStack** framework called **ServiceStack.Text**, which claims to be faster, but you should probably value compatibility and documentation over speed. The same applies to other JSON libraries such as Jil (`https://github.com/kevin-montrose/Jil`) and **NetJSON** (`https://github.com/rpgmaker/NetJSON`), which can be even faster than ServiceStack in benchmarks.

If you are after pure performance, and you control all of the endpoints, then you probably will want to use a binary protocol. However, this may limit future interoperability with third-party endpoints that you don't control. Therefore, it's best to only use these internally.

It would be a bad idea to build your own custom message protocol on top of UDP. So, if you want to use binary serialization, you should look at something such as **protobuf-net**, which is a protocol that buffers implementation for .NET. You may also wish to consider Microsoft's Bond framework (`https://github.com/Microsoft/bond`) or Amazon's Ion (`https://amzn.github.io/ion-docs/index.html`). You may need to tune these tools for best performance, for example, by changing the default buffer size.

SIMD CPU instructions

Single Instruction Multiple Data (SIMD) is a technique that is available on many modern processors and can speed up execution by parallelizing calculations even in a single thread on one core. SIMD takes advantage of additional instructions available on CPUs to operate on sets of values (vectors) rather than just single values (scalars).

The most common instruction set for this is called **Streaming SIMD Extensions 2 (SSE2)** and it has been around for over 15 years since its debut with the Pentium 4. A newer instruction set called **Advanced Vector Extensions (AVX)** offers superior performance over SSE2 and has been around for over five years. So, if you're using a reasonably recent x86-64 CPU, then you should have access to these extra instructions.

 Some ARM CPUs (such as those in the Raspberry Pi 2 and 3) contain a similar technology called **NEON**, officially known as **Advanced SIMD**. This is not currently supported in .NET, but may be in the future. An official open source library project in C is hosted at `http://projectne10.org/`.

You can use the following Boolean property to test if SIMD is supported:

```
Vector.IsHardwareAccelerated
```

This property is JIT-intrinsic, and the value is set by RyuJIT at runtime.

You can instantiate a generic typed `Vector` or use one of the two/three/four dimensional convenience classes. For example, to create a single precision floating point vector, you could use the following generic code:

```
var vectorf = new Vector<float>(11f);
```

To create a single precision floating point 3D vector instead, you could use this code:

```
var vector3d = new Vector3(0f, 1f, 2f);
```

A two-dimensional double precision floating point vector can be a good substitute for a `Complex` structure. It will give higher performance on hardware-accelerated systems. `Vector2` only supports single precision floating point numbers, but you can use the generic type to specify the real and imaginary components of the complex number as a double. `Complex` only supports double precision floating point numbers but, if you don't need high precision, you could still use the `Vector2` convenience class. Unfortunately, this means that it's not simply a drop-in replacement, but the math is different anyway.

You can now use standard vector mathematics, but modifying your algorithms to take advantage of vectors can be complex and isn't something you should typically be doing in a web application. It can be useful for desktop applications but, if a process takes a long time in a web request, it's often best to run it in the background and then it doesn't need to be as quick.

We will cover this distributed architecture approach in the next chapter. For this reason, we won't be going into any more detail on SIMD, but you can read more about it if you wish, now that you have a taste of it. You can read some background information at `https://en.wikipedia.org/wiki/SIMD` and you can find the documentation for the .NET implementation on MSDN at `http://msdn.microsoft.com/en-us/library/dn858218`. You could also take a look at the example console application, which is available for download along with this book, as a simple starter for ten.

Parallel programming

While SIMD is good at increasing the performance of a single thread running on one core, it doesn't work across multiple cores or processors and its applications are limited. Modern scaling means adding more CPUs, not simply making a single thread faster. We don't just want to parallelize our data as SIMD does; we should actually focus more on parallelizing our processing, as this can scale better.

There are various .NET technologies available to help with parallel processing so that you don't have to write your own threading code. Two such parallel extensions are **Parallel LINQ (PLINQ)**, which extends the LINQ operations you're familiar with, and the **Task Parallel Library (TPL)**.

Task Parallel Library

One of the main features of the TPL is to extend loops to run in parallel. However, you need to be careful with parallel processing, as it can actually make your software slower while doing simple tasks. The overheads involved with marshalling the multiple tasks can dwarf the execution of the workload for trivial operations.

For example, take the following simple `for` loop:

```
for (int i = 0; i < array.Length; i++)
{
    sum += array[i];
}
```

The array in the preceding `for` loop contains 100,000 integers, but adding integers is one of the easiest things a CPU can do and using a `for` loop on an array is a very quick way of enumerating. This accumulation will complete in under a tenth of a millisecond on a reasonably modern machine.

You may think that you would be able to speed this up by parallelizing the operation. Perhaps you could split the array, run the summation on two cores in parallel and add the results.

You might use the following code to attempt this:

```
Parallel.For(0, array.Length, i =>
{
    Interlocked.Add(ref sum, array[i]);
});
```

 You must use an interlocked add or you will get an incorrect summation result. If you don't, the threads will interfere with each other, corrupting the data when writing to the same location in memory.

However, this code actually runs over 42 times slower than the first example. The extra overhead, the complexity of running many threads, and locking the variable so that only one thread can write to it at a time is just not worth it in this case.

Parallelization can be useful for more complex processes, especially if the body of the loop performs some slow operation such as accessing the file system. However, blocking I/O operations may be better dealt with by using asynchronous access. Parallel access can cause contention, because access may eventually have to be performed in series at some point, for example, at the hardware level.

If we want to perform a more processor-intensive operation, such as hashing multiple passwords, then running the tasks in parallel can be beneficial. The following code performs a PBKDF2 hash on each password in a list and then calculates the Base64 representation of the result:

```
foreach (var password in passwords)
{
    var pbkdf2 = new Rfc2898DeriveBytes(password, 256, 10000);
    Convert.ToBase64String(pbkdf2.GetBytes(256));
}
```

We're not using the output in this example, but you may be doing this to upgrade the security of passwords in your database by migrating them to a more resilient key-stretching algorithm. The input may be plaintext passwords or the output of a legacy one-way hash function, for example MD5 or an unsalted SHA.

We can improve the speed of this on a multicore system by using the `Parallel.ForEach` loop, using code such as the following:

```
Parallel.ForEach(passwords, password =>
{
    var pbkdf2 = new Rfc2898DeriveBytes(password, 256, 10000);
    Convert.ToBase64String(pbkdf2.GetBytes(256));
});
```

This will speed up the process, but by how much will depend on many factors, such as the number of passwords in the list, the number of logical processors, and the number of CPU cores. For example, on a Core i5 CPU with two cores but four logical processors, having only two passwords in the list does not result in a massive improvement (only 1.5 times quicker). With four passwords (or more) in the list, the improvement is better (about 1.9 times quicker). There is still some overhead, so you can't get double the speed with twice the CPU cores.

We can see the reason for this difference by looking at the CPU utilization in the task manager during benchmarking.

With only two passwords to hash, the CPU graph looks like the following:

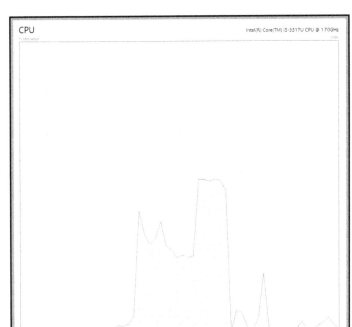

In the preceding graph, we can see that initially, when hashing in series, the CPU is running at about 25%, fully using one logical CPU. When hashing two passwords in parallel, it uses 50%, running on two logical processors. This doesn't translate into a twofold increase in speed due to the intrinsic overheads and the nature of **hyper-threading**.

 Hyper-threading is a technology that typically exposes two logical processors to the OS for each physical core. However, the two logical CPUs still share the execution resources of their single core.

Although there are two cores on the CPU die, hyper-threading exposes four logical CPUs to the OS. As we only have two threads, because we are hashing two passwords, we can only use two processors. If the threads are executed on different cores, then the speed increase can be good. But if they are executed on processors sharing the same core, then performance won't be as impressive. It is still better than single-threaded hashing due to scheduling improvements, which is what hyper-threading is designed for.

When we hash four passwords at the same time, the CPU graph looks like the following:

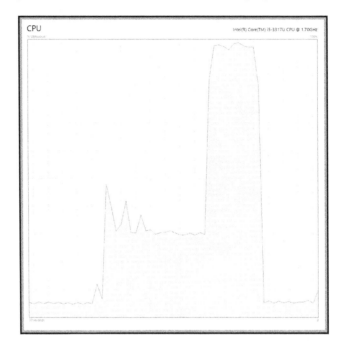

We can see that now the initial 25% usage jumps to almost full utilization and we are making use of most of the processor. This translates to just under a doubling of the performance as compared to hashing in sequence. There are still significant overheads involved, but, as the main operation is now so much quicker, the tradeoff is worth it.

Parallel LINQ

There are other ways to take advantage of parallel programming, such as LINQ expressions. We could rewrite the previous example as a LINQ expression and it might look something like the following:

```
passwords.AsParallel().ForAll(p =>
{
    var pbkdf2 = new Rfc2898DeriveBytes(p, 256, 10000);
    Convert.ToBase64String(pbkdf2.GetBytes(256));
});
```

You can enable these features with the `AsParallel()` method. The `ForAll()` method has the same purpose as the loops in previous examples and is useful if the order is unimportant. If ordering is important, then there is an `AsOrdered()` method that can help solve this. However, this can reduce the performance gains due to the extra processing involved.

This example performs similarly to the previous one that used a parallel loop, which is unsurprising. We can also limit the number of operations that can occur in parallel, using the `WithDegreeOfParallelism()` method as follows:

```
passwords.AsParallel().WithDegreeOfParallelism(2).ForAll(p =>
{
    var pbkdf2 = new Rfc2898DeriveBytes(p, 256, 10000);
    Convert.ToBase64String(pbkdf2.GetBytes(256));
});
```

This preceding example limits the hashes to two at a time and performs similarly to when we only had two passwords in the list, which is to be expected. This can be useful if you don't want to max out the CPU, because there are other important processes running on it.

You can achieve the same effect with the TPL by setting the `MaxDegreeOfParallelism` property on an instance of the `ParallelOptions` class. This object can then be passed into overloaded versions of the loop methods as a parameter, along with the main body.

It's important, when you're using parallel LINQ to query datasets, that you don't lose sight of the best place for the query to be performed. You may speed up a query in the application with parallelization, but the best place for the query to occur may still be in the database, which can be even faster. To read more on this topic, refer back to `Chapter 7`, *Optimizing I/O Performance*, and `Chapter 5`, *Fixing Common Performance Problems*.

Parallel benchmarking

Let's have a look at the output of a simple .NET Core console application, which benchmarks the techniques that we have just discussed. It shows one situation where parallelization doesn't help and actually makes things worse.

It then shows another situation where it does help.

When calculating a sum by accumulating 100,000 random integers between zero and ten, the quickest way is to use an array in a simple `foreach` loop. Using parallelization here makes the process much slower and, if used naively, without locking, will give an incorrect result, which is much worse.

When performing a more computationally intensive workload, such as a PBKDF2 hashing function on multiple passwords, parallelization can help significantly. The time is almost halved, as it is running across two cores. The final operation, which limits the number of threads, can take a varying amount of time on different runs. This is likely due to the threads sometimes sharing a core and sometimes running on different cores. It can be almost as quick as using all logical cores, depending on the work.

The CPU graph for the benchmark looks like the following:

The initial parallel summations max out the CPU and are very inefficient. Next, the single-threaded hashing uses only one logical processor (25%), but the other, later hashes make almost full use of both the cores. The final hashing, limited to two passwords at a time, only makes use of half the CPU power.

Parallel programming limitations

Performance problems with web applications don't typically mean increasing speed for a single user on the system in isolation. It's easy to make a web app perform when there's only one user, but the challenge lies in maintaining that single user performance as the number of users scales up and you have wall-to-wall requests.

The parallel programming techniques discussed in this section have limited use in scaling web applications. You already have a parallelized system, as each user request will be allocated its own resources. You can simply add more instances, agents, or machines to meet demand. The problem then is in distributing work efficiently between them and avoiding bottlenecks for shared resources. We'll cover this in greater depth in the next chapter.

Multithreading and concurrency

In the previous section on parallel programming we briefly covered using an `Interlocked.Add` to avoid errors when writing to the same location in memory from multiple threads. Concurrency and locking are the hardest things to get right when it comes to multithreaded programming. Getting it wrong can hurt performance and even cause incorrect calculations.

As locking it is so often an area where mistakes are made, we will include a short primer. This is by no means extensive but will help you identify areas where you may need to be careful.

Locking

Locking is a way of ensuring that a resource can only be used by a single thread at one time. Every thread that wishes to use the locked item must wait its turn, so that operations are performed sequentially. This series processing ensures consistency but can also slow a system down if there is significant waiting for locks to be released.

Locking is also applicable to databases and you may have used it in SQL, but here we will cover it in relation to C# and multithreading in .NET. There are many low level constructs and primitives that can be used for locking. However, we will be taking a more practical approach and showing the high-level locking syntax commonly used in .NET programming.

The standard way to implement locking in C# is with the `lock` statement. This is similar to the `using` statement in that it is syntactic sugar that wraps the underlying implementation. It helps you to avoid forgetting to implement all of the boilerplate code that is necessary, similar to how a `using` statement ensures disposal of objects. It is easy to forget the requirements of exception handling and cause a memory leak or deadlock.

A **deadlock** is where you make a mistake in your locking implementation and create a situation where nothing can acquire or release a lock. This can cause your program to get stuck in an infinite loop and hang.

Let's examine a simple locking example. Consider the following trivial method.

```
private static void DoWork(ref int result)
{
    for (int i = 0; i < 1000000; i++)
    {
        result++;
    }
}
```

We call this method twice on separate threads and wait for them both to finish, using the following code.

```
var result = 0;
var t1 = Task.Run(() => { DoWork(ref result); });
var t2 = Task.Run(() => { DoWork(ref result); });
Task.WaitAll(t1, t2);
```

What will the `result` variable be after this? It won't be two million, as it should be. Doing this without locking will cause corruption and an erroneous result.

We have used `Task.WaitAll(t1, t2)` here so that the code can run in the `Main` method of a console app. However, it is generally preferable to use `await Task.WhenAll(t1, t2)` if within an `async` method. In much the same way, `await Task.Delay(100)` is preferable to `Thread.Sleep(100)`. In C# 7.1 you can have an `async Main` method for a console application, so this is not a concern.

To use a `lock`, first we need to declare and initialize an object for it to use. We've done this at the class level and defined it like so.

```
private static object l = new object();
```

We can now use this object to `lock` an operation, but where should we perform this lock for the best performance? Let's try inside the loop, with the following code.

```
for (int i = 0; i < 1000000; i++)
{
    lock (l)
    {
        result++;
    }
}
```

This performs correctly and we get the right result, but it is slow. In this example, a better way to do this would be to lock outside the loop. This improved version is shown in the following code.

```
lock (l)
{
    for (int i = 0; i < 1000000; i++)
    {
        result++;
    }
}
```

This performs significantly quicker, as we are only locking twice rather than two million times. This is an extreme example and for a real workload there should be a tuning exercise to find the optimal locking strategy.

Under the hood, a `lock` statement uses a `Monitor` internally to implement the lock. You don't normally need to worry about this unless you have special requirements. It is easier and safer to use `lock` rather than directly using `Monitor`. There is also `Mutex` (for spanning processes) and `Semaphore` (where you lock a pool of resources rather than a single object).

The `Interlocked.Add` used previously wraps a special CPU instruction. This allows a value to be altered atomically at the processor level. If it is not used then different bytes of the same value could be altered by different threads, corrupting the result. In our preceding example it would be quicker to use `Interlocked.Increment(ref result)`. However, our code is just to simulate a much more complex workload, where this wouldn't apply, and using `Interlocked` wouldn't be a suitable solution.

Not locking when there are multiple threads is something to avoid, as is locking in the wrong place. Let's look at some other things that are sensible to avoid next.

Practices to avoid

We've shown some ways of speeding up software, but it's often better to illustrate what not to do and how things can go wrong. Web applications generally perform well if no bad practices have been followed and here we'll highlight a few things you should watch out for.

Reflection

Reflection is the process of programmatically inspecting your code with other code, and digging into its internals at runtime. For example, you could inspect an assembly when it is loaded to see what classes and interfaces it implements so that you can call them. It is generally discouraged and should be avoided if possible. There are usually other ways to achieve the same result that don't require reflection, although it is occasionally useful.

Reflection is often bad for performance, and this is well-documented, but, as usual, it depends on what you're using it for. What is new is that there are significant changes to reflection for .NET Core. The API has changed and it is now optional. So, if you don't use reflection, you don't have to pay the performance penalty.

There is an extra method on the reflection API now, so, whereas previously you would have called something like `myObject.GetType().GetMembers()`, you now need to call it as `myObject.GetType().GetTypeInfo().GetMembers()` by inserting the new `GetTypeInfo()` method, which is in the `System.Reflection` namespace.

If you must use reflection, then it is best not to perform it repeatedly or in a tight loop. However, it would be fine to use it once during the startup of your application. However, if you can avoid using it entirely, you can benefit from some of the new improvements in .NET Core.

Regular expressions

A **regular expression (regex)** can be very useful, but can perform badly and is typically misused in situations where another solution would be better. For example, a regex is often used for email validation when there are much more reliable ways to do this.

If reusing a regex repeatedly, you may be better off compiling it for performance by specifying the `RegexOptions.Compiled` option in the constructor. This only helps if you're using the regex a lot and doing so involves an initial performance penalty. So, ensure that you check whether there is actually an improvement and it isn't now slower.

The `RegexOptions.IgnoreCase` option can also affect performance, but it may in fact slow things down, so always test for your inputs. Compiling has an effect on this too and you may want to use `RegexOptions.CultureInvariant` in addition, to avoid comparison issues.

Be wary of trusting user input to a regex. It is possible to get them to perform a large amount of backtracking and use excessive resources. You shouldn't allow unconstrained input to a regex, as they can be made to run for hours.

Regexes are often used for email address validation, but this is usually a bad idea. The only way to fully validate an email address is to send an email to it. You can then have the user click a link in the email to indicate that they have access to that mailbox and have received it. Email addresses can vary a lot from the common ones that people are regularly exposed to, and this is even truer with the new top-level domains being added.

Many of the regexes for email address validation found online will reject perfectly valid email addresses. If you want to assist the user, and perform some basic email address validation on a form, then all you can sensibly do is check that there is an @ symbol in it (and a . after that) so that the email is in the form x@y.z. You can do this with a simple string test and avoid the performance penalty and security risk of a regular expression.

String concatenation in tight loops

As strings are immutable and can't change, when you concatenate a string a new object is created. This can cause performance problems and issues with memory use if you do it a lot inside a tight loop.

You may find it better to use a string builder or another approach. However, don't fret too much about this, as it only applies at a large scale. Always test to see if it is genuinely a problem and don't micro-optimize where you don't need to.

It's good general advice to work out where your code is spending most of its time, and focus your optimization there. It's obviously much better to optimize code executed millions of times inside a loop than code that only runs occasionally.

Dynamic typing

C# is a statically typed language and variable types are checked at compile time, but it does have some dynamic features. You can use the `dynamic` type and objects such as `ExpandObject` to get some of the features of a dynamically typed language. The `var` type is not in fact dynamic, and is simply inferred at compile time.

Dynamic typing has a performance and safety penalty, so it is best avoided if you can find another way to solve your problem. For example, the `ViewBag` in ASP.NET MVC is dynamic, so it is best not to use `ViewBag`, and use a well-defined view model instead. This has many other benefits apart from performance, such as safety and convenience.

Synchronous operations

Synchronous methods block execution, and should be avoided if possible, especially if they are slow or access I/O. We've covered asynchronous (async for short) operations in previous chapters. Understanding how to use async is important for modern high-performance programming, and new language features make it more accessible than ever. If an `async` method is available, then it should generally be used in preference to the synchronous blocking version.

The `async` and `await` keywords make asynchronous programming much easier than it used to be, but, as covered in `Chapter 5`, *Fixing Common Performance Problems*, the effects on web applications are not always visible for a lone user. These convenient features allow you to serve more users simultaneously by returning threads to the pool during downtime, while waiting for operations to complete. The threads can then be used to service other users' requests, which allows you to handle more users with fewer servers than otherwise.

Async methods can be useful, but the big gains come not from writing asynchronous code, but from having an asynchronous architecture. We will cover distributed architecture in the next chapter, when we discuss message queuing.

Exceptions

Exceptions should, as the name suggests, be reserved for exceptional circumstances. Exceptions are slow and expensive and shouldn't be used as flow control in business logic if you know that an event is likely to occur.

This isn't to say that you shouldn't use exception handling, as you should. However, it should be reserved for events that are genuinely unexpected and rare. If you can predict ahead of time that a condition may occur then you should handle it explicitly.

For example, the disk becoming full and your code not being able to write a file because there is no space is an exceptional situation. You would not expect this to normally happen, and you can just `try` the file operation and `catch` any exceptions. However, if you are trying to parse a date string or access a dictionary, then you should probably use the special `TryParse()` and `TryGetValue()` methods and check for null values rather than just relying on exception handling.

Summary

In this chapter, we discussed some techniques that can improve the performance of code execution and dug into the projects that make up .NET Core and ASP.NET Core. We explored data structures, serialization, hashing, parallel programming, and how to benchmark to measure relative performance. We also covered how to perform multithreading, concurrency, and locking with C#.

Linear performance characteristics are easier to scale and code that does not exhibit this behavior can be slow when the load increases. Code that has an exponential performance characteristic or has erratic outliers (which are rare but very slow when they occur) can cause performance headaches. It is often better to aim for code that, while being slightly slower in normal cases, is more predictable and performs consistently over a large range of loads.

The main lesson here is to not blindly apply parallel programming and other potentially performance-enhancing techniques. Always test to make sure that they make a positive impact, as they can easily make things worse. We aim for the situation where everything is awesome but, if we're not careful, we can make everything awful by mistake.

In the next chapter, you'll learn about caching and message queuing. These are two advanced techniques that can significantly improve the performance of a system.

9
Learning Caching and Message Queuing

Caching is incredibly useful and can be applied to almost all layers of an application stack. However, it's hard to always get caching working correctly. So, in this chapter, we will cover caching at the web, application, and database levels. We will show you how to use a reverse proxy server to store the results of your rendered web pages and other assets. We'll also cover caching at lower levels, using an in-memory data store to speed up access. You will learn how to ensure that you can always flush (or bust) your cache if you need to force the propagation of updates.

This chapter also covers asynchronous architecture design using message queuing and abstractions, which encapsulate various messaging patterns. You will learn how to perform a long running operation (such as video encoding) in the background, while keeping the user informed of its progress.

You will learn how to apply caching and message queuing software design patterns to slow performing operations so that they don't have to be performed in real time. You'll also learn about the complexity that these patterns can add, and understand the trade-offs involved. We'll see how to combat these complexities and mitigate the downsides in Chapter 10, *The Downsides of Performance-Enhancing Tools*.

The topics covered in this chapter include the following:

- Web caching background
- JavaScript service workers
- Varnish proxy and IIS web servers

- Redis and Memcached in-memory application caching
- Message Queuing and messaging patterns
- RabbitMQ and its various client libraries

Why caching is hard

Caching isn't hard because it's difficult to cache something. Caching is indefinitely easy; the hard part is invalidating the cache when you want to make an update. There's a well-used quote from the late Phil Karlton of Netscape, which goes as follows:

> *"There are only two hard things in Computer Science: cache invalidation and naming things."*

There are also many humorous variants on it, as used previously throughout this book. This sentiment may be a slight exaggeration, but it highlights how complex removing your *done-computer-stuff ™* from your *quick-things-box 2.0 ™* is perceived to be. Naming things is genuinely very hard though.

Caching is the process of storing a temporary snapshot of some data. This temporary cache can then be used instead of regenerating the original data (or retrieving it from the canonical source) every time it is required. Doing this has obvious performance benefits, but it makes your system more complicated and harder to conceptualize. When you have many caches interacting, the results can appear almost random, unless you are disciplined in your approach.

When you are reasoning about caching (and message queuing), it is helpful to dispel the idea that data only exists in a single consistent state. It is easier if you embrace the concept that data has a freshness and is always stale by some amount. This is, in fact, always the case, but the short time frames involved in a small system mean that you can typically ignore it in order to simplify your thinking. However, when it comes to caching, the timescales are longer, so freshness is more important. A system at scale can only be eventually consistent, and various parts of it will have a different temporal view of the data. You need to accept that data can be in motion; otherwise, you're just not thinking four-dimensionally!

As a trivial example, consider a traditional static website. A visitor loads a page in their browser, but this page is now instantly out of date. The page on the server could have been updated just after the visitor retrieved it, but they will not know, as the old version will remain in their browser until they refresh the page.

If we extend this example to a database-backed web application, such as an ASP.NET or WordPress website, then the same principle applies. A user retrieves a web page generated from data in the database, but it could be out of date as soon as it is loaded. The underlying data could have changed, but the page containing the old data remains in the browser.

By default, web apps typically regenerate HTML from the DB for every page load, but this is incredibly inefficient if the data has not changed. It is only done like this so that when a change is made, it shows up immediately when the page is refreshed.

However, a user may have an old page in their browser, and you have limited control over this. So you may as well cache this page on the server as well and only remove it when the underlying data in the database changes. Caching the rendered HTML like this is often essential for maintaining performance at a scale beyond simply a small number of users.

Web caching

The first category of caching that we'll discuss is at the web level. This involves storing the final output of your web stack as it will be sent to users so that, when requested again, it's ready to go and doesn't need to be regenerated. Caching at this stage removes the need for expensive database lookups and CPU-intensive rendering at the application layer. This reduces latency and decreases the workload on your servers, allowing you to handle more users and serve each user rapidly.

Web caching typically occurs on your web servers or on reverse proxy servers, which you have put in front of your web servers to shield them from excessive load. You might also choose to hand this task over to a third party, such as a CDN. Here, we will cover two pieces of web server and proxy server software, IIS and Varnish. However, many more web caching and load balancing technologies are available, for example, NGINX or HAProxy.

Caching at the web layer works best for static assets and resources such as JavaScript, CSS, and images. Yet, it can also work for anonymous HTML, which is rarely updated but regularly accessed, such as a homepage or landing page, which is unauthenticated and not customized for a user.

We touched upon proxy servers in Chapter 5, *Fixing Common Performance Problems* and covered web layer caching a little in Chapter 6, *Addressing Network Performance*. However, in this chapter, we'll go into more detail on web caching.

Caching background

Before we delve into the implementation details, it helps to understand a little about how caching works on the web. If you take the time to study the mechanisms at work, then caching will be less confusing and not as frustrating as if you had just dived straight in.

It is helpful to read and understand the relevant HTTP specifications. However, don't assume that software always strictly adheres to these web standards even if it claims to.

First, let's look at a typical network setup that you may be traversing with your HTTP traffic. The following diagram illustrates an example of a common configuration for a web application:

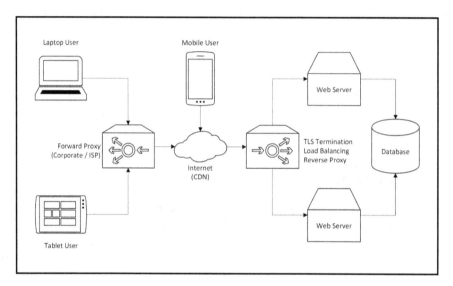

As seen in the preceding diagram, the laptop and tablet users are connecting through a caching forward proxy server (which may be on a corporate network or at an ISP). The mobile user is connecting directly over the internet. However, all the users are going through a CDN before reaching your infrastructure.

After your firewall (not shown), there is an appliance that terminates the TLS connections, balances the load between web servers, and acts as a caching reverse proxy. These functions are often performed by separate devices, but we've kept things simple here.

Copies of your resources will be kept on your web servers, your reverse proxy, your CDN, any forward proxies, and in the browsers on all user devices. The simplest way to control the caching behavior of these resources is to use in-band signaling and add HTTP headers to your content, declaring cache control metadata only in a single place.

It's good practice to apply the same standard HTTP caching techniques to your own web servers and proxies even though you could customize them and flush their caches at will. This not only cuts down on the amount of configuration that you have to do, and avoids duplicated work, but it also ensures that any caches that you don't control should behave correctly too. Even when using HTTPS, the browser will still perform caching and there may also be transparent corporate proxies or meddling ISP captive portals in the way.

HTTP headers

HTTP caching involves setting cache control headers in your responses. There are many of these headers, which have been added over the years from different standards and various versions of the protocol. You should know how these are used, but you should also understand how the uniqueness of a cacheable resource is determined, for example, by varying the URL or by altering only a part of it, such as query string parameters.

Many of these headers can be categorized by the function and the version of HTTP that they were introduced with. Some headers have multiple functions and some are non-standard, yet are almost universally used. We won't cover all of these headers, but we will pick out some of the most important ones.

There are broadly two types of caching header categories. The first defines an absolute time during which the cache can be reused without checking with the server. The second defines rules that the client can use to test with the server if the cache is still valid.

Most instructional headers (those that issue caching commands) fit into one of these two header categories. In addition to these, there are many purely informational headers, which provide details about the original connection and client that may otherwise be obscured by a cache (for example, the original client IP address).

Some headers, such as `Cache-Control`, are part of the latest standard, but others, such as `Expires`, are typically used only for backward compatibility, in case there is an ancient browser or an old proxy server in the way. However, this practice is becoming increasingly unnecessary as infrastructure and software are upgraded.

The latest caching standard in this case is HTTP/1.1, as HTTP/2 uses the same caching directives (RFC 7234). Some headers date from HTTP/1.0, which is considered a legacy protocol. Very old software may only support HTTP/1.0. Standards may not be implemented correctly in all applications. It is a sensible idea to test that any observed behavior is as expected.

The Age header is used to indicate how long (in seconds) a resource has been in a cache. On the other hand, the ETag header is used to specify an identifier for an individual object or a particular unique version of that object.

The Cache-Control header tells caches if the resource may be cached. It can have many values including a max-age (in seconds) or no-cache and no-store directives. The confusing, yet subtle, difference between no-cache and no-store is that, no-cache indicates that the client should check with the server before using the resource whereas no-store indicates that the resource shouldn't be cached at all. To prevent caching, you should generally use no-store.

The ASP.NET Core ResponseCache action attribute sets the Cache-Control header and is covered in Chapter 6, *Addressing Network Performance*. However, this header may be ignored by some older caches. Pragma and Expires are older headers used for backward compatibility and they perform some of the same functions that the Cache-Control header now handles.

The X-Forwarded-* headers are used to provide more information about the original connection to the proxy or load balancer. These are non-standard, but widely used, and are standardized as the combined Forwarded header (**RFC 7239**). The Via header also provides some proxy information, and Front-End-Https is a non-standard Microsoft header, which is similar to X-Forwarded-Proto. These protocol headers are useful for telling you whether the original connection used HTTPS when this is stripped at the load balancer.

 If you are terminating the TLS connections at a load balancer or proxy server and are also redirecting users to HTTPS at the application level, then it is important to check the Forwarded headers. You can get stuck in an infinite redirection loop if your web servers desire HTTPS but only receive HTTP from the load balancer. Ideally, you should check all varieties of the headers, but if you control the proxy, you can decide what headers to use.

There are lots of different HTTP headers that are involved in caching. The following list includes the ones that we haven't covered here. The large number of headers should give you an idea of just how complicated caching can be:

- If-Match
- If-Modified-Since
- If-None-Match
- If-Range
- If-Unmodified-Since

- Last-Modified
- Max-Forwards
- Proxy-Authorization
- Vary

Cache busting

Cache busting (also known as cache bursting, cache flushing, or cache invalidation) is the hard part of caching. It is easy to put an item in a cache, but if you don't have a strategy ahead of time to manage the inevitable change, then you may come unstuck.

Getting cache busting correct is usually more important with web-level caching. This is because, with server-side caching (which we'll discuss later in this chapter), you are in full control and can reset if you get it wrong. A mistake on the web can persist and be difficult to remedy.

In addition to setting the correct headers, it is helpful to vary the URL of resources when their content changes. This can be done by adding a timestamp, but often, a convenient solution is to use a hash of the resource content and append this as a parameter. Many frameworks, including ASP.NET Core, use this approach. For example, consider the following JavaScript tag in a web page:

```
<script src="js/site.js"></script>
```

If you make a change to `site.js`, then the browser (or proxy) won't know that it has altered and may use a previous version. However, it will re-request it if the output is changed to something like the following:

```
<script src="js/site.js?v=EWaMeWsJBYWmL2g_KkgXZQ5nPe-a3Ichp0LEgzXczKo">
</script>
```

Here the `v` (version) parameter is the **Base64 URL encoded**, SHA-256 hashed content of the `site.js` file. Making a small change to the file will radically alter the hash due to the **avalanche effect**.

 Base64 URL encoding is a variant of standard Base64 encoding. It uses different non-alphanumeric characters (+ becomes – while / changes to _) and percent encodes the = character (which is also made optional). Using this safe alphabet (from RFC 4648) makes the output suitable for use in URLs and filenames.

In ASP.NET Core, you can easily use this feature by adding the `asp-append-version` attribute with a value of `true` in your Razor views, as follows:

```
<script src="~/js/site.js" asp-append-version="true"></script>
```

Service workers

If you are writing a client-side web app rather than a simple dynamic website, then you may wish to exert more control over caching using new browser features. You can do this by writing your cache control instructions in JavaScript (technically **ECMAScript**). This gives you many more options when it comes to a visitor using your web app offline.

A **service worker** gives you greater control than the previous AppCache API. It also opens the door to features such as mobile web app install banners (which prompt a user to add your web app to their home screen). However, it is still a relatively new technology.

Service workers are a new experimental technology, and as such, are currently only supported in some recent browsers (partially in Chrome, Firefox, and Opera). You may prefer to use the previous deprecated AppCache method (which is almost universally supported) until adoption is more widespread. Information on current browser support is available at http://caniuse.com/#feat=serviceworkers and http://caniuse.com/#feat=offline-apps (for AppCache). A more detailed service worker breakdown is available at https://jakearchibald.github.io/isserviceworkerready/.

A service worker can do many useful things (such as background synchronization and push notifications), but the interesting parts, from our point of view, are the scriptable caches, which enable offline use. It effectively acts as an in-browser proxy server and can be used to improve the performance of a web application in addition to allowing interaction without an internet connection (after initial installation, of course).

There are other types of **web workers** apart from service workers (for example, audio workers, dedicated workers, and shared workers), but we won't go into these here. All web workers allow you to offload work to a background task so that you don't make the browser unresponsive (by blocking the main UI thread with your work).

Service workers are asynchronous and rely heavily on JavaScript **promises**, which we'll assume you are familiar with. If you're not, then you should read up on them, as they're useful in many other contexts involving asynchronous and parallel scripting.

Service workers require the use of HTTPS (yet another good reason to use TLS on your entire site). However, there is an exception for `localhost`, so you can still develop locally.

Service worker example

To install a service worker, first create a file for it (which is served over HTTPS). In the following example, this file is called `service-worker.js`. Then, inside a `<script>` tag on your HTML page (also served over HTTPS), add the following JavaScript code:

```
if ('serviceWorker' in navigator) {
    navigator.serviceWorker.register('service-worker.js', {
        scope: '/'
    });
}
```

The preceding code snippet first checks to see whether the service workers are supported, and if they are, it registers your worker. You can now fetch resources and add them to the cache. An interesting performance-enhancing use case for this is prefetching resources (that the user may need) ahead of time and putting them in the cache. Scope is an optional parameter and isn't strictly necessary in this case, as the file is in the root of the domain. We've shown it only to demonstrate usage, but it may be useful to specify this if the file was in a subfolder.

Before going any further, you should check that your worker has been installed correctly. In Chrome, you can open the special URL `chrome://inspect/#service-workers` to see any active service workers. For example, after opening `https://instabail.uk/` in one tab, you can open the service worker inspector in another; you should see something like the following screenshot:

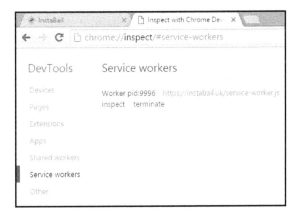

You can also visit `chrome://serviceworker-internals` in Chrome to see the status of all service workers that have been registered, even if the sites aren't still open. For example, even after closing `https://instabail.uk/` you should continue to see something like the following screenshot:

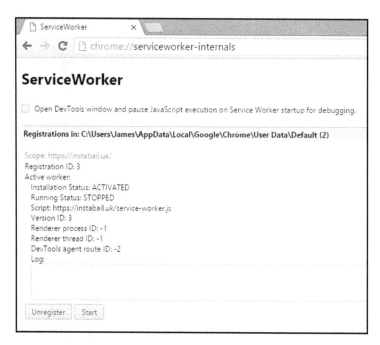

You can remove service workers by clicking the **Unregister** button. If the service is running, you will have **Stop** and **Inspect** buttons in place of **Start**. This page may be removed or merged into the inspector in a future version of Chrome.

Now you can start adding the content to your service worker JavaScript file. We first need to install the worker and cache some files, which is done with an event listener, as shown in the following code:

```
self.addEventListener('install', function (event) {
    event.waitUntil(
        caches.open('cache-v01').then(function (cache) {
            return cache.addAll([
                '/',
                '/Content/bootstrap.min.css'
            ]);
        })
    );
});
```

We have named our cache `cache-v01`, and provided an array of resources to cache. You will probably have more entries here and define the array outside of the function, but we have kept things simple here for clarity.

Don't cache your homepage if it dynamically renders live content. You may also want to use cache-busting parameters for resources, as mentioned previously.

We can then add a `fetch` event listener to perform the magic of caching and fetching resources:

```
self.addEventListener('fetch', function (event) {
    event.respondWith(
        caches.match(event.request)
            .then(function (response) {
                if (response) return response;
                var myReq = event.request.clone();
                return fetch(myReq).then(
                    function (response) {
                        var myResp = response.clone();
                        caches.open('cache-v01')
                            .then(function (cache) {
                                cache.put(event.request, myResp);
                            });
                        return response;
                    }
                );
            }
        )
    );
});
```

First we check if the requested resource is in the cache and if it is, we return this. With promises, you can chain the `then` functions together and fall through them. If there is a cache miss due to the resource not being in the cache, we perform a `fetch` to our server to get the resource and return this. We then add the resource to the others by putting it in the same cache. We clone the request and response, because they are streams and can only be consumed once.

The `fetch` function is the modern version of an **XMLHttpRequest (XHR)** and is used to retrieve data over the network. You can't use a synchronous XHR inside of a service worker, as they're designed to be asynchronous.

You can inspect your service worker and the caches in more detail by using the browser developer tools (*F12*). On the **Resources** tab, select **Service Workers** and you will see something like the following screenshot:

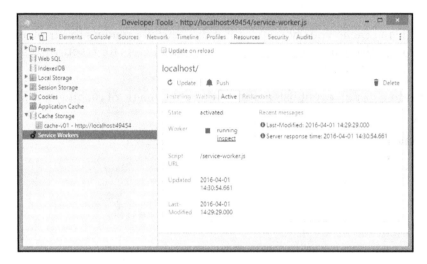

If you select **Cache Storage,** you will see the contents of the cache, which will look something like the following:

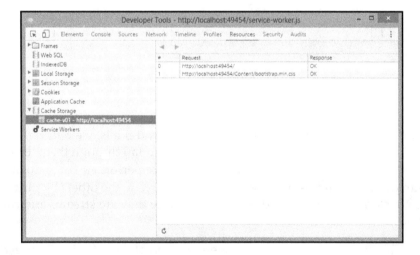

You can refresh the cache and delete items by right-clicking. **Application Cache**, above **Cache Storage**, will show the deprecated AppCache resources. As you navigate around, your site pages will be added to the cache (these pages should be suitable for caching, as they won't be requested from the server again if using our demo code).

After this, once you refresh the cache view, you should see more entries listed, which may look something like the following screenshot:

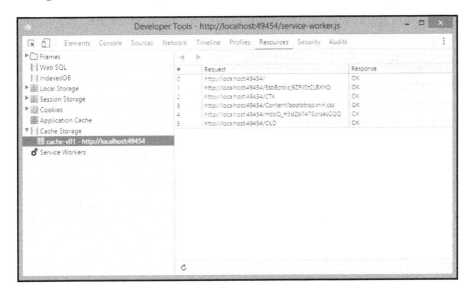

You can see that the cache entries are listed alphabetically and not in the order in which they were added to the cache. These pages will now be a snapshot, fixed at the point in time that they were retrieved. This may not be the functionality that you want!

For simplicity, the service worker that we've built here is a trivial example and you would likely want to expand it to at least handle the case where the network `fetch` fails by adding a `catch` statement. For example, you could serve a previously cached offline fallback page in its place. You should also check that you're not caching error pages from the server, so test the response status code.

You also need to carefully consider your cache invalidation strategy. Service workers give you the tools to build this, as they don't make as many assumptions as the HTML5 AppCache did. For example, you can now programmatically delete entries from the cache.

We'll leave it here for client-side script controlled caching, but you may want to look into this in more detail, especially once the specification has stabilized and browser support is more widespread. There are many other new features now available in JavaScript, which make async programming like this easier than it used to be. For example, arrow functions, which are similar to LINQ lambda expressions in C#.

Remember to measure your results for performance. Service workers can slow things down if you don't use their features, as they add an extra step to the process.

Web and proxy servers

Caching from a server's point of view is intimately linked to client-side caching in the browser. In addition to storing resources on the server, the headers that you set will be used to control caches everywhere.

The HTTP headers that you set are used by both proxy servers and browsers, including not only standard browsing, but also fetching from a service worker. For example, if the `Cache-Control` header specifies `no-store`, then you won't be able to add the resource to a cache from your worker.

IIS

Internet Information Services (**IIS**) is Microsoft's web server. It can be used to serve content from your ASP.NET application or as a proxy server, along with many other things such as FTP. IIS supports output caching, with the `OutputCache` action attribute. You can also use `ResponseCache` to set the correct headers, as covered in `Chapter 6`, *Addressing Network Performance*.

ASP.NET Core 2.0 now supports debugging from Visual Studio 2017 when using IIS on Windows. You can attach to the process and step through code much as you can with a traditional ASP.NET project. Testing on the full version of IIS is a good idea if that is what you plan to use in production. Testing with Kestrel or IIS Express can only go so far and you should aim to be as live-like as possible early on.

IIS can also be used as a proxy, for example, in front of the Kestrel web server on a single machine. However, when caching for multiple web servers, you may be better off using dedicated proxy server software such as Varnish.

Varnish

Varnish is a free reverse proxy server that runs on Unix-like operating systems such as **Linux** and **FreeBSD**. You can install it with your package manager (for example, `apt` or `yum`) or provision a proxy server with DevOps software such as **Chef** or **Puppet**. To configure Varnish, you use a **domain-specific language** (**DSL**) called **Varnish configuration language** (**VCL**).

 You can read more about Varnish at `http://varnish-cache.org/`.

You shouldn't need to configure Varnish too much if you are using HTTP caching headers correctly. However, you can also use the custom HTTP PURGE method to remove entries from the cache, which works with the Squid proxy software too. You may occasionally see a cryptic **guru meditation** error if Varnish is not properly configured, but you should be able to track down the issue in the Varnish logs. It could indicate that no healthy web servers are available.

Varnish configuration is beyond the scope of this book, but it's very well documented on the Varnish website. If you don't want to run your own proxy server, then you could use a CDN. You may still want your own proxy in addition to using a CDN, as large CDNs, with many **points of presence** (**PoP**), might request the same resource via each PoP, and not share assets across them. This can be an issue if you pay a lot for bandwidth, although some CDNs have a feature (often called origin shielding) that can help with this.

Working with a content delivery network

A CDN is commonly used in two ways, as a proxy for offloading your content or as a hosting provider for common third-party libraries and frameworks. You can use a dynamic CDN service, such as CloudFlare or Akamai, for the first use case, but the second situation (using a static CDN from Google or Microsoft) is more common and that's what we'll cover here.

Although using a CDN for your libraries, such as jQuery and Twitter bootstrap, is becoming less useful with the adoption of HTTP/2, it can still be helpful for reducing your hosting costs. Also, if you use a popular CDN and library, then a user may already have a copy of some required assets. For example, if the user has been to another site that uses jQuery from Google's CDN, then it may already be in their browser cache.

It is essential to have a fallback copy of whatever files you require from a CDN. This is easier than ever with the Razor view engine support built into ASP.NET Core.

The following code shows how jQuery is included in the default MVC Razor layout, for non-development environments. Both the CDN and local versions are specified along with a test:

```
<script src="https://ajax.aspnetcdn.com/ajax/jquery/jquery-2.2.0.min.js"
        asp-fallback-src="~/lib/jquery/dist/jquery.min.js"
        asp-fallback-test="window.jQuery"
        crossorigin="anonymous"
        integrity="sha384-
K+ctZQ+LL8q6tP7I94W+qzQsfRV2a+AfHIi9k8z8l9ggpc8X+Ytst4yBo/hH+8Fk">
</script>
```

The preceding code snippet not only renders the standard `<script>` tag for the Microsoft CDN, but also adds the following inline JavaScript afterwards, which includes the local version if the CDN load fails:

```
(window.jQuery||document.write("\u003Cscript
src=\u0022\/lib\/jquery\/dist\/jquery.min.js\u0022
crossorigin=\u0022anonymous\u0022 integrity=\u0022sha384-
K\u002BctZQ\u002BLL8q6tP7I94W\u002BqzQsfRV2a\u002BAfHIi9k8z8l9ggpc8X\u002BY
tst4yBo\/hH\u002B8Fk\u0022\u003E\u003C\/script\u003E"));
```

Previously, you would have had to do this manually, usually in a hurry when your CDN went down. This new helper also works for other scripts and CSS files. For more examples, take a look at `_Layout.cshtml` in the default template.

It's important to use a secure HTTPS connection to CDN resources in order to avoid mixed content warnings or script loading errors in browsers. Most popular CDNs support HTTPS and for added safety you should use SRI hashes (as in the preceding examples). For additional information on CDNs, see `Chapter 6`, *Addressing Network Performance*.

When not to cache

There are certain situations when you shouldn't cache pages or at least you need to be very careful with how you go about it. As a general rule of thumb, caching the rendered output of an authorized page is a bad idea. In other words, if a user has logged into your site, and you are serving them customized content (which could easily be sensitive), then you need to consider caching very carefully.

If you accidentally serve one user's cached content to another, then at best, it will be annoying, as the personalization will be incorrect. At worst, you could expose private information to the wrong person and potentially get into legal trouble.

This is similar to the general rule of not universally enabling CORS if you serve authenticated content. It can be done successfully, but you need to understand the mechanisms in order to configure it to work safely.

Cross-Origin Resource Sharing (CORS) is generally used as a way of allowing JSON APIs to be accessed from JavaScript in a webpage on another domain. Without this, the browser will prevent communication between scripts that don't share the same origin.

For caching, you will need a unique identifier in the URL that can't be guessed. Some dynamic cache control systems, used by network appliances and CDNs, can make use of cookies for this, but it's beyond normal HTTP-based cache control. It is similar to how you might need sticky sessions on a load balancer, because your application was not designed to be stateless.

For authenticated caching, it may be better to not cache at the web level and instead cache at the application level and below. This allows you to cache smaller discrete chunks rather than a whole page, which can enhance reusability.

Application layer caching

Application level (or layer) caching means storing reusable data temporarily inside your infrastructure, but not in the main database. This can be in the memory of your application or web servers, but with multiple servers, this tends to be in a distributed in-memory store such as Memcached or Redis.

You can, of course, use both in-memory stores on your web servers and a centralized cache. However, if you have multiple web servers, then you will need a way to synchronize the caches. You can use **publish/subscribe (pub/sub)** messaging for this, which we will cover later in this chapter.

The following diagram shows a simple centralized caching setup. In a real situation, you will probably have multiple clustered cache servers:

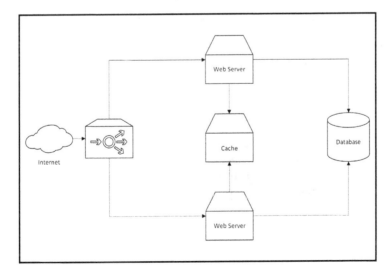

The web servers can now ask the cache if the data they need is in there before going to the database. This reduces load on the DB and is often quicker, as the data will be in memory if present. If there is a cache miss and the database does need to be queried, then the result can be written to the cache for other servers to use.

Redis

Redis is a popular in-memory store that can also persist data to disk for permanent storage. It runs best on Linux, but a version is available on Windows for development purposes. Redis additionally supports pub/sub messaging, which can be useful for cache invalidation. You can read more about Redis at `http://redis.io/`.

You may wish to use the Windows version of Redis for local development work, but still deploy to the supported version on Linux. You can get the Windows version at `http://github.com/MSOpenTech/redis` or you could run the Linux version in a virtual machine, perhaps using **Docker** or **Vagrant**.

Redis cache is provided as a service on both Azure and AWS (**ElastiCache** offers both Memcached and Redis). You don't need to manage your own server, but because the technology is not cloud-specific, you won't get locked in if you want to migrate in the future.

As Redis keeps the entire dataset in memory but is also able to persist to disk it can be suitable as a primary data store, unlike Memcached. However, it is more commonly used only as a cache, especially if a cloud service is used and it's paired with a cloud database such as **Azure SQL Database** or AWS **Relational Database Service** (**RDS**).

There are two recommended .NET C# clients for Redis: ServiceStack.Redis and StackExchange.Redis. The Stack Exchange client is used heavily on sites such as Stack Overflow and is easier to use correctly than the the ServiceStack one. You can read more about it at `http://github.com/StackExchange/StackExchange.Redis` and install it via NuGet.

If using caching at the application layer, then you will probably need to write a significant amount of custom code. You will also need to work out what format to serialize your data into for storage in the cache. If serving directly to browsers, then JSON could be useful. But if is to be used internally, then you may prefer a binary format such as MS Bond or protocol buffers.

See `Chapter 8`, *Understanding Code Execution and Asynchronous Operations*, for more on serialization formats and libraries.

Database result set caching

Caching at the database level is similar to application level caching, and it uses similar infrastructure, but requires less custom code. You can use the caching features built into an O/RM, which may make it easier to retrofit.

When we talk about database caching here, we are not referring to caching within the database engine itself. DBs use extensive performance-enhancing techniques, such as query caching, and hold lots of their data in memory. However, this is abstracted away from the developer and the caching we mention here refers to storing the output of a query in an application cache. This is similar to, but subtly different from, the previous section, where you will be storing custom objects.

In the context of O/RMs (such as NHibernate and Entity Framework), this is known as second-level caching. First-level caching generally already happens per session, by default, and is used to help avoid things like *select N+1* problems. Second-level caching operates at a level higher than individual transactions and allows you to share cached data across multiple database sessions over your entire application.

Message queuing

A **message queue** (**MQ**) is an asynchronous and reliable way of moving data around your system. It is useful for offloading work from your web application to a background service, but can also be used to update multiple parts of your system concurrently. For example, distributing cache invalidation data to all of your web servers.

MQs add complexity and we will cover managing this in `Chapter 10`, *The Downsides of Performance-Enhancing Tools*. However, they can also assist in implementing a **microservices architecture** where you break up your monolith into smaller parts, interfaced against contracts. This can make things easier to reason about within large organizations, where different teams manage the various parts of the application. We will discuss this in more detail in the next chapter, as queues aren't the only way of implementing this style of architecture. You can build microservices with many transport technologies, for example HTTP APIs can be used.

Coffee shop analogy

If using MQs, then you may need to implement extra reconciliation logic for errors occurring in the background. This is best explained with a coffee shop analogy.

If you purchase a takeaway coffee, perhaps in a branch of a popular multinational chain of franchised caffeinated beverage outlets (that dislikes paying tax), then your drink is prepared asynchronously to the payment processing. Typically, you place your order and a barista will start to prepare your coffee, before you have paid for it. Additionally, you will normally pay before receiving your drink. There are many things that could go wrong here, but they are rare enough for the extra cost to be worth it, as it speeds up the ordinary workflow.

For example, you may find that you are unable to pay after placing your order, but the coffee creation process has already begun. This will result in wasted stock, unless there is another customer waiting for whom it could be used. Or perhaps, after you have paid, the barista discovers that a key ingredient for your order is missing. They could either offer you a refund, or negotiate a different drink.

Although more complex, this process is clearly superior to performing the actions in series. If you had to demonstrate that you had the means to pay, your drink was made, and then you completed paying, only one customer could be served at a time. Assuming there are enough staff, payment processing and drink preparation can be performed in parallel, which avoids a long queue of customers.

Running a coffee shop in this way makes intuitive sense and yet, in a web application, it is common to have a relatively long-running transaction complete before informing the user of the result. In some situations, it may be better to assume the action will succeed, inform the user of this immediately and have a process in place in case it goes wrong.

For example, payment processing gateways can be slow and unreliable, so it may be better to charge a user's credit card after accepting an order. However, this means that you can no longer handle a failure by showing the user an error message. You will have to use other methods of communication.

When you order items on Amazon, they take payment details immediately, but they process the payment in the background and send you emails with the results. If the payment fails, they would need to cancel the order fulfilment and notify you. This requires extra logic, but is quicker than processing the payment transaction and checking stock before confirming the order.

Message queuing styles

Broadly speaking, there are two styles of message queuing. These styles are with and without a central broker. With a broker, all messages go through a hub, which manages the communication. Examples of this style include **RabbitMQ**, **ActiveMQ**, and MS **BizTalk**.

There are also broker-less styles (that don't use a broker), where communication between nodes is direct. An example of this style includes ZeroMQ (**ØMQ**), which has a native C# port called **NetMQ**.

Cloud queuing services, including **Azure Service Bus**, Azure Queue storage, and AWS **Simple Queue Service** (**SQS**), are also available. However, as with all non-generic cloud services, you should be wary of getting locked in. There are cloud providers of standard RabbitMQ hosting, which makes migration to your own infrastructure easier down-the-line if you don't initially want to run your own server. For example, CloudAMQP offers RabbitMQ hosting on multiple cloud platforms.

RabbitMQ implements the **Advanced Message Queuing Protocol** (**AMQP**), which helps to ensure interoperability between different MQ brokers, for example, to allow communication with the **Java Message Service** (**JMS**). Azure Service Bus also supports AMQP, but a big benefit of RabbitMQ is that you can install it on your development machine for local use, without an internet connection.

There is also **Microsoft Message Queuing** (**MSMQ**), which is built into Windows. While this is useful for communication between processes on a single machine, it can be tricky to get it working reliably between multiple servers.

Common messaging patterns

There are two types of common messaging patterns: point-to-point unicast and publish/subscribe. These send messages to a single recipient and many recipients respectively.

Unicast

Unicast is the standard message queuing approach. A message is sent from one service process or software agent to another. The queuing framework will ensure that this happens reliably and will provide certain guarantees about delivery.

This approach is dependable, but doesn't scale well as a system grows because each node will need to know about all its recipients. It would be better to loosely couple system components together so that they don't need to have knowledge about any of the others.

This is often achieved by using a broker, which has three main advantages:

- By using a broker, you can decouple processes from each other so that they aren't required to know about the system architecture or be alive at the same time. They only care about the message types and the broker takes care of routing the message to the correct destination.
- Broker queues enable an easy distribution of work pattern, especially when combining multiple producers. You can have multiple processes consuming the same queue and the broker will allocate messages to them in a round-robin fashion. This is a simple way of building a parallel system, without having to do any asynchronous programming or worrying about threads. You can just run multiple copies of your code, perhaps on separate machines if constrained by hardware, and they will run simultaneously.
- You can easily broadcast or multicast a particular type of message, perhaps to indicate that an event has occurred. Other processes that care about this event can listen to the messages without the publisher knowing about them. This is known as the pub/sub pattern.

Pub/sub

Pub/sub, as the name suggests, is where a software agent publishes a message onto a queue, and other agents can subscribe to that type of message to receive it. When a message is published, all subscribers receive it, but crucially the publisher does not require any knowledge of the subscribers or even need to know how many there are (or even if there are any at all).

Pub/sub is best done with the broker style of message queuing architecture. It can be done without a broker, but it is not particularly reliable. If your use case can tolerate message loss, then you may be able to get away without a broker. But, if you require guaranteed delivery, then you should use one. Using the RabbitMQ broker also allows you to take advantage of exchanges which can perform complex routing of messages.

If you don't want to lose messages, then you need to carefully design your pub/sub system (even if using a broker). A published message that has no subscribers may simply disappear into the ether without a trace and this might not be what you want.

The following diagram shows the differences between simple message forwarding, work distribution, and pub/sub:

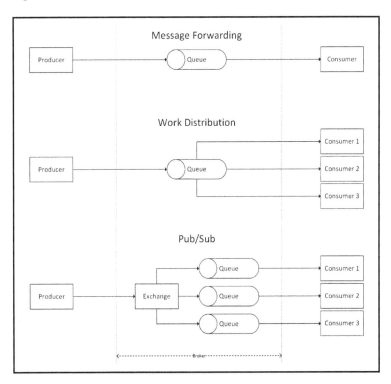

Clearly, if you require a reliable broker, then it needs to be highly available. Typically, you would cluster multiple brokers together to provide redundancy. Using a broker also allows you to write custom rules to define which subscribers receive what messages. For example, your payment system may only care about orders, but your logging server may want to get all messages from all systems.

You will want to monitor not only your broker servers but also the length of the queues. In other words, the number of messages in each queue should always be steady and close to zero. If the number of messages in a queue is steadily growing then this might indicate a problem, which your operations team will need to resolve. It may be that your consumers can't process messages faster than your producers are sending them and you must construct additional consumers. This could be automated and your monitoring software could spin up an extra instance to scale your system, meeting a temporary spike in demand.

RabbitMQ

RabbitMQ is a free and open source message queuing server. It's written in Erlang, which is the same robust language that WhatsApp uses for its messaging backend.

RabbitMQ is currently maintained by Pivotal (whose labs also make the Pivotal Tracker agile project management tool), but it was originally made by LShift. It was then acquired by VMware before being spun out as a joint venture. It's distributed under the **Mozilla Public License** (**MPL**) v1.1, an older version of the license that the Firefox web browser uses.

The messaging server can be used from many different languages and frameworks such as Java, Ruby, and .NET. This can make it helpful for linking diverse applications together, for example, a Rails app that you want to interface with an ASP.NET Core app or C# service.

 You can read more about RabbitMQ and download builds from `http://www.rabbitmq.com/`.

RabbitMQ is more modern than systems such as MSMQ and includes features such as an HTTP API and a web admin management interface. Along with HTTP and AMQP, it also supports **Simple Text Orientated Messaging Protocol** (**STOMP**) and **MQTT**, which is useful for lightweight **Internet of Things** (**IoT**) hardware applications. All of these protocols improve interoperability with other messaging systems and they can normally be secured using standard TLS.

The web management interface shows you how many messages are flowing through your queues, and how they are configured.

It also allows you to administer your queues (tasks such as purging or deleting messages) and looks something like the following screenshot:

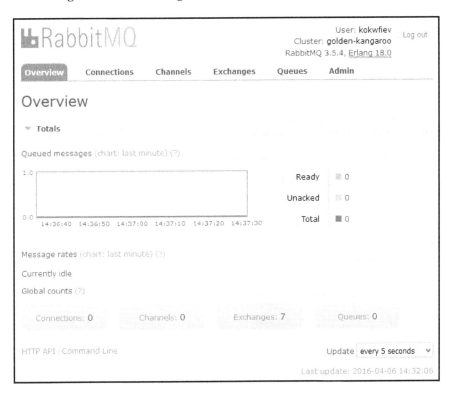

Queuing frameworks and libraries

You will typically want to use a prebuilt client library or framework to interact with your message queues. There are official libraries in many different languages for the various queuing systems, which offer low-level access. For example, RabbitMQ has an official .NET/C# client library.

However, there are also other opinionated clients and frameworks, which offer a higher level of abstraction for common messaging tasks. For example, **NServiceBus** (**NSB**), which supports RabbitMQ, MSMQ, SQL Server, and Azure, is a commercial offering.

A free alternative to NSB is **MassTransit** (http://masstransit-project.com/), which is a lightweight service bus and distributed application framework. It has also spun out the super-convenient **Topshelf** framework (http://topshelf-project.com/), which makes creating Windows services really easy.

Neither yet runs on .NET Core, but the work to port both of these projects is in progress.

 Library and framework support for .NET Core and ASP.NET Core is progressing rapidly, so check `http://anclafs.com/` for the latest information. Feel free to help out and contribute to this list or to any of the open source projects that need porting.

One interesting feature of MassTransit (and NSB) is support for sagas. A saga is a complex state machine that allows you to model the story of an entire workflow. Rather than defining individual messages and documenting how they all fit together, you can implicitly capture the golden path and error flows within a saga.

There is an excellent open source library called **EasyNetQ**, which makes implementing pub/sub on RabbitMQ trivial. You can read about it at `http://easynetq.com/`. Both the official RabbitMQ client and EasyNetQ now support .NET Core.

You could also look into using **RestBus**, which is a RabbitMQ library that supports ASP.NET Core. You can read more about it at `http://restbus.org/`, and it additionally supports Web API and ServiceStack.

Summary

In this chapter, we investigated the various tools and methods used for caching and message queuing. These two techniques offer different ways of improving the performance of your system by moving data to other locations and not having one massive monolith do everything.

These are both advanced topics and difficult to cover in such a small space. Hopefully, you have been introduced to some fresh ideas that can help you with solving problems in different ways. You can also visit the author's website at `https://unop.uk/` for the coverage of more topics. If you have discovered a new technology that you think will assist, you're encouraged to read the documentation and specifications for all of the implementation details.

However, before you dive in, you should understand that advanced techniques are complex and have downsides, which can reduce your development speed. In the next chapter, we'll learn about these downsides and discover approaches for managing complexities, such as microservices.

10
The Downsides of Performance-Enhancing Tools

A lot of the topics that we covered in this book improve performance at a cost. Your application will become more complicated and harder to understand or reason about. This chapter discusses these trade-offs and how to mitigate their impact.

You should implement many of the approaches that you learned so far in this book only if you require them and not just because they are interesting or challenging. It's often preferable to keep things simple if the existing performance is good enough.

You will learn how to make pragmatic choices about what technologies and techniques you should use. You'll also see how to manage the complexities if you choose to use advanced methods.

The topics covered in this chapter include the following:

- Managing complexity with frameworks and architecture
- Building a healthy culture to deliver high performance
- Distributed debugging and performance logging
- Understanding statistics and stale data

Many books and guides only focus on the positives of new tools and frameworks. However, nothing comes for free, and there is always a penalty, which may not be immediately obvious.

You may not feel the effects of the choices that you make for a long time, particularly in technical architecture. You might not discover that a decision was bad until you try to build on it, perhaps years later.

Managing complexity

One of the main problems with performance-enhancing techniques is that they typically make a system more complicated. This can make a system harder to modify and it may also reduce your productivity. Therefore, although your system runs faster, your development is now slower.

We commonly find this complexity problem in enterprise software, although usually for different reasons. Typically, many unnecessary layers of abstraction are used, supposedly to keep the software flexible. Ironically, this actually makes it slower to add new features. This may seem counter-intuitive until you realize that simplicity makes change easier.

 There's a satirical enterprise edition of the popular programmer interview coding test *FizzBuzz*, which is available on GitHub (via the short URL `http://www.fizzbuzz.enterprises/`). It's a good inspiration for how to not do things.

If you don't need a feature yet, then it's often best to leave it out rather than building it just in case you might need it in the future. The more code you write, the more bugs it will have, and the harder it will be to understand. Over-engineering is a common negative psychological trait that is easy to fall victim to if you aren't aware of it, and marketers often exploit this.

For a non-software example, four-wheel drive SUVs are sold to people who will never need their off-road capabilities on the false premise that it may potentially come in useful someday. Yet the financial, safety, environmental, and parking convenience costs outweigh this supposed benefit because it's never used.

We often term this development advice from the **extreme programming (XP)** philosophy, **You Aren't Going to Need It (YAGNI)**. Although we sometimes use slightly different words, the meaning is the same. YAGNI advocates keeping things simple and only building what you immediately need.

This doesn't mean that you should make your software hard to modify. It's still important to stay flexible just don't add features before you need them. For example, adding an abstract base class when there is only a single implementation may be an overkill. You could easily add it along with the second implementation, if and when you build it.

It's difficult to move fast and not break things when doing so. How you achieve high reliability in addition to a consistently good development speed will depend on many things that are specific to your situation, such as your team size, organizational structure, and company culture.

One method is to embrace change and develop a system where you can refactor your code in confidence. Using a statically-compiled language such as C# is a good start, but you should also have a comprehensive test suite to avoid regressions.

You should design a system so that it is loosely coupled, which means that you can change parts in isolation without a lot of knock-on effects. This also makes it easier to build unit tests, which are invaluable in preventing functional regressions when refactoring.

We will cover testing and automation with a **Continuous Integration** (**CI**) workflow in the next chapter. In this chapter, we will talk more about the various architectural styles that can help you maintain your application.

Understanding complexity

When learning about new ways of doing things, you should avoid doing them without understanding the reasons. You should know the benefits and downsides, and then measure the changes to prove that they are what you expect. Don't just blindly implement something and assume it improves the situation. Try to avoid **cargo cult programming** and always objectively evaluate a new approach.

Cargo cult programming is the practice of emulating something successful but failing to understand the reasons of why it works. Its name comes from the cargo cults of the Pacific, who built dummy airstrips after World War II to encourage cargo delivery. We use it to describe many things where correlation has been confused with causation. One example is a company encouraging long hours to deliver a project because they have heard of successful projects where employees worked long hours. However, they fail to understand that the successful project and long hours are both independent byproducts of a highly motivated and competent workforce, and they are not directly related.

It's important to keep the code readable, not just for others on your team or new members but also for your future self (who will have forgotten how something works and why it was written in the way it was). This doesn't simply mean writing helpful explanatory comments in the code, although this is a very good practice. It also applies to sourcing control comments and keeping the documentation up to date.

Readability also involves keeping things simple by only making them as complex as they need to be and not hiding functionality in unnecessary layers of abstraction, for example, by not using clever programming techniques to reduce the file line count when a standard structure (for example, a loop or an `if` statement) would be more readable and only slightly longer.

It helps to have a standard way of doing things in your team to avoid surprises. Using the same method everywhere can be more valuable than finding a better way of doing it and then having lots of different ways. If there is consensus, then you can go back and retrofit the better method everywhere you need it.

Complexity reduction

There are various solutions to manage the complexity that performance-enhancing techniques can add. These usually work by reducing the amount of logic that you need to think about at any time by hiding the complications.

One option is to use frameworks that standardize how you write your application, which can make it easier to reason about. Another approach is to use an architecture that allows you to only think about small parts of your code base in isolation. By breaking up a complex app into manageable chunks, it becomes easier to work with.

This idea of modularity is related to the **single responsibility principle** (**SRP**), which is the first of the **SOLID** principles (the others are open/closed, Liskov substitution, interface segregation, and dependency inversion). It is also similar to the higher-level **Separation of Concerns** (**SoC**) and to the simplicity of the Unix philosophy. It is better to have many tools that each do one thing well, rather than one tool that does many things badly.

Frameworks

Frontend frameworks have become popular in recent years. Facebook's **React** is a library designed to reliably build web application views in JavaScript, although the patent licensing is controversial. The aim is to help large teams work on a project by simplifying the data flow and standardizing the approach. React can be integrated with ASP.NET Core using the **ReactJS.NET** project (`https://reactjs.net/`).

This is not to be confused with **React Native**, used to build cross-platform apps that share code across iOS, Android, and the **Universal Windows Platform** (**UWP**). If you prefer coding in C#, then you can build your cross-platform mobile apps with **Xamarin**. However, we won't go further into any of these technologies in this book. Visit the author's website (`https://unop.uk/`) to read about ReactJS.NET and Xamarin.Forms.

On the backend, we have the server-side frameworks of .NET Core and ASP.NET Core. Along with C# features, these provide convenient ways of simplifying historically complicated features. For example, the `async` and `await` keywords hide a lot of the complicated logic associated with asynchronous programming, and lambda functions concisely express intent.

We covered many of these features earlier in this book, so we won't go over them again here. We also highlighted libraries that can make your life easier by hiding boilerplate code for complex operations, for example, `EasyNetQ` and `RestBus`.

Hiding a complex process is never perfect, and you will occasionally come across abstractions that leak some of their implementation detail. For example, when handling exceptions, you may find that the issue you're interested in is now wrapped in an aggregate exception. If you're not careful, your error logs may no longer contain the detail that you desire.

 It's good practice not to log the individual properties of an exception, as exceptions already have built-in logic to output all of the relevant information. Simply log an exception as a string and you will get the message and stack trace, including any inner exceptions.

What we have yet to talk about in detail is the architecture of a web application. Splitting a monolithic system up into discrete parts can not only improve performance, but if done right it can also make it easier to maintain.

Architecture

In the previous chapter, when discussing message queuing, we briefly covered the microservices architecture. This style is a more modern reimagining of the traditional **Service Oriented Architecture** (**SOA**), and although using reliable MQ communication is preferred, we can also perform this with **Representational State Transfer** (**REST**) HTTP APIs.

Typically, we build a traditional web app as a single application or monolith. This is common if the app has grown organically over an extended period of time, and this is a perfectly acceptable practice. It's a poor decision to over-engineer too early before there is any need, which may never materialize.

Excessive popularity is a nice problem to have, but don't optimize for this prematurely. This isn't an excuse to make things unnecessarily slow, so be sure to understand the trade-offs involved.

Using a monolithic architecture is not an excuse to build something badly, and you should plan for expansion, even if you do not implement it immediately. You can keep things simple while still allowing for future growth. Although the application is a single unit, you should split the code base into well-organized modules, which are linked together in a simple, logical, and easy-to-understand way. Refer to the SOLID principles mentioned previously.

If a monolithic application can't easily scale to meet user demand and is performing poorly as a result, then you can split it up into smaller separate services. You may also wish to split an app up if it has become too cumbersome to iterate on quickly and the development speed has slowed.

Monolith versus microservices

The following diagram shows some differences between a typical monolith and a microservices architecture:

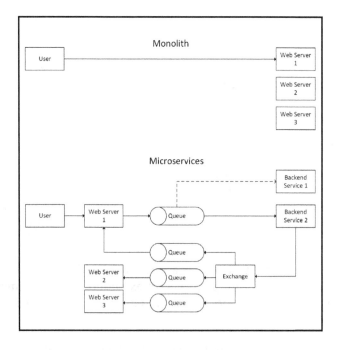

Here, the user makes a request to an application running on a web farm. We have omitted firewalls, load balancers, and databases for clarity, but multiple web servers are shown to illustrate that the same code base runs on multiple machines.

In the initial monolith architecture, the user communicates directly with a single web server. This is ideally per request/response pair. However, if the application is poorly designed and holds the state in memory, then **sticky sessions** may cause the load to pool on certain servers.

The second example in the diagram, that is, the microservices architecture, is obviously more complicated but also more flexible. The user again sends a request to a web server, but instead of doing all the work, the server puts a message onto a queue.

The work in this queue is distributed between multiple backend services, of which the first one is busy, so a second service picks up the message. When the service completes, it sends a message to an exchange on the message broker, which uses a pub/sub broadcast to inform all the web servers.

One added piece of complexity is that the architecture should have already sent the response to the user's original web request, so you need to consider the **user experience** (**UX**) more carefully. For example, you can display a progress indicator and update the status of this with an asynchronous WebSocket connection.

Architecture comparison

The monolith approach is simple, and you can just add more web servers to handle additional users. However, this approach can become cumbersome, as an application (and the development team) grows larger because the slightest change requires a full redeployment to each web server.

In addition, a monolith is easy to scale vertically (up) but hard to scale horizontally (out), which we covered previously. However, a monolith is easier to debug, so you need to be careful and have good monitoring and logging. You don't want any random outage investigation to turn into a murder mystery hunt because of unnecessarily implemented microservices.

Historically, Facebook had a deployment process that consisted of slowly compiling their PHP code base to a gigantic gigabyte-scale binary (for runtime performance reasons). They then needed to develop a modified version of BitTorrent to efficiently distribute this huge executable to all of their web servers. Although this was impressive infrastructure engineering, it didn't address the root cause of their **technical debt** problem, and they have since moved on to better solutions, such as the **HipHop Virtual Machine** (**HHVM**), which is similar to the .NET CLR

If you wish to practice continuous delivery and deploy multiple times a week (or even many times a day), then it's advantageous to break your web application up. You can then maintain and deploy each part separately, communicating with each other using messages against an agreed API.

This separation can also help you use agile development methodologies—for example, using many smaller teams rather than big teams because smaller teams perform better.

Your instrument of control to scale a monolith is very crude, as all the work is done in one place. You can't scale some parts of your app independently to the other components of the application. You can only scale the whole thing, even if the high load is concentrated in a small part. This is analogous to a central bank only having control of a single interest rate as a lever, which affects many things at once. If your app is distributed, then you only need to scale the part that requires it, avoiding over-provisioning and reducing costs.

A well-used (and often rephrased) quote from Abraham Maslow goes:

> *"I suppose it is tempting, if the only tool you have is a hammer, to treat everything as if it were a nail."*

This is known as the law of the instrument, and it is related to confirmation bias. If you only have one tool, then you are likely to use this tool for everything and only see things that support your existing ideas. This commonly applies to tools and frameworks, but it can also apply to scaling techniques.

The first step towards modularity may be to split a big web application into many smaller web apps so that you can deploy them separately. This strategy can have some benefits, but it also has many limitations. Some logic may be unsuitable to host in a web app, for example, long-running processes, such as those monitoring a filesystem or used to manipulate media.

You may also find that you need to duplicate code that was shared in the original monolith. If you adhere to the **Don't Repeat Yourself** (**DRY**) doctrine, then you might extract this functionality to a library. Yet, now you have dependencies and versioning to manage. You'll also need processes to build, package, and host your library in a private repository, all of which can slow down development and reduce your agility.

 Sometimes, we also refer to DRY as **Duplication Is Evil** (**DIE**), and this is the sensible idea that an implementation should only occur in a unique location. If other code requires this functionality, then it should call the original function and not have copied code pasted in. This means that you only need to make a change in a single place to apply it everywhere.

A more advanced approach is to extract functionality into a separate service, which can handle many different web applications. If designed correctly, then this service won't need to have any knowledge of these apps and will simply respond to messages. This allows you to add a new web app without making changes to the code of the other applications or services.

Refactoring

Refactoring a monolith into services can be tricky if the application has become a tightly coupled big-ball-of-mud, but if it's been well-built (with plenty of test coverage and loosely coupled code), then it shouldn't be too taxing. There's a big difference between a well-built monolith and a big-ball-of-mud made with little thought.

It's worth expanding on test coverage, as unit tests are essential for successful refactoring without introducing regressions or new bugs. Unit tests allow you to refactor and tidy up in confidence, and they prevent the creation of code that is fragile, which developers are afraid to touch. We will cover testing in a greater detail, including automation, in Chapter 11, *Monitoring Performance Regressions*.

Both of these design patterns may appear superficially similar, but internally it's a different story. The following diagram illustrates the differences between a well-architected monolith and a messy big-ball-of-mud.

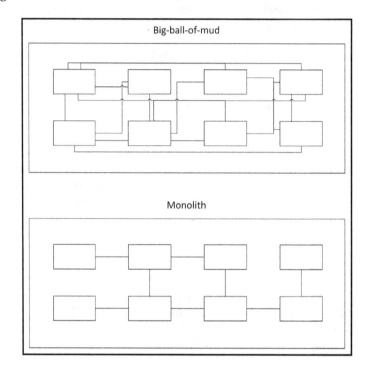

The large boxes represent the code running on each web server (the **Web Server N** boxes from the monolith example in the earlier diagram). From the outside, they look the same, but the difference is in the internal coupling of the code.

The big-ball-of-mud is a tangled mess with code referencing other functions throughout the application. The monolith is well-structured with a clear separation of concerns between different modules.

Changes to the code in the big-ball-of-mud can have unexpected side-effects because the other parts of it may rely on the implementation details of what you are modifying. This makes it brittle, difficult to alter, and developers may be afraid of touching it.

The well-built monolith is easy to refactor and split out into separate services because the code is neatly-organized. It uses abstract interfaces to communicate between modules, and code doesn't reach into another class's concrete implementation details. It also has excellent coverage with unit tests, which run automatically on every check-in/push.

Tools are also very useful in refactoring and testing. We covered the Visual Studio IDE and ReSharper plugin previously, but there are many more tools for testing. We will cover more testing tools, including automation, in `Chapter 11`, *Monitoring Performance Regressions*.

Although both are a single code base, the quality of the monolith is much higher because it is internally well-distributed. Good design is important for future-proofing, as it allows for expansion. The monolith hasn't been split up too early (before scaling was required), but the design makes this easy to do later. In contrast, the big-ball-of-mud has accumulated a large amount of technical debt, which it needs to pay off before we can make any further progress.

Technical debt (or tech debt for short) is the concept of not finishing a job or cutting corners, which could lead to more difficulties until it is paid back. For example, failing to properly document a system will make it more difficult for new developers. Tech debt is not necessarily a bad thing if it is deliberately taken on in full knowledge, logged, and paid back later. For example, waiting to write the documentation until after a release can speed up the delivery. However, tech debt that is not paid back or is accumulated without knowledge (simply due to sloppy coding) will get worse over time and cause bigger issues later.

The best way to deliver a high-quality and flexible application (that's easy to refactor) is to have a competent and conscientious development team. However, these attributes can often be more about culture, communication, and motivation than simply skill or raw talent. Although this isn't a book about team management, having a healthy culture is very important, so we'll cover a little of this here. Everyone in an operations and software development department can help create a positive and friendly culture, even if you usually need a buy-in from higher up as well.

A culture of high performance

If you want to achieve high performance, then it's important to foster a company culture that encourages this and recognizes performance as vital. Culture can't just come from the bottom (only involving engineers). Culture needs to come from the top, and the management must buy in to the performance prerogative.

This section is not very technical, so feel free to skip it if you don't care about management or the human side of software development.

A blameless culture

The most important attributes of a high performance culture are that it should be open and blameless. Everyone needs to be focused on achieving the best possible outcomes through measuring and learning. Attributing fault to individuals is toxic to delivering great software, and this is not only the case when it comes to performance.

If something goes wrong, then it is a process problem, and the focus should be on improving it and preventing the repetition of mistakes in the future, for example, by automating it. This is similar to how safety-critical industries such as air travel behave, as they recognize that blaming people discourages them from raising issues early, before a disaster occurs.

A related philosophy is the Japanese process of Kaizen, which encourages continuous improvement by everyone. The car manufacturer Toyota pioneered Kaizen practices to improve the efficiency of their production line, and most automotive companies and many other different industries have since adopted them.

Some industries also have processes to encourage whistle-blowing that protect the individual raising concerns. However, if this is required in web application development, then it's a sure sign that the culture needs work. Developers should feel that they are able to directly raise concerns bypassing their line manager without consequence. If everyone's opinion is respected, then this shouldn't even be necessary.

Intellectual dishonesty

If team members get defensive when ideas are challenged, then this is a sign that things may not be working well. Everybody makes mistakes and has gaps in their knowledge, a truth the best engineers embrace. You should strive for a culture where everyone is open to new ideas and is always asking questions.

If people are unable to accept constructive criticism and have their ideas challenged, then they may lack confidence and may be covering up a lack of competence. Experienced developers know that you never stop learning; they admit their ignorance and are always open to offers of improvement.

Being closed to suggestions alters the behavior of others, and they will stop raising small issues early. This results in open secrets about poor quality, and the first that is known about a problem is at release time, at which point everything is much worse (or on fire).

This is not an excuse to be nasty to people, so always try to be nice and gently explain the reasons behind your criticism. It's easy to find fault in anything, so always propose an alternative approach. If you are patient, then a reasonable person will be grateful for the learning opportunity and appreciate gaining experience.

A good rule to follow is *don't be a jerk* and treat others as you would like to be treated; so be kind and think about how you would feel if the situation were reversed. Just remember that being nice is not always compatible with doing the right thing.

A little self-deprecation can go a long way to making you more approachable rather than simply dictating the one-true-way. However, you should make it clear when something is a joke or tongue in cheek, especially when dealing with cultures that are more direct, or when communicating textually.

It is always a bad idea to generalize (no exceptions, ever). However, as one example, North Americans are often less subtle than, and not as sarcastic as, the British (who also spell some words differently, and some would say, more correctly). Obviously, use your own judgment because this may be terrible advice and could cause offense or, even worse, a full-on diplomatic incident. Hopefully, it is self-evident (or maybe not) that this whole paragraph is tongue-in-cheek.

People who have integrity and confidence in their ideas can afford to be modest and self-deprecating, but internal company culture can influence this too. A particularly bad practice is to conduct performance reviews by *laddering* (also known as stack ranking), which involves putting everyone in order, relative to everybody else. This is toxic because it rewards people who focus more on marketing themselves than those who recognize the deficiencies in their technical skills and try to improve them. In the pathological case, all of the best people are forced out, and you end up with a company full of sociopathic sharp suits, who are technically illiterate or even morally bankrupt.

Slow down to go faster

Sometimes, the company must allow the development team to slow down on feature delivery in order to focus on performance and resolving the technical debt. They should be given time to be thoughtful about design decisions so that they can cogitate avoiding premature generalization or careless optimization.

Performance is a significant selling point of software, and it is much easier to build quality throughout the development process than in a polishing phase at the end. There is a significant body of evidence that suggests good performance improves your **Return on Investment (RoI)** and creates customers. This is especially true on the web, where poor performance decreases conversion rate and search engine ranking.

Having a healthy culture is not only important for the runtime performance of your software but also for the speed at which you can develop it. The team should be encouraged to behave rigorously and write precise, but also concise, code.

You get what you measure, and if you only measure the rate of feature delivery or, even worse, simply the **Lines of Code** (**LoC**) written, then the quality will suffer. This will hurt you in the long run and is a false economy.

False economies are when you make short-term cost saving measures that actually lose you more money in the long term. Examples of this are skimping on hardware for developers or interrupting someone in the middle of coding with something trivial, which could easily wait until later, and forcing them to switch contexts.

Another non-software example is a shortsighted government making cuts to investment in research and sacrificing long-term growth for short-term savings. Or a country leaving an economic union on the promise that the membership fee would be spent on something better, despite the fee being dwarfed by the long-term losses to the economy.

Hardware is significantly cheaper than a developer's time. Therefore, if everyone on your team doesn't have a beefy box and multiple massive monitors, then productivity is being needlessly diminished. Even over a decade ago, Facebook's software developer job adverts listed dual 24-inch widescreen monitors as a perk.

From the ground up

In a healthy and progressive culture, it can be tempting to rewrite poor-quality software from scratch, perhaps in the latest trendy framework, but this is usually a mistake. Released software is battle-hardened (no matter how badly it was built), and if you rewrite it, then you will probably make the same mistakes again, for example, reimplementing bugs that you have already patched. This is especially true if the software was not built with good unit test coverage, which can help prevent regressions.

The only case where you could reasonably rewrite an application from the ground up is if you had deliberately made a prototype to explore the problem space with the sole intention of throwing it away. However, you should be very careful because if you've actually built a **Minimum Viable Product** (**MVP**) instead, then these prototyes that are in fact MVPs have a habit of sticking around for a long time and forming the foundations of larger applications.

A better approach to a full rewrite is to add tests to the application (if it doesn't already have them) and gradually refactor it to improve the quality and performance.

If you built an application in such a way as to make it difficult to unit test, then you can start with **user interface** (**UI**) tests, perhaps using a headless web browser. We will cover testing more, including performance testing, in the next chapter.

Shared values

Culture is really just a set of shared values, including things such as openness, sustainability, inclusivity, diversity, and ethical behavior. It can help having these values formally documented so that everyone knows what you stand for.

You may have a progressive open salary policy so that others can't use secret earning information as a tool to pay people less. However, this would need to apply universally, as it's unhealthy to have multiple conflicting cultures because this can precipitate an us-versus-them attitude.

There's plenty more to say about culture, but, as you can see, there are many competing concerns to balance. The most important idea is to make intentional and thoughtful trade-offs. There isn't one correct choice, but you should always be conscious of the consequences and appreciate how tiny actions can alter the team's performance.

The price of performance

Developers should have an idea of the available budget for performance and understand the cost of the code that they write, not just in execution throughput but in readability, maintainability, and power efficiency. Throwing more cores at a unit of work is not nearly as good as refactoring it to be simpler.

Efficiency has become increasingly important, especially with the rise of mobile devices and cloud computing time-based usage billing. Parallelizing an inefficient algorithm may solve a performance problem in the time domain, but it's a crude brute-force approach, and altering the underlying implementation may be better.

Less is often more and sometimes doing nothing is the best approach. Software engineering is not only about knowing what to build but what not to build. Keeping things simple helps the others on your team use your work. You should aim to avoid surprising anyone with non-obvious behavior. For example, if you build an API then you should give it conventional defaults. If the operation could potentially take a long time, then make and name the methods as async to indicate this fact.

You should aim to make it easy to succeed and hard to fail when building on your code. Make it difficult to do the wrong thing; for example, if a method is unsafe, name it to document this fact. Being a competent programmer is only a small part of being a good developer; you also need to be helpful and proficient at communicating clearly.

In fact, being an expert programmer can be a downside if you don't deliberately keep things simple to aid the understanding of the others in your team. You should always balance performance improvements against the side-effects, and you shouldn't make them at the expense of future development efficiency without good reason.

Distributed debugging

Distributed systems can make it difficult to debug problems, and you need to plan for this in advance by integrating technology that can help with visibility. You should know what metrics you want to measure and what parameters are important to record.

As you run a web application, it isn't a case of deploy and forget, as it might be with mobile apps or desktop software. You will need to keep a constant automated eye on your application to ensure that it is always available. If you monitor the correct performance metrics, then you can get early warning signs of problems and can take preventative action. If you only measure the uptime or responsiveness, then the first that you may know of a problem is an outage notification, probably at an unsociable hour.

You may outsource your infrastructure to a cloud-hosting company so that you don't have to worry about hardware or platform failures. However, this doesn't completely absolve you of responsibility, and your software will still need continuous monitoring. You may need to architect your application differently to work in harmony with your hosting platform and scale or self-heal when issues arise.

If you design your system correctly, then your web application will run itself, and you'll rarely get notified of actions that require your attention. If you can successfully automate all of the things, rather than babysitting a live deployment, then that's more time you can use to build the future.

In a distributed architecture, you can't simply attach a debugger to the live web server, not that this is a good idea even when possible. There is no one live server anymore; there are now many live servers and even more processes. To get a holistic picture of the system, you will need to simultaneously examine the state of multiple modules.

There are many tools that you can use to help with centralizing your debug information. You can retrofit some of them. However, to get the most out of them, you should decide what to measure upfront and build telemetry capabilities into your software from the start.

Logging

Logging is vital in a high-performance application, so while it is true that logging adds some overhead and can slow down execution, omitting it would be short-sighted and a false economy. Without logging, you won't know what is slow and requires improvement. You will also have other concerns, such as reliability, for which logging is essential.

Error logging

You may be familiar with the excellent ASP.NET package called **Error Logging Modules and Handlers** (**ELMAH**), used to catch unhandled exceptions (http://elmah.github.io/). ELMAH is great for existing applications, as you can drop it into a live-running web app. However, it's preferable to have error logging built into your software from the start.

Unfortunately, ELMAH does not yet support ASP.NET Core, but there is a similar package called **Error Logging Middleware** (**ELM**). Adding this to your web application is just as simple as installing Glimpse, but it doesn't have all the features of ELMAH. ELM isn't really suitable for production use, but it can still be useful locally to aid debugging.

First, add the `Microsoft.AspNetCore.Diagnostics.Elm` NuGet package to your project. You can use the graphical tooling of your IDE to do this (the methods will vary depending on what IDE you are using, for example Visual Studio or VS Mac). Alternatively, you can use the following command in the Terminal, which works on all the supported platforms:

```
dotnet add package Microsoft.AspNetCore.Diagnostics.Elm
```

This will add a line to the `.csproj` file, which should look something like the following:

```
<PackageReference Include="Microsoft.AspNetCore.Diagnostics.Elm"
Version="0.2.2" />
```

The way packages are referenced in .NET Core 2.0 is different from .NET Core 1.0. They are no longer specified in a JSON file and although you can edit the XML project file manually, it is easier to use the supplied tooling. You can use the `dotnet migrate` command to upgrade an old `project.json`-based solution to an `msbuild`-based `.csproj` one.

Then, in the `ConfigureServices` method of the `Startup` class, add the following line of code:

```
services.AddElm();
```

You also need to add the following lines to the `Configure` method of the same class:

```
app.UseElmPage();
app.UseElmCapture();
```

You may want to put these lines of code inside the `if` statement that tests for `env.IsDevelopment()`, so that they are only active on your workstation.

You can now visit the `/Elm` path of your web application in your browser to see the logs, as shown in the following screenshot. Use the search box to filter results, click on **v** at the end of each line to expand the entry's details, and click on **^** to collapse it again:

ASP.NET Core Logs

Debug ∨		filter	Clear Logs

Path	Method	Host	Status Code					Logs		
RequestId:OHL6P3SPPCKF2...			08-01-2017 20:52:...	0 Critical	0 Error	0 Warning	1 Information	0 Debug		∨

			Date	Time	Name	Severity	State	Error	
									^
			08/01/17	20:52:44	Microsoft.AspNetCore.H...	Debug	Beginning RequestId:OHL...		
			08/01/17	20:52:44	Microsoft.AspNetCore.H...	Information	Request starting HTTP/1....		
/ima... GET loca... 304			08/01/17	20:52:44	Microsoft.AspNetCore.Di...	Debug	Beginning Request: ...		
			08/01/17	20:52:44	Microsoft.AspNetCore.St...	Information	The file /images/ba...		
			08/01/17	20:52:44	Microsoft.AspNetCore.Di...	Debug	Completed Request...		
			08/01/17	20:52:44	Microsoft.AspNetCore.H...	Information	Request finished in 0.333...		
			08/01/17	20:52:44	Microsoft.AspNetCore.H...	Debug	Completed RequestId:OH...		

Path	Method	Host	Status Code				Logs		
/ima...	GET	loca...	304	08-01-2017 20:52:...	0 Critical	0 Error	0 Warning	3 Information	0 Debug ∨
/ima...	GET	loca...	304	08-01-2017 20:52:...	0 Critical	0 Error	0 Warning	3 Information	0 Debug ∨
/ima...	GET	loca...	304	08-01-2017 20:52:...	0 Critical	0 Error	0 Warning	3 Information	0 Debug ∨
/js/s...	GET	loca...	304	08-01-2017 20:52:...	0 Critical	0 Error	0 Warning	3 Information	0 Debug ∨

When using ELM, ELMAH, or even the default error pages, you should be careful not to show detailed exceptions or stack traces to real users. This isn't simply because they're unfriendly and unhelpful but because they are a genuine security concern. Error logs and stack traces can reveal the internal workings of your application, which malicious actors can exploit.

You can use the website, ASafaWeb (`https://asafaweb.com/`), to check if you are unknowingly revealing more information about your app than you should be. It focuses more on traditional ASP.NET applications, but it's still useful.

As you have probably noticed when running your app in a Terminal, you also get any log entries streamed to the console (depending on the logging level that you have configured). You can pipe this output to anything you like and this is a very common pattern for Unix applications to use. Treating logs as event streams and simply writing them to `stdout` is one of the factors of twelve-factor apps.

Twelve-factor apps are a way of designing web applications so that they are well-suited to running in a cloud-hosting environment. These rules were conceived by the team at Heroku as good practices to follow. They focus on Linux, but this is now a great option for hosting ASP.NET Core web applications.

You can read about the other eleven factors on the website dedicated to twelve-factor apps at `https://12factor.net/`. The factor regarding logs is number eleven (`https://12factor.net/logs`).

ELM is fairly basic, but it can still be useful. However, there are better solutions already built into the default templates, such as integrated support for logging and **Application Insights**.

Application Insights

Application Insights is a telemetry service that allows you to monitor the performance of your application and view requests or exceptions. You can use it with Azure, but it will also work locally without needing an Azure account. However, if you're not hosting on Azure, then you may wish to use something else.

In Visual Studio 2017, you can right-click your web app project, click **Add**, and then click **Application Insights Telemetry**. You can then click the start button and register your app. However, keep in mind the privacy and cost implications of using Azure. You can use the SDK locally by clicking the understated link at the bottom of the register page.

This practice of designing a user interface to encourage a particular behavior from users that may not be in their best interest is called a **dark pattern**. Microsoft is betting big on Azure, so it is understandable that much of their software is designed to funnel you into a Microsoft online account and Azure. However, you don't need to use VS or Windows to build software with .NET Core, and it's also fairly easy to switch off the telemetry in the SDK and development tools.

Build and run the project, and then open the **Application Insights Search** window to see the output. Navigate around the web app in your browser, and you will see records starting to appear, which should look something like the following:

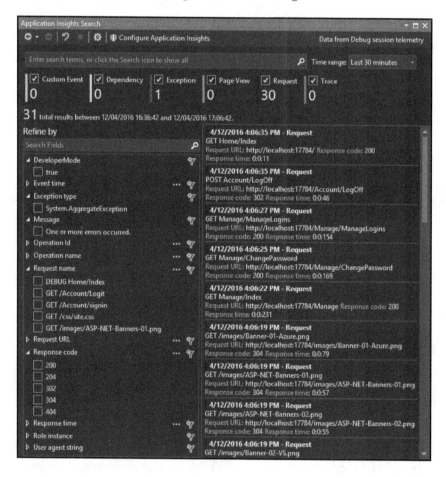

If you don't see any records in the output, then you may need to update the NuGet package (`Microsoft.ApplicationInsights.AspNetCore`) or click on the search icon.

You can filter by event type, for example, requests or exceptions, and there are more detailed filters to refine your search. You can select an individual record to see more details, which will look something like this:

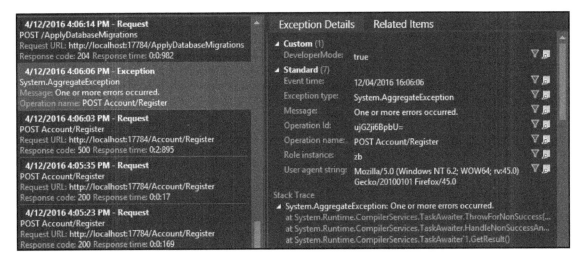

One of the more interesting things that this can tell you is whether your application is triggering any external events. For example, you can see whether your app has made a web API request to a URL on another domain and how much this action has slowed it down by.

We don't have enough space to cover Application Insights in more detail here, and if you're not using Azure, then you will want to consider other options anyway. You can read more about it online at `https://docs.microsoft.com/en-us/azure/application-insights/app-insights-asp-net-core`.

Integrated logging

Logging is now built into ASP.NET Core and so is **dependency injection** (**DI**), and both are included in the default templates. This reduces the barrier to entry, and it's now trivial to use these helpful technologies in even the smallest of projects.

Previously, you were required to add logging and DI libraries before you started, which could put many people off using them. If you didn't already have a standard choice for both, then you would need to wade through the plethora of projects and research the merits of each.

 You can still use your preferred libraries if you are already acquainted with them. It's just that there are now sensible defaults, which you can override.

Logging is added to your app in the `Program` class, but the way this is done is slightly different in ASP.NET Core 2.0 from what it was in ASP.NET Core 1.0. In the templates, it is added when the `CreateDefaultBuilder` method is called, which easily sets up sensible defaults. If you want to customize this, then the syntax is different from the previous version. You no longer call a logger factory, and there is a `ConfigureLogging` method instead. Refer to the documentation (`https://docs.microsoft.com/en-us/aspnet/core/fundamentals/logging?tabs=aspnetcore2x`) for the full details if you want to use something other than the default configuration.

Logging is configured in the `Startup` class, and if you use the standard web application template, then this will already be included for you. The logger factory reads settings from the `appsettings.json` file. Here, you can configure the logging level, and by default, the relevant section looks as follows:

```
"Logging": {
  "IncludeScopes": false,
  "Debug": {
    "LogLevel": {
      "Default": "Warning"
    }
  },
  "Console": {
    "LogLevel": {
      "Default": "Warning"
    }
  }
}
```

In the development mode, the following settings will be used to override these (from `appsettings.Development.json`):

```
"Logging": {
  "IncludeScopes": false,
  "LogLevel": {
    "Default": "Debug",
    "System": "Information",
    "Microsoft": "Information"
  }
}
```

This sets a very chatty log level, which is useful for development, but you will probably want to only log warnings and errors when you run this in production.

 Along with logging, useful development debugging tools included by default in the `Startup` class include a developer exception page, which is like an advanced version of the old **Yellow Screen Of Death** (**YSOD**) ASP.NET error page. Also included is a database error page, which can helpfully apply EF migrations and which mitigates a common pitfall of the previous EF code-first migration deployments.

To add the logger to your MVC home controller via constructor injection, you can use the following code (after adding `using Microsoft.Extensions.Logging;` to your `using` statements at the top of the file):

```
private readonly ILogger Logger;
public HomeController(ILoggerFactory loggerFactory)
{
    Logger = loggerFactory.CreateLogger<HomeController>();
}
```

After this, you can use `Logger` to log events inside action methods, as follows:

```
Logger.LogDebug("Home page loaded");
```

There are many more logging levels and overloaded methods available so that you can log additional information, for example, exceptions. We won't go into any more detail here, but you don't simply have to log text events; you can also record execution times (perhaps with a stopwatch) or increment counters to see how often certain events occur. Next, we'll see how to view these numbers centrally and read them correctly.

For more examples of how to use logging, you can examine the default account controller (if you've included individual user account authentication in the template).

Centralized logging

Logging is great. However, in a distributed system, you will want to feed all of your logs and exceptions into a single location, where you can easily analyze them and generate alerts. One potential option for this is Logstash (`https://www.elastic.co/products/logstash`), which we fleetingly mentioned in `Chapter 4`, *Measuring Performance Bottlenecks*.

If you prefer a more modular approach and want to record performance counters and metrics, then there is **StatsD**, which listens for UDP packets and pushes to Graphite for storage and graphing. You can get it at `https://github.com/etsy/statsd` and there are a few .NET clients listed on the wiki, along with a sample C# code in the main repository. Another open source option for collecting logs is Fluentd (`https://www.fluentd.org/`).

You may wish to use message queuing for logging so that you can quickly put a logged event into a queue and forget about it rather than directly hitting a logging server. If you directly call an API (and aren't using UDP), then make sure that it's asynchronous and non-blocking. You don't want to slow down your application by logging inefficiently.

There are also cloud options available, although the usual caveats about lock-in apply. AWS has **CloudWatch**, which you can read more about at `https://aws.amazon.com/cloudwatch/`. Azure Diagnostics is similar, and you can integrate it with Application Insights; read more at `https://docs.microsoft.com/en-us/azure/monitoring-and-diagnostics/azure-diagnostics`.

There are other cross-platform cloud services available, such as New Relic or Stackify, but these can be quite expensive and you may wish to keep your logging within your own infrastructure. You could shoehorn the data into analytics software, such as **Google Analytics** or the privacy-focused Piwik (which is open source and can be self-hosted), but these are less suitable because they're designed for a slightly different purpose.

Statistics

When interpreting your collected metrics, it helps to know some basic statistics in order to read them correctly. Taking a simple *mean* average can mislead you and may not be as important as some other characteristics.

When instrumenting your code to collect metadata, you should have a rough idea of how often particular logging statements will be called. This doesn't have to be exact, and a rough order of magnitude approximation (or **Fermi estimate**) will usually suffice.

The question you should try to answer is how much of the data should be collected—all of it or a random sample? If you need to perform sampling, then you should calculate how big the sample size should be. We covered sampling in relation to SQL in `Chapter 7`, *Optimizing I/O Performance*, and the idea is similar here. Performance statistics require the same level of rigor as benchmarking does, and you can easily be misled or draw incorrect conclusions.

StatsD includes built-in support for sampling, but there are many other approaches available if you want to investigate them. For example, online streaming algorithms and reservoirs are two options. The important thing to keep in mind for performance is to use a fast **random number generator** (**RNG**). As, for sampling, this doesn't need to be cryptographically secure; a **pseudorandom number generator** (**PRNG**) is fine. In .NET, you can use `new Random()` for a PRNG rather than the more secure option of `RandomNumberGenerator.Create()`. See `Chapter 8`, *Understanding Code Execution and Asynchronous Operations*, for more examples of how to use both of these.

When looking at your results, the outliers may be more interesting than the average. Although the median is more valuable than the mean, in this case, you should really look at the percentiles, for example, the 90th, 95th, and 99th percentiles. These data points can represent only a small fraction of your data, but at scale, they can occur frequently. You want to optimize for these worst case scenarios because if your users experience pages loads taking over five seconds 10% of the time (even though the average looks fast), then they may go elsewhere.

There's much more to say about statistics, but beyond the basics there are diminishing returns. If your math is rusty, then it is probably wise to have a refresher (Wikipedia is great for this). Then, you can explore some more advanced techniques, for example, the high-performance **HyperLogLog** (**HLL**) algorithm, which can estimate the size of a large set of elements using very little memory.

Redis supports the HLL data structure (with the `PFADD`, `PFCOUNT`, and `PFMERGE` commands). For more on different data structures, refer to `Chapter 8`, *Understanding Code Execution and Asynchronous Operations*.

This is only a brief introduction to performance logging, but there is much more for you to explore. For example, if you want to standardize your approach, then you can look into APDEX (`http://www.apdex.org/`), which sets a standard method to record the performance of applications and compute scores.

Managing stale caches

It's worth providing a quick reminder to still consider simple issues after all of this complexity. It is far too easy to get lost in the details of a complicated bug or performance tweak and miss the obvious.

A good technique to help with this is *rubber duck debugging*, which gets its name from the process of explaining your problem to a rubber duck on your desk. Most of us have experienced solving a problem after asking for help, even though the other person hasn't said anything. The process of explaining the problem to someone (or something) else clarifies it, and the solution becomes obvious.

If something appears to not be working after a fix, then check simple things first. See whether the patch has actually been delivered and deployed. You may be seeing stale code from a cache instead of your new version.

When managing caches, versioning is a useful technique to help you identify stale assets. You can alter filenames or add comments to include a unique version string. This can be **Semantic Versioning (SemVer)**, an ISO date and timestamp, or a hash of the contents. For more on cache busting, refer to `Chapter 9`, *Learning Caching and Message Queuing*.

SemVer is a great way of versioning your code because it implicitly captures information on compatibility and breaking changes. You can read more about SemVer at `semver.org`.

Summary

In this chapter, we saw how there are always downsides to every decision and every choice has a cost attached because nothing comes for free. There are always trade-offs involved, and you need to be aware of the consequences of your actions, which may be small and subtle.

The key lesson is to take a thoughtful and rigorous approach to adding any performance-enhancing technique. Measurement is crucial to achieving this, but you also need to know how data can mislead you if you collect or interpret it incorrectly.

In the next chapter, we will continue with the measurement theme and learn how to use tests to monitor performance regressions. You will see how to use testing (including unit testing), automation, and continuous integration to ensure that once you solve a performance problem, it stays that way.

11
Monitoring Performance Regressions

This chapter will cover writing automated tests to monitor performance, along with adding the tests to a **Continuous Integration** (**CI**) and deployment system. By constantly checking for regressions, you'll avoid building a slow application accidentally. We'll also cover how to safely load test a system without forcing it offline and how to ensure that the tests mimics real-life usage as far as possible.

Topics covered in this chapter include the following:

- Profiling
- Load testing
- Automated testing
- Performance monitoring
- Continuous integration and deployment
- Realistic environments and production-like data
- UI testing with selenium and phantom headless browsers
- A/B testing for conversion optimization
- Cloud services and hosting
- DevOps

You will see how to automate performance monitoring and testing so that you don't need to remember to keep doing it manually. You'll learn how to catch regressions early, before they cause trouble, and how to safely back them out for rework.

Profiling and measurement

We started this book by highlighting the importance of measurement and profiling by covering some simple techniques in `Chapter 4`, *Measuring Performance Bottlenecks*. We continued this theme throughout, and we'll end the book on it as well because it's impossible to overstate how important measuring and analyzing reliable evidence is.

Previously, we covered the use of Glimpse to provide insights into the running of your web application. We also demonstrated the Visual Studio diagnostics tools and the Application Insights **Software Development Kit** (**SDK**). There's another tool that's worth mentioning-- the Prefix profiler, which you can get at `https://stackify.com/prefix/`.

Prefix is a free web-based ASP.NET profiler that supports ASP.NET Core. There's a live demo on their website (at `http://demo.prefix.io/`) if you want to quickly check it out, and it looks like the following:

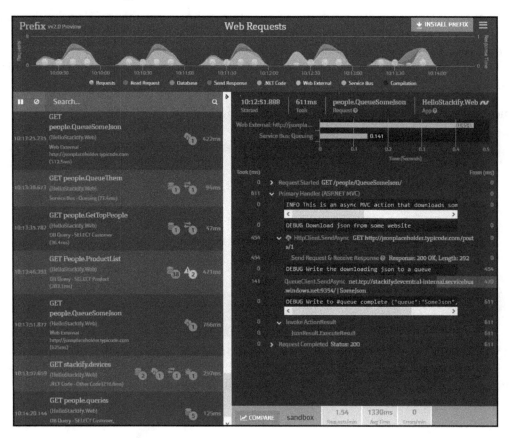

You may also want to look at the **PerfView** performance analysis tool from Microsoft, which is used in the development of .NET Core. You can download PerfView from `http://microsoft.com/download/details.aspx?id=28567` as a ZIP file that you can just extract and run. It is useful to analyze the memory of .NET applications, among other things. PerfView looks like this when you launch it:

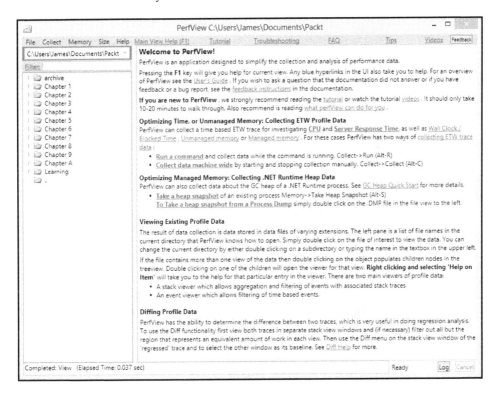

You can use PerfView for many debugging activities, for example, to take a snapshot of the heap or force GC runs. We don't have space for a detailed walk-through here, but the included instructions are good, and there are blogs on MSDN with guides and many video tutorials on *Channel 9* at `https://channel9.msdn.com/Series/PerfView-Tutorial` if you need more information.

> **Sysinternals** tools (`https://docs.microsoft.com/en-us/sysinternals/`) can also be helpful, but as they do not focus much on .NET, they are less useful in this context.

While tools such as these are great, what would be even better is to build performance monitoring into your development workflow. Automate everything that you can, make performance checks transparent and routine, and run by default.

Manual processes are bad because you can skip steps, and you can easily make errors. You wouldn't dream of developing software by emailing files around or editing code directly on a production server, so why not automate your performance tests too.

Change control processes exist to ensure consistency and reduce errors. This is why using a **source control management** (**SCM**) system such as Git, Mercurial, or even the legacy **Team Foundation Version Control** (**TFVC**) is essential. It's also extremely useful to have a build server and perform CI builds on every push, or even have fully-automated CD deployments.

Git is now the default version control system in TFS and support has been built into Visual Studio. TFVC is discouraged unless you have very specific requirements. You can read more about the differences between the two systems (along with a comparison of their distributed or centralized designs) at `https://www.visualstudio.com/en-us/docs/tfvc/comparison-git-tfvc`. If you want to migrate from TFVC to Git, then there is a guide at `https://www.visualstudio.com/learn/migrate-from-tfvc-to-git/`.

 Source control allows multiple people to work on a file simultaneously and merge the changes later. It's like Word's *track changes* feature, but actually usable. We assume that we're preaching to the converted and you already use source control. If not, stop reading right now and go install an SCM system.

If the code deployed in production differs from what you have on your local workstation, then you have very little chance of success. This is one of the reasons why SQL **stored procedures** (**SPs/sprocs**) are difficult to work with, at least without rigorous version control. It's far too easy to modify an old version of an SP on a development DB, accidentally revert a bug fix, and end up with a regression. If you must use SPs, then you will need a versioning system, such as ReadyRoll (which Redgate has now acquired).

As this isn't a book on **Continuous Delivery** (**CD**), we will assume that you are already practicing CI and have a build server, such as JetBrains, TeamCity, TFS, ThoughtWorks GoCD, and CruiseControl.net, or a cloud service such as AppVeyor. Perhaps you're also automating your deployments using a tool such as Octopus Deploy or TFS. Maybe you even have your own internal NuGet feeds, using software such as The Motley Fool's Klondike or a cloud service such as MyGet (which also supports npm, Bower, and VSIX packages).

NuGet packages are a great way of managing internal projects. In Visual Studio 2017, you can see the source code of packages and debug into them. This means no more huge solutions, containing a ludicrous number of projects that are hard to navigate and slow to build in Visual Studio.

Bypassing processes and doing things manually will cause problems even if you are following a script. If it can be automated, then it probably should be, and this includes testing.

Testing

Testing is essential to producing high-quality and well-performing software. The secret to productive testing is to make it easy, reliable, and routine. If testing is difficult or tests regularly fail because of issues unrelated to the software (for example, environmental problems), then tests will not be performed or the results will be ignored. This will cause you to miss genuine problems and ship bugs that you could have easily avoided.

There are many different varieties of testing, and you may be familiar with the more common cases used for functional verification. In this book, we will mainly focus on tests pertaining to performance. However, the advice here is applicable to many types of testing.

Automated testing

As mentioned previously, the key to improving almost everything is automation. Tests that are only run manually on developer workstations add very little value. Of course, it should be possible to run the tests on desktops, but this shouldn't be the official result because there's no guarantee that they will pass on a server (where the correct functioning matters more).

Although automation usually occurs on servers, it can be useful to automate tests that run on developer workstations too. You can do this live unit testing in Visual Studio 2017 Enterprise Edition, and in other versions, you could use a plugin such as **NCrunch**. This runs your tests as you work, which can be very useful if you practice **test-driven development** (**TDD**) and write your tests before your implementations.

One way of enforcing testing is to use gated check-ins in TFS, but this can be a little draconian, and if you use an SCM such as Git, then it's easier to work on branches and simply block merges until all the tests pass. You want to encourage developers to check-in early and often because this makes merges easier.

Therefore, it's a bad idea to have features in progress sitting on workstations for a long time (generally no longer than a day).

Continuous integration

CI systems automatically build and test all your branches and feed this information back to your version control system. For example, using the GitHub API, you can block the merging of pull requests until the build server reports a successfully tested merge result.

Both **Bitbucket** and **GitLab** offer free CI systems called pipelines, so you may not need any extra systems in addition to the one for source control, because everything is in one place. GitLab also offers an integrated Docker container registry, and there is an open source version that you can install locally. For more on Docker, refer back to the earlier chapters or the *Hosting* section covered later in this chapter.

You can do something similar with **Visual Studio Team Services** for CI builds and unit testing. Visual Studio also has Git services built into it.

This process works well for unit testing because unit tests must be quick so that you get early feedback. Shortening the iteration cycle is a good way of increasing productivity, and you'll want the lag to be as small as possible.

However, running tests on each build isn't suitable for all types of testing because not all tests can be quick. In this case, you'll need an additional strategy so as not to slow down your feedback loop.

 There are many unit testing frameworks available for .NET, for example, NUnit, xUnit, and MSTest (Microsoft's unit test framework, now with a revamped v2), along with multiple graphical ways of running tests locally, such as the Visual Studio Test Explorer and the ReSharper plugin. People have their favorites, but it doesn't really matter what you choose because most CI systems will support all of them.

Slow testing

Some tests are slow, but even if each test is fast, they can easily add up to a lengthy time if you have a lot of them. This is especially true if they can't be parallelized and need to be run in sequence, so you should always aim to have each test stand on its own without any dependencies on others.

It is good practice to divide your tests into rings of importance so that you can at least run a subset of the most crucial ones on every CI build. However, if you have a large test suite or some tests that are unavoidably slow, then you may choose to run these only once a day (perhaps overnight) or every week (maybe over the weekend).

Some testing is simply slow by nature and performance testing can often fall into this category, for example, load testing or **user interface** (**UI**) testing. We usually class this as integration testing, rather than unit testing because they require your code to be deployed to an environment for testing and the tests can't simply exercise the binaries.

To make use of such automated testing, you will need to have an automated deployment system in addition to your CI system. If you have enough confidence in your test system, then you can even have live deployments happen automatically. This works well if you also use **feature switching** to control the rollout of new features.

We won't go into the implementation details of CI or automated deployments in this book. However, we will cover feature switching, how to apply performance testing to CI processes, and what to do when you discover a regression.

Fixing performance regressions

If you discover a performance issue at the unit testing stage, then you can simply rework this feature, but it's more likely that these problems will surface in a later testing phase. This can make it more challenging to remedy the problem because the work may already have been built upon and may have other commits on top of it.

The correct course of action is often to back out regressions immediately, or at least as soon as possible, upon discovery. Delays will only make the issue harder to fix later, which is why it's important to get fast feedback and highlight problems quickly.

It's important to be disciplined and always remove regressions, even though it may be painful. If you let the occasional minor regression in, then you can easily become sloppy and let more serious ones in over time because of the precedent it sets.

Load testing

Load testing is the process of discovering how many concurrent users your web app can support. You generally perform it on a test environment with a tool that gradually ramps up a simulated load, for example, JMeter (`http://jmeter.apache.org/`). Perhaps, you'd prefer using a JMeter-compatible cloud service, such as BlazeMeter, or an alternative, such as **Loader.io**, if your test systems are web-facing.

Load testing can take a significant amount of time depending on the scale of your service because it can be configured to continue until the test environment gets unacceptably slow for users or falls over and becomes unresponsive. You need to be extremely careful with load testing and not only from the point of view of accidentally testing your live systems to destruction while they're in use.

You also need to be wary of getting false results, which may mislead you into concluding that your system can handle more load than it actually will. Balancing these two competing concerns of safety and realism can be difficult. It's important to get realistic results, but you need to balance this against not stressing your production environment and impacting the experience of real users.

Realism

Keeping it real is an important principle of performance testing. If you don't use a realistic environment and workload, then your results may be worse than having no data because they could mislead you into bad decisions. When you have no information, you at least know that you're in the dark and just guessing.

We'll cover workloads and feature switching shortly, including an example of how to implement your own simple version from scratch. First, let's look at how to make your test environments representative of production.

Realistic environments

Using a test environment that is as close to production (or as live-like) as possible is a good step toward ensuring reliable results. You can try and use a smaller set of servers and then scale your results up to get an estimate of live performance. However, this assumes that you have an intimate knowledge of how your application scales and what hardware constraints will be the bottlenecks.

A better option is to use your live environment or, rather, what will become your production stack. You first create a staging environment that is identical to live, then you deploy your code to it, and then you run your full test suite, including a comprehensive performance test, ensuring that it behaves correctly. Once you are happy, then you simply swap the staging and production, perhaps using DNS or Azure **staging slots**.

The following diagram shows how you first release to staging and go live simply by making staging become production:

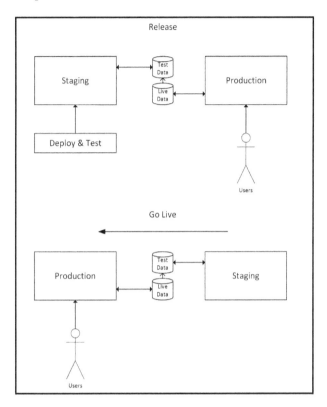

Your old live environment now either becomes your test environment, or if you use immutable cloud instances, then you can simply terminate it and spin up a new staging system. This concept is known as *blue-green deployment*, but unfortunately, specific implementation instructions are beyond the scope of this book. See the author's website at `https://unop.uk/` for more on cloud hosting in AWS and Azure.

You don't necessarily have to move all the users across at once, in a big bang; you can move over a few first in order to test whether everything is correct. We'll cover this shortly, in the *Feature switching* section of this chapter.

Realistic workloads

Another important part of performing realistic testing is to use real data and real workloads. Synthetic data often won't exercise a system fully or find exotic edge cases. You can use **fuzzing** to generate random data, but if you have a production system, then you can simply use the data from this and parse your logs to generate a realistic workload to replay.

Obviously, don't replay actions onto a live system that could modify user data, and be wary of data privacy concerns or any action that could generate an external event, for example, sending a mass email or charging a credit card.

You can use a dedicated test system, but you still need to be careful to stub out any external APIs that don't have a test version.

Another approach is to use dummy users for your testing if you don't mind your users discovering the fakes and possibly interacting with them. One case of this approach is Netflix's cult *Example Show*, which is a homemade video of an employee running around their office grounds with a laptop.

Feature switching

An alternative to fake users or test environments is to run performance tests on your real live environment using genuine users as they interact with your web application. You can use feature switching to gradually roll out a new feature to a small subset of your user base and monitor the system for excessive load. If everything seems normal, then you can continue the rollout; otherwise, you can rollback.

> You may hear similar ideas referred to by other names, such as **feature flags**, **feature toggles**, **canary releases**, or **branch by abstraction**. Some of these may have subtly different meanings, but the general guiding principle of gradually releasing a change is much the same.

The following diagram shows how you could progressively migrate users to a new feature by deploying it but not initially enabling it. Your first users could be members of staff so that any issues are detected early:

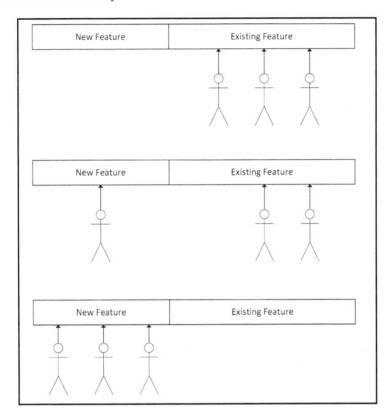

Once all the users start consuming the new feature, then you can safely remove the old feature (and the feature switch itself). It's a good idea to regularly tidy up like this to avoid clutter and make later work easier.

If you discover that your system experiences excessive load as you slowly increase the percentage of users on the new feature, then you can halt the rollout and prevent your servers from becoming overloaded and unresponsive. You then have time to investigate and either back out of the change or increase the available resources.

One variation on this theme is when a new feature requires a data migration and this migration is computation or networking-intensive, for example, migrating user-submitted videos to a new home and transcoding them in the process. In this case, the excessive load that you are monitoring will only be transient, and you don't need to back out of a feature. You only need to ensure that the rate of migration is low enough to not excessively tax your infrastructure.

Although the new feature is usually branched to in code, you can instead perform switching at the network level if you use blue-green deployment. This is known as a canary release and can be done at the DNS or load-balancer level. However, specific implementation details are again beyond the remit of this book. See the author's website at `https://unop.uk/` for more on DNS.

You can find many open source feature switching libraries online or you could write your own, which we will show you how to do later. `FeatureToggle` is a feature switching library for .NET and it supports .NET Core as of version 4 (`https://github.com/Jason-roberts/FeatureToggle`). There are also paid cloud services available, such as `LaunchDarkly`, which offer easy management interfaces.

 Library and framework support for .NET Core and ASP.NET Core change rapidly, so check `https://github.com/jpsingleton/ANCLAFS` for the latest information.

To illustrate feature switching, let's build our own extremely simple implementation for an ASP.NET Core web application. To start with, we take the default existing homepage view (`Index.cshtml`) and make a copy (`IndexOld.cshtml`). We then make our changes to `Index.cshtml`, but these aren't important for the purposes of this demo.

In `HomeController.cs`, we change the logic to return the new view in a relatively small percentage of time or the old one, otherwise. The original code was simply the following:

```
public IActionResult Index()
{
    return View();
}
```

We change this action to return the new view in a quarter of the cases, as follows:

```
public IActionResult Index()
{
    var rand = new Random();
    if (rand.Next(99) < 25)
    {
        return View();
    }
    return View("IndexOld");
}
```

This code picks a random number out of a hundred, and if it is less than 25, then it loads the new view. Clearly, you wouldn't hardcode values like this, and you would probably use a database to store configuration and control it with a web admin page.

If you load the page in a browser, then three out of four times, you should get the original page, which looks like the following:

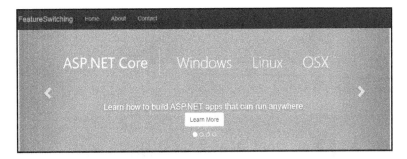

However, roughly one out of every four pages loads; you will get the new page, which looks like the following:

We removed the carousel and cut the number of image loads in half. You can see the difference in the browser developer tools, for example, the Firefox performance analysis for the original looks like the following:

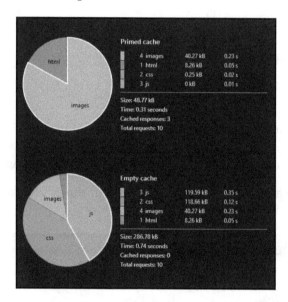

Whereas, the performance analysis for the new version looks like this:

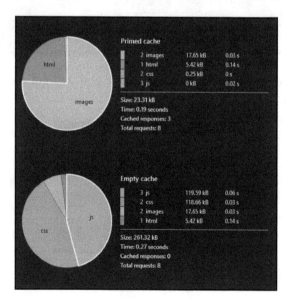

You can see that the number of **images** has decreased, which has reduced the page size and the total number of requests required.

 These measurements were taken with the hosting environment set to `Production`. If you remain with the default of `Development`, then your results will differ. Refer to the following documentation page to know how to change this:
https://docs.microsoft.com/en-us/aspnet/core/fundamentals/environments

Once the new view has been progressively rolled out to all users (with no performance problems), the action method code can be reverted to the original state and the old view deleted. Obviously, this is a trivial example. Hopefully, you can now see how feature switching can be performed.

Using feature switching to roll out in this way works well for performance testing, but you need to be confident that your new code is functionally correct or at least safe to deploy. However, in certain circumstances, you can also test the functionality by extending this approach and performing experiments.

Experimenting for science

If you take the feature switching rollout to its logical conclusion, then you can switch on a new refactored version for a small percentage of users but not actually expose the output. You will run the existing version in parallel as a control and show this to the user. However, you will collect the results of both the versions, including performance data. You can then compare them to ensure that the new version (hopefully with a higher performance) is correct and consistent with the existing behavior.

GitHub has an open source Ruby library, called `Scientist`, which can be used to successfully refactor permissions and for merging code. In the process, GitHub discovered existing legacy bugs, found missing features, optimized database queries, and swapped a search system. `Scientist` not only displays the correctness of the new code but also its performance relative to the old implementation.

 An important concern with `Scientist` (or any method using this experimentation approach) is to not change data. All operations should be read-only and should have no side effects; otherwise, you will perform the modification more than once, which could have undesirable consequences.

There's a .NET port of `Scientist` by GitHub employee Phil Haack, called *Scientist.NET*, and you can get it at `https://github.com/github/Scientist.net`. It supports .NET Core and you can install it via NuGet, where it's just called `Scientist`. Check `http://ANCLAFS.com` for the latest information.

This idea of experimenting on users is similar to the marketing concept of **A/B testing**, which is used to discover conversion effectiveness. However, with `Scientist`, you don't typically show the users different outputs or even intend the output to change, you just record the new output for the subset of users that you have it enabled for.

A/B testing

A/B testing is similar to feature switching, but we usually use it to test the effectiveness of different web page designs and how they affect the *conversion funnel* analytics. We normally use it for digital marketing rather than for software development because it's less about what is correct and more about what the customers prefer. However, the underlying technical principals are comparable to feature switching and experimentation.

In a simple example, you serve half your visitors the old version of a page and the other half, a new version designed to increase engagement. You then record how many visitors click through or perform some action on each variant. If the new version performs better, then you keep it and roll it out to everyone. However, if it converted worse, you roll back to the old version and try again.

You can see that this is very similar to how feature switching works, and you can use the same tools to do both. The only difference is regarding what you are measuring--user analytics or the health of your infrastructure.

A/B testing is not normally used for backend features and is simply used to assess UI alternatives. However, it is different to functionally test your web interface, so let's cover the basics of UI testing now.

User interface testing

There's one area of an application that is traditionally difficult to test, and that's the **UI**. This is particularly the case for **Graphical User Interfaces** (**GUIs**), as used in web applications. One reason for this is that users typically have a lot of flexibility in how they display their interface, and this is especially true for web browsers. A naive pixel-based testing approach is going to be extremely fragile.

You need to design your application to be easily testable, and the UI is no exception. While it is possible to test the UI of a poorly-designed legacy application, and this may even be the easiest testing approach, if you consider UI testing upfront, then life will be a lot easier. For example, including sensible IDs on your HTML **Document Object Model** (**DOM**) elements makes testing much more straightforward and less fragile.

Checking your application from a web browser perspective can be a useful additional step on top of automated unit and integration testing. You can use it not only to test for functional correctness and regressions but also to measure client-side performance, which is increasingly important. There are many UI testing tools available, most of which you can integrate into your CI build pipeline to automate testing.

Web UI testing tools

One of the most popular web testing tools is **Selenium**, which allows you to easily write tests and automate web browsers using **WebDriver**. Selenium is also useful for many other tasks apart from testing, and you can read more about it at `http://docs.seleniumhq.org/`.

> WebDriver is a protocol to remotely control web browsers, and you can read about it at `https://w3c.github.io/webdriver/webdriver-spec.html`.

Selenium uses real browsers, the same versions your users will access your web application with. This makes it excellent to get representative results, but it can cause issues if it runs from the command line in an unattended fashion. For example, you may find your test server's memory full of dead browser processes that have timed out.

You may find it easier to use a dedicated headless test browser, which while not exactly the same as what your users will see, is more suitable for automation. Of course, the best approach is to use a combination of both, perhaps running headless tests first and then running the same tests on real browsers with WebDriver.

One of the most well-known headless test browsers is **PhantomJS**. This is based on the **WebKit** engine, so it should give you similar results to Chrome and Safari. PhantomJS is useful for many things apart from testing, such as capturing screenshots, and you can drive it with many different testing frameworks. As the name suggests, you can control PhantomJS with JavaScript, and you can read more about it at `http://phantomjs.org/`.

WebKit is an open source engine for web browsers, which was originally part of the **KDE** Linux desktop environment. It is mainly used in Apple's Safari browser, but a fork called **Blink** is used in Google Chrome, Chromium, and Opera. You can read more at webkit.org.

Other automatable testing browsers, based on different engines, are available, but they have some limitations. For example, **SlimerJS** (https://slimerjs.org/) is based on the **Gecko** engine used by Firefox, but is not fully headless.

You probably want to use a higher-level testing utility rather than scripting browser engines directly. One such utility that provides many useful abstractions is **CasperJS** (http://casperjs.org/), which supports running on both PhantomJS and SlimerJS.

Another is **Capybara**, which allows you to easily simulate user interactions in Ruby. It supports Selenium, WebKit, **Rack**, and PhantomJS (via Poltergeist), although it's more suitable for Rails apps. You can read more at http://teamcapybara.github.io/capybara/.

There is also **TrifleJS** (http://triflejs.org/), which uses the .NET WebBrowser class (the Internet Explorer **Trident** engine), but this is a work in progress. Additionally, there's **Watir** (http://watir.com/), which is a set of Ruby libraries targeting Internet Explorer and WebDriver. However, neither have been updated in a while, and IE has changed a lot recently.

 Microsoft Edge (codenamed Spartan) is the new version of IE, and the Trident engine was forked to **EdgeHTML**. The JavaScript engine (Chakra) was open sourced as **ChakraCore** (https://github.com/Microsoft/ChakraCore).

It shouldn't matter too much what browser engine you use, and PhantomJS will work fine as a first pass for automated tests. You can always test with real browsers after using a headless one, perhaps with Selenium or with PhantomJS using WebDriver.

 When we refer to browser engines (WebKit/Blink, Gecko, or Trident/EdgeHTML), we generally mean only the rendering and layout engine, not the JavaScript engine (SFX/Nitro/FTL/B3, V8, SpiderMonkey, or Chakra/ChakraCore).

You'll probably still want to use a utility such as CasperJS to make writing tests easier, and you'll likely need a test framework, such as **Jasmine** (https://jasmine.github.io/) or **QUnit** (http://qunitjs.com/) too. You can also use a test runner that supports both Jasmine and QUnit, such as **Chutzpah** (http://mmanela.github.io/chutzpah/).

You can integrate your automated tests with many different CI systems, for example, Jenkins or JetBrains TeamCity. If you prefer a cloud-hosted option, then there's Travis CI (`https://travis-ci.org/`) and AppVeyor (`http://appveyor.com/`), which is also suitable for building .NET apps.

You may prefer to run your integration and UI tests from your deployment system, for example, to verify a successful deployment in Octopus Deploy. There are also dedicated, cloud-based web application UI testing services available, such as BrowserStack (`https://www.browserstack.com/`).

Automating UI performance tests

Automated UI tests are clearly great at checking for functional regressions but they are also useful for performance testing. You have programmatic access to the same information provided by the network inspector in the browser developer tools.

You can integrate the **YSlow** (`http://yslow.org/`) performance analyzer with PhantomJS, enabling your CI system to check for common web performance mistakes on every commit. YSlow came out of Yahoo!, and it provides rules used to identify bad practices, which can slow down web applications for users. It's a similar idea to Google's PageSpeed Insights service (which you can automate via its API).

However, YSlow is pretty old, and things have moved on in web development recently, for example, HTTP/2. A modern alternative is *the coach* from **sitespeed.io**, and you can read more at `https://github.com/sitespeedio/coach`. You should check out their other open source tools too, such as the dashboard at `https://dashboard.sitespeed.io/`, which uses Graphite and Grafana.

You can also export the network results (in industry standard HAR format) and analyze them however you like, for example, visualizing them graphically in waterfall format, as you might do manually with your browser developer tools.

> The **HTTP Archive (HAR)** format is a standard way of representing the content of monitored network data for exporting to other software. You can copy or save as HAR in some browser developer tools by right-clicking a network request.

Staying alert

Whenever you perform testing, particularly UI or performance testing, you will get noisy results. Reliability is not perfect, and there will always be failures that are not due to bugs in the code. You shouldn't let these false positives cause you to ignore failing tests, and although the easiest course of action may be disabling them, the correct thing to do to make them more reliable.

> The scientifically minded know that there is no such thing as a perfect filter in binary classification, and always look at the precision and recall of a system. Knowing the rate of false positives and negatives is important to get a good idea of the accuracy and tradeoffs involved.

To avoid testing fatigue, it can be helpful to engage developers and instill a responsibility to fix failing tests. You don't want everyone thinking that it's somebody else's problem. It should be easy to see who broke a build by the commit in version control, and it's then their job to fix the failing test (and buy biscuits).

You can have a bit of fun with this and create something a little bit more interesting than a wall-mounted dashboard. Although having **information radiators** is useful if you don't get desensitized to them. There's plenty of cheap **Internet of Things** (**IoT**) hardware available today, which allows you to turn some interesting objects into build failure alarms. For example, an **Arduino**-controlled traffic light, an **ESP8266**-operated foam-missile turret, or a Raspberry Pi-powered animatronic figure. See the author's website (https://unop.uk/) for ideas.

DevOps

The practice of **DevOps** is when development, operations, and quality-assurance testing teams all collaborate seamlessly. Although DevOps is more of a cultural consideration, there is still plenty of tooling that can help with automation. We have covered much of this previously and the only missing pieces left now are to provision and configure infrastructure, then monitor it while in use.

When using automation and techniques such as feature switching, it is essential to have a good view of your environments so that you know the utilization of all the hardware. Good tooling is important when monitoring, and you want to easily be able to see the vital statistics of every server. This will consist of at least the CPU, memory and disk space consumption, and you will want alarms set up to alert you if any of these metrics stray outside of their allowed bands.

DevOps tooling

One of the primary themes of DevOps tooling is defining infrastructure as code. The idea is that you shouldn't manually perform a task, such as setting up a server, when you can create software to do it for you. You can then reuse these provisioning scripts, which will not only save you time but will also ensure that all of the machines are consistent and free of mistakes or missed steps.

Provisioning

There are many systems available to commission and configure new machines. Some popular configuration-management automation tools are **Ansible** (https://www.ansible.com/), **Chef** (http://chef.io/), and **Puppet** (http://puppet.com/).

Not all of these tools work great on Windows servers, partly because Linux is easier to automate. However, you can run ASP.NET Core on Linux and still develop on Windows, using Visual Studio and testing in a VM or container. Developing for a VM is a great idea because it solves the problems in setting up environments and issues where it "works on my machine" but not in production.

> **Vagrant** (http://vagrantup.com/) is a great command-line tool to manage developer VMs. It allows you to easily create, spin up and share developer environments.

If you create your infrastructure as code, then your scripts can be versioned and tested, just like your application code. We'll stop before we get too far off topic, but the point is that if you have reliable environments, which you can easily verify, instantiate, and perform testing on, then CI is a lot easier.

Monitoring

Monitoring is essential, especially for web applications, and there are many tools available to help with it. A popular open source infrastructure-monitoring system is **Nagios** (http://nagios.org/). Another more modern open source alerting and metrics tool is **Prometheus** (https://prometheus.io/).

If you use a cloud platform, then there will be monitoring built in, for example, AWS CloudWatch or Azure Diagnostics. There are also cloud services to directly monitor your website, such as **Pingdom** (https://www.pingdom.com/), **Uptime Robot** (https://uptimerobot.com/), **Datadog** (https://www.datadoghq.com/), and **PagerDuty** (https://www.pagerduty.com/).

You probably already have a system in place to measure availability, but you can also use the same systems to monitor performance. This is not only helpful to ensure a responsive user experience, but it can also provide early warning signs that a failure is imminent. If you are proactive and take preventative action, then you can save yourself a lot of trouble reactively fighting fires.

This isn't a book on operations, but it helps to consider application support requirements at design time. Development, testing, and operations aren't competing disciplines, and you will succeed more often if you work as one team rather than simply throwing an application over the fence and saying it "worked in test, ops problem now".

Hosting

It's well worth considering the implications of various hosting options because if developers can't easily access the environments they need, then this will reduce their agility. They may have to work around an availability problem and end up using insufficient or unsuitable hardware, which will hamper progress and cause future maintenance problems. Or their work will simply be blocked and delivery set back.

Unless you are a very large organization, hosting in-house is generally a bad idea for reliability, flexibility, and cost reasons. Unless you have some very sensitive data, then you should probably use a data center.

You can co-locate servers in a data center, but then you need staff to be on call to fix hardware problems. Or you can rent a physical server and run your application on *bare metal*, but you may still need remote hands to perform resets or other tasks on the machine.

The most flexible situation is to rent self-service virtual machines, commonly known as cloud hosting. There are many hosting companies that offer this, but the big players are Amazon, Google, and Microsoft.

Microsoft's Azure is the obvious choice for a .NET shop and it has improved immensely since launch compared to its original offering. Its **Platform as a Service (PaaS)** to host .NET applications is the most polished and the easiest to get running on quickly. It also offers lots of extra services that go beyond simple VMs.

However, .NET Core and ASP.NET Core are new types of framework, which are not aimed solely at C# developers, who would usually pick the default option offered by Microsoft. The targeted market is developers who may be used to choosing alternative platforms and open source frameworks. Therefore, it makes sense to cover other options, which people new to .NET may be more familiar with.

The difference between PaaS and **Infrastructure as a Service** (**IaaS**) is that PaaS is higher level and provides a service to run applications, not computers. IaaS simply provides you with a VM. However, with PaaS, this is abstracted away, and you don't need to worry about setting up and updating an instance.

Amazon Web Services (**AWS**) is the most established cloud host, and it started by only offering IaaS, although they now offer PaaS options. For example, **Elastic Beanstalk** supports .NET. Even though Windows (and SQL Server) support has improved, it is still not first class, and Linux is clearly their main platform.

However, now that .NET Core and SQL Server run on Linux, this may be less of a problem. You will pay a premium for Windows server instances, but you're also charged more for some enterprise Linux distributions (**Red Hat** and **SUSE**). However, you can run other Linux distributions, such as **Ubuntu** or **CentOS** without paying a premium.

Google Cloud Platform used to consist of **App Engine** (**GAE**), which was quite a restrictive PaaS, but it is getting more flexible. They now offer a generic IaaS called **Compute Engine** (**GCE**), and there's a new flexible version of GAE, which is more like GCE. These new offerings are useful, as you couldn't traditionally run .NET on GAE, and they also provide other products such as pre-emptible VMs and a cloud CDN (with HTTPS at no extra cost).

Azure may still be the best choice for you, and it integrates well with other Microsoft products, such as Visual Studio. However, it is worth having healthy competition because this keeps everyone innovating. It's definitely a good idea to frequently look at the pricing of all options, (which changes regularly) because you can save a lot of money depending on the workload that you run.

If you are eligible for Microsoft's BizSpark program, then you can get three years of Azure credits (suitable to host a small application). You also get a Visual Studio subscription for free software licenses (previously called an MSDN subscription).

Whatever hosting provider you choose to use, it is sensible to avoid vendor lock-in and use services that are generic, which you can easily swap for an alternative. For example, using hosted open source software, such as PostgreSQL, Redis, or RabbitMQ, rather than an equivalent custom cloud provider product. You could also take a resilient multi-cloud approach to protect yourself from an outage of a single provider. See the author's website (`https://unop.uk/`) for comparisons of cloud-hosting providers.

Docker is a great technology for this purpose because many different cloud services support it. For example, you can run the same container on Azure Container Service, Docker Cloud, AWS EC2 Container Service, and Google's **Kubernetes** Container Engine.

Docker also runs on Windows (using Hyper-V), and in Visual Studio 2017 you can deploy to and debug a container. This can run ASP.NET Core on Linux, and when you are ready to deploy, you can just push to production and have confidence that it will work as it did on your machine. You can read more about Docker on Windows at `http://docker.com/ Microsoft`.

 When choosing a cloud (or even a region), it's important to not only consider the monetary cost. You should also factor in environmental concerns, such as the main fuel used for the power supply. For example, some regions can be cheaper, but this may be because they use dirty coal power, which contributes to climate change and our future security.

Summary

In this chapter, you saw how you might integrate automated testing into a CI system in order to monitor for performance regressions. You also learned some strategies to roll out changes and ensure that tests accurately reflect real life. We also briefly covered some options for DevOps practices and cloud-hosting providers, which together make continuous performance testing much easier.

In the next chapter, we'll wrap-up everything that we covered throughout this book and suggest some areas for further investigation. We'll reinforce our learnings so far, give you some interesting ideas to think about, contemplate possible futures for .NET, and consider the exciting direction the platform is taking.

12
The Way Ahead

This chapter sums up what you learned in this book. It refreshes the main tenets of performance, and it reminds you that you should always remain pragmatic. We'll recap why you shouldn't optimize just for its own sake and why you should always measure the problems and results. This chapter also introduces more advanced and exotic techniques that you may wish to consider learning about if you need more speed or are a serious performance enthusiast.

The topics covered in this chapter include the following:

- Summary of the previous chapters
- The native tool chain
- Alternative CPU architectures, such as ARM
- Advanced hardware (GPUs, FPGAs, and ASICs)
- Machine learning and AI
- Big data and MapReduce
- The Orleans virtual actor model
- Custom transport layers
- Advanced hashing functions
- Library and framework support
- The future of ASP.NET Core

We'll reinforce how to assess and solve performance issues by refreshing your memory of the lessons in the previous chapters. You'll also gain awareness about other advanced technology available to assist you in delivering high performance, which you may wish to investigate further. Finally, we'll highlight what libraries and frameworks support .NET Core and ASP.NET Core, and we'll try to hypothesize the possible future directions for these exciting platforms.

Reviewing what we learned

Let's briefly recap what we covered earlier in this book.

In Chapter 1, *What's New in ASP.NET Core 2?*, we covered what has changed in the second version of ASP.NET Core compared with the first major release, and we highlighted some of the new features available in C# 6.0 and C# 7.0. Then, in Chapter 2, *Why Performance Is a Feature*, we discussed the basic premise of this book and showed you why you need to care about the performance of your software. In Chapter 3, *Setting Up Your Environment*, we demonstrated how to get started with ASP.NET Core on Windows, macOS, and Linux.

In Chapter 4, *Measuring Performance Bottlenecks*, we showed you that the only way you can solve performance problems is to carefully measure your application. Then, in Chapter 5, *Fixing Common Performance Problems*, we looked at some of the most frequent performance mistakes and how to fix them.

After this, we went a little deeper in Chapter 6, *Addressing Network Performance*, and dug into the networking layer that underpins all web applications. Then, in Chapter 7, *Optimizing I/O Performance*, we focused on input/output and how this can negatively affect performance.

In Chapter 8, *Understanding Code Execution and Asynchronous Operations*, we jumped into the intricacies of C# code and looked at how its execution can alter performance. Then in Chapter 9, *Learning Caching and Message Queuing*, we initially looked at caching, which is widely regarded to be quite hard. Then, we investigated message queuing as a way to build a distributed and reliable system.

In Chapter 10, *The Downsides of Performance-Enhancing Tools*, we concentrated on the negatives of the techniques that we previously covered, as nothing comes for free. Then in Chapter 11, *Monitoring Performance Regressions*, we looked at measuring performance again but, in this case, from an automation, **Continuous Integration** (**CI**), and DevOps perspective.

Further reading

If you've read this far, then you will probably want some pointers for other things to research and read up on. For the rest of this chapter, we'll highlight some interesting topics that you may want to look into further but we couldn't cover fully in this book. You can also visit the author's website (at https://unop.uk/) for coverage of more topics.

Going native

One of the problems with the old ASP.NET is that it was really slow, which is why one of the main guiding principles of ASP.NET Core has been performance. Impressive progress has already been made, but there are plenty of more opportunities for further enhancements.

One of the most promising areas is the native tool chain, which has unfortunately been delayed. However, it should be shipped after .NET Core 2.0, and it is already in use for UWP apps on the Windows Store. This is different from the self-contained publishing and cross compilation already available in .NET Core, as it compiles to machine-native binaries rather than portable IL instructions.

Previously, if you wanted to call unmanaged native code from managed .NET code, you would have had to use **Platform Invoke (PInvoke)**, but this had performance overheads and safety concerns. Even if your native code was faster, the overheads often meant that it was not worth bothering about.

The native tool chain should give native levels of performance but with the safety and convenience of a managed runtime. Ahead-of-time compilation is fascinating and very technical, but the upshot is that if we know the target architecture, then it can provide a performance boost. We can also trade a slower compilation for faster execution, as it doesn't have to happen at runtime.

It is also possible to optimize for different processors that may offer special performance features and instructions—for example, targeting low-energy ARM chips instead of the usual Intel-style processors.

Processor architecture

Typically, when writing desktop or server software, you will target an Intel-based architecture such as x86 or x64. However, ARM-based chips are gaining popularity, and they can offer fantastic power efficiency. If the software is specially optimized for them, then they can also offer excellent performance.

For example, the **Scratch** graphical programming language, used to teach computing, has been optimized for the Raspberry Pi 3, and it now runs roughly twice as fast as it does on an Intel Core i5. Other software applications have also been optimized for the ARM processor, for example, the Kodi open source media player.

ARM Holdings is simply an intellectual property company and they don't make any processors themselves. Other companies, such as Apple and Broadcom, license the designs or architecture and fabricate their **System on a Chip** (**SoC**) products.

This means that there are many different chips available, which run multiple versions of the ARM architecture and instruction set. This fragmentation can make it harder to support, unless you pick a specific platform.

Windows 10 IoT (Internet of Things) Core runs on the Raspberry Pi (version 2 and 3) and it can be set up using the standard **New Out Of the Box Software** (**NOOBS**) installer. Windows 10 IoT Core is not a full desktop environment to run normal applications, but it does allow you to make hardware projects and program them with C# and .NET. However, for web applications, you would want to run .NET Core on a Linux distribution, such as Raspbian (the main Raspberry Pi OS, based on **Debian**).

Hardware is hard

We previously mentioned additional hardware that can be used for computation in `Chapter 8`, *Understanding Code Execution and Asynchronous Operations*, including **Graphics Processing Units** (**GPUs**), **Field Programmable Gate Arrays** (**FPGAs**), and **Application Specific Integrated Circuits** (**ASICs**).

Not only can these devices be used for specific processing tasks, but their storage can be used as well. For example, you can borrow the RAM from a GPU if the main memory is exhausted. However, this technique is not required as much as it used to be when memory was more limited.

You may have heard of RAM SANs, which were SANs using standard RAM for permanent storage (with a battery backup). However, these have become less relevant as SSDs (based on flash memory) improved in speed and increased in capacity to the point of replacing mechanical drives for many common tasks.

You can still purchase high-performance SANs, but they will probably be based on flash memory rather than RAM. If you use RAM as your main storage (for example, with Redis), then it is important that you use **Error-Correcting Code** (**ECC**) memory. ECC RAM is more expensive, but it is better suited for server use. However, some cloud instances don't use it, or it is hard to find out whether it's even offered, because it isn't listed in the specifications. You may well get away without this, as in reality, corruption is very rare, but you should still have reconciliation routines to catch these and other errors.

One application of custom computation hardware is **machine learning** (**ML**), specifically the deep learning branch of ML using multilevel neural networks. This technology has seen impressive advances in recent years and this has led to things such as self-driving vehicles. ML applications can make very good use of non-CPU processing, particularly GPUs, and NVIDIA provides many tools and libraries to help with this.

Google built a custom ASIC, called a **Tensor Processing Unit** (**TPU**), to accelerate their TensorFlow machine learning library and cloud services. You can read more at `https://www.tensorflow.org/` and `https://cloud.google.com/ml-engine/`.

Machine learning

Not only can you use **Artificial Intelligence** (**AI**) to replace drivers and other jobs, such as call center staff or even some doctor's tasks, but you can also use some basic ML in your own web applications to provide product suggestions relevant to your customers or to analyze marketing effectiveness, just like Amazon or Netflix do.

You don't even need to build your own ML systems, as you can use cloud services such as **Azure ML**. This allows you to use a graphical drag-and-drop interface to build your ML systems, although you can also use Python and R.

You still need to know a little bit about data science, such as the elementary principles of binary classification and training data, but even then, it significantly reduces the barrier to entry. Yet, if you want to fully explore ML and big data possibilities, then you probably need a dedicated data scientist.

You can try out Azure ML at `https://studio.azureml.net/`, and you don't even need to register. The following screenshot shows an example of what it looks like:

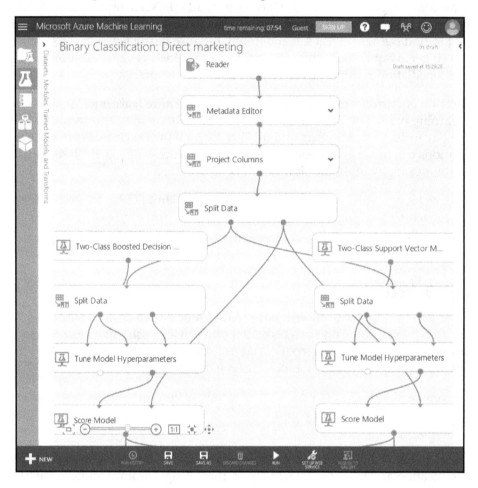

If you don't want to build a recommendation engine for yourself, then there is a ready-to-use recommendations API available in Azure. Azure also offers APIs for facial and speech recognition, emotion and sentiment analysis, content moderation, text/voice translation, and plenty more. The models in some of these systems have been trained on large amounts of data, so they can be used without building your own corpus.

Big data and MapReduce

Big data is probably an overused term these days, and what is sometimes described as big is usually more like medium data. Big data is when you have so much information that it is difficult to process, or even store, on a single machine. Traditional approaches often break down with big data, as they are not adequate for the huge automatically-acquired datasets that are common today. For example, the amount of data constantly collected by IoT sensors or by our interactions with online services can be vast.

One caveat of big data and ML is that, although they are good at finding correlations in large sets of data points, you cannot use them to find causations. You also need to be mindful of data privacy concerns and be very careful of not judging someone before they have acted, based only on a predicted predisposition.

> Anonymizing data is incredibly difficult and is not nearly as simple as removing personal contact details. There have been many cases of large *"anonymized"* datasets being released, where individuals were later easily identified from the records.

One technology that is useful for analyzing big data is **MapReduce**, which is a way of simplifying an operation such that it is suitable to run in parallel on a distributed infrastructure. A popular implementation of MapReduce is Apache Hadoop, and you can use this in Azure with **HDInsight**, which also supports related tools, including Apache Spark and Apache **Storm**. Other options to handle large datasets include Google's Cloud Bigtable or **BigQuery**.

You can see the available options for Azure HDInsight in the portal. Spark is shown in the following screenshot:

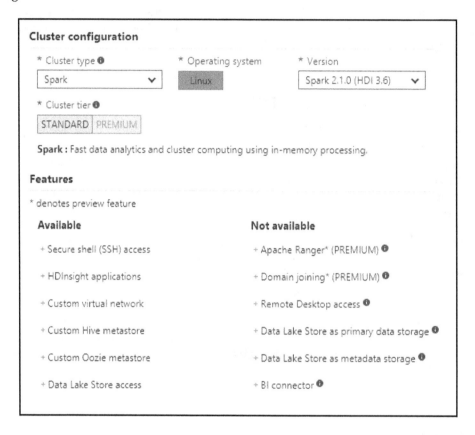

You can see from this screenshot that Spark is available only on Linux. Hadoop is more established and is also available on Windows, as shown in the following screenshot:

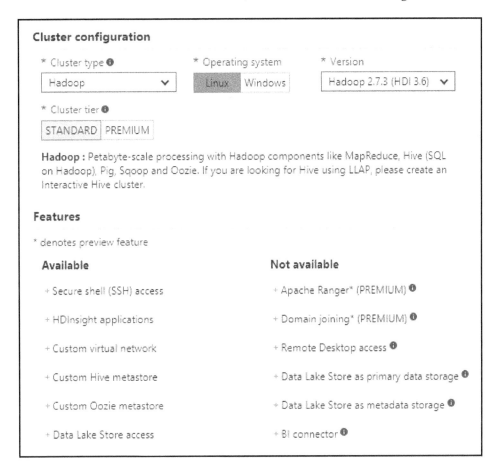

The next screenshot shows that Storm is also available but not on the premium cluster tier (the same as Spark):

You can read more about HDInsight at `https://docs.microsoft.com/en-us/azure/hdinsight/`.

Orleans

Another interesting project is an open source framework from Microsoft called **Orleans**, which is a distributed virtual actor model that was used to power the cloud services of some Halo Xbox games. What this means is that if you build your system by separating your logic into separate actors, this allows it to easily scale based on the demand.

In Orleans, actors are known as grains, and you can write them in C# by inheriting from an interface. These are then executed by an Orleans server called a **silo**. Grains can be persisted to storage, such as SQL or **Azure Tables**, to save their state and to reactivate later. Orleans can also make use of the Bond serializer for greater efficiency.

Unfortunately, Orleans does not currently support .NET Core. Support is planned for version 2.0 of Orleans, which is currently a work in progress. Orleans allows you to write simple and scalable systems with low latency, and you can read more at `http://dotnet.github.io/orleans/`.

Custom transports

In `Chapter 6`, *Addressing Network Performance*, we started with an introduction to TCP/IP and briefly mentioned **User Datagram Protocol** (**UDP**). We also covered **Transport Layer Security** (**TLS**) encryption and how to minimize the impact of secure connections while still reaping performance benefits.

UDP is simpler and quicker than **Transmission Control Protocol** (**TCP**), but you either need to not care about reliable delivery (multiplayer games and voice/video chat) or build your own layer to provide this. In `Chapter 10`, *The Downsides of Performance-Enhancing Tools*, we highlighted **StatsD**, which uses UDP to avoid blocking latency while logging to a remote central server.

There are alternatives to TLS if you aren't constrained to a browser, but if you're developing a web application, this will probably only apply inside your server infrastructure. For example, the WhatsApp messaging app uses **Noise Pipes** and Curve25519 from the Noise Protocol Framework (`http://noiseprotocol.org/`) between the smartphone app and its servers, in addition to the Signal Protocol for end-to-end encryption.

Using Noise Pipes instead of TLS increases performance because fewer round trips are required to set up a connection. Another option with similar benefits is the **secure pipe daemon** (**spiped**), as used by and created for the secure Linux/BSD backup software, **Tarsnap**. However, you do need to pre-share the keys, but you can read more about this at `http://www.tarsnap.com/spiped.html`.

Advanced hashing

We covered hashing functions a fair amount in this book, especially in Chapter 8, *Understanding Code Execution and Asynchronous Operations*. This area is constantly advancing and it's useful to keep an eye on the future to see what's coming. Although today it is reasonable to use a member of the SHA-2 family for quick hashing and PBKDF2 for slow (password) hashing, this is unlikely to always be the case.

For fast hashing, there is a new family of algorithms called **SHA-3**, which should not be confused with SHA-384 or SHA-512 (which are both in the SHA-2 family). SHA-3 is based on an algorithm called Keccak, which was the winner of a competition to find a suitable algorithm for the new standard. Other finalists included Skein (http://skein-hash.info/) and BLAKE2 (http://blake2.net/), which is faster than MD5 but actually secure.

An algorithm called Argon2 won a similar competition for password hashing (http://password-hashing.net/). To see why this matters, you can visit https://haveibeenpwned.com/ (run by .NET security guru Troy Hunt) to see whether your details are in one of the large numbers of data breaches. For example, LinkedIn was breached and didn't use secure password hashing (only an unsalted SHA-1 hash). Consequently, most of the plain text passwords were cracked and recovered. Therefore, if a LinkedIn account password was reused on other sites, then these accounts can be taken over.

It's a very good idea to use a password manager and create strong unique passwords for every site. It is also beneficial to use two-factor authentication (sometimes also called two-step verification) if available. For example, you can do this by entering a code from a smartphone app in addition to a password. This is particularly useful for email accounts, as they can normally be used to recover other accounts.

Library and framework support

There have been some significant changes to .NET Core and ASP.NET Core between versions 1.0 and 2.0. Sensibly, many popular libraries and frameworks were waiting for .NET Standard 2.0, before adding support.

Obviously, a book is a bad place to keep up with the changes, so the author has put together a GitHub repository to display the latest compatibility information. You can find the *ASP.NET Core Library and Framework Support* list at http://anclafs.com/.

If you would like to update anything or add a library or framework, then please send a pull request. The repository is located at `https://github.com/jpsingleton/ANCLAFS` and it includes a lot of useful tools, libraries, frameworks, and more. We mentioned many of these earlier in this book, and the following sample is just a small selection of what is listed, because package support will grow over time:

- Scientist.NET
- FeatureToggle
- MiniProfiler
- Glimpse
- Prefix
- Dapper
- Simple.Data
- EF Core
- Hangfire
- ImageResizer
- DynamicImage
- ImageSharp
- RestBus
- EasyNetQ
- RabbitMQ client
- MassTransit
- Topshelf
- Nancy
- Orleans

The future

A quote often attributed to the physicist Niels Bohr goes as follows:

> *Prediction is very difficult, especially about the future.*

However, we'll have a go at this anyway, starting with the more straightforward bits. The official ASP.NET Core roadmap lists SignalR support shipping with version 2.1. SignalR is being rewritten, as many lessons were learned with large deployments, and improvements were needed.

There is also the continued progress of the .NET Standard specification, created to enhance portability between .NET Core, the .NET Framework, and Mono. For example, .NET Core 2.0 and .NET Framework 4.6.1 both implement .NET Standard 2.0. This means that projects written in either can use libraries that adhere to the .NET Standard 2.0 spec. As .NET Standard 2.0 is now finalized, any increase in the API surface area will use a higher version number. The .NET Standard is analogous to the HTML5 spec, which is implemented to varying degrees by different browsers. You probably won't need to worry too much about this unless you are writing a library or a NuGet package. Refer to the documentation at `https://docs.microsoft.com/en-gb/dotnet/standard/net-standard` if you are.

You may have wondered why .NET 4.7 isn't currently mentioned in the .NET Standard docs. Expect this to change and for the various frameworks to continue to converge. However, you may not want to upgrade to a new version too early, as there have been a few serious bugs in the new releases. For example, there was a nasty bug in 4.6 that passed the wrong values to method parameters. There was also a horrible error in 4.6.2 where the max-age header was set to a huge value, which could result in assets being cached in proxies for over 2000 years! Hot-fixes (or quality updates) are usually released for these issues, so make sure that you stay on top of them and don't simply rely on the version number.

From a language point of view, C# 7.1 and 7.2 offer some small improvements, and 8.0 will contain some bigger new features. The intention is to add some high-performance, low-level code features for optimizing games and other performance-sensitive operations. These are the things for which you previously had to use unsafe code, and the plan is to make them safe to use but still quick. Other language features up for inclusion are default implementations of interfaces, which are available in Java and Swift. This allows you to update an interface without breaking all the classes that implement it. It also makes for a cleaner map from Xamarin to the Android and iOS platform APIs. C# 7.1 allows an `async` main method, and in the future, you may be able to `await` a `foreach` loop or a `using` statement too. The final list is subject to change, so check the C# language design repository on GitHub (`https://github.com/dotnet/csharplang`) nearer the time, or even get involved.

Microsoft has said that it will listen to user feedback and use it to drive the direction of the platforms, so you have a voice. They also use the telemetry gathered from the SDK tooling to decide on platform support and release some of this data periodically. As the code is all open source, you can help shape the future by adding the features that you want. Much of the F# development comes from the community, and it will be good to see it supported better in ASP.NET Core and related tooling. For example, the FSharp.Data web scraping tool was a community contribution. Take a look at GitHub and jump in.

Further into the future is harder to predict, but there has been a steady stream of projects being open sourced by Microsoft, from the early offerings of ASP.NET MVC to the Xamarin framework for cross-platform app development. The XAML Standard is taking shape and the prospect of a universal UI framework that works across all major desktop and mobile operating systems is an alluring one.

It's an exciting time to be working with C# and .NET, especially if you want to branch out from web development. The Unity game engine is part of the .NET foundation, and there are some interesting developments in **Virtual Reality** (**VR**) and **Augmented Reality** (**AR**) hardware. For example, Microsoft Hololens, Oculus Rift, Samsung Gear VR, and HTC Vive are all unbelievably better than the basic VR that came out a couple of decades ago.

It's also a great time to be looking at IoT, which, while it may still be looking for its killer app, has so much more cheap and powerful hardware available for use. A Raspberry Pi Zero W costs only $10 with a camera connector and WiFi/Bluetooth. With a computer such as the Raspberry Pi 3, which offers almost desktop-class performance and WiFi/Bluetooth for $35, anyone can now easily learn to code (perhaps in C# or .NET) and make things.

The following is the wisdom of Alan Kay:

> *The best way to predict the future is to invent it.*

So, get out there and make it! And make sure that you share what you've done.

Summary

We hope that you enjoyed this book and learned how to make your web applications well-performing and easy to maintain, particularly when you use C#, ASP.NET Core, and .NET Core. We tried to keep as much advice as possible applicable to general web app development, while gently introducing you to the latest open source frameworks from Microsoft and others.

Clearly, a topic such as this changes quite rapidly, so keep your eyes open online for updates. Hopefully, a lot of the lessons in this book are generally good ideas and they will still be sensible for a long time to come.

Always keep in mind that optimizing for its own sake is pointless, unless it's literally an academic exercise. You need to measure and weigh the benefits against the downsides; otherwise, you may end up making things worse. It is easy to make things more complex, harder to understand, difficult to maintain, or all of these.

It's important to instill these pragmatic performance ideas into the team culture, or else teams won't always adhere to them. However, above all, remember to still have fun!

Index

asynchronous (async) methods 99
asynchronous availability 17
asynchronous operations
  about 99, 100
  background queuing 100
  tools 100
Augmented Reality (AR) 315
Authenticated Encryption with Additional Data
  (AEAD) 136
automated testing 281
Availability Zone (AZ) 161
AWS Relational Database Service (RDS) 240
Azure Application Gateway 151, 160
Azure CDN 115
Azure Diagnostics
  reference 272
Azure Load Balancer 160
Azure ML
  about 305
  reference 306
Azure Service Bus 243
Azure SQL Database 240

B

background queuing 100
bad practices, avoiding for web application
  exceptions 221
  reflection 219
  regular expressions 219
  string concatenation, in tight loops 220
  synchronous operations 221
bcrypt 28
BenchmarkDotNet
  about 93
  reference 93, 194
big data 307
BigQuery 307
Bitbucket 282
bitmap (BMP) 118
BizTalk 243
Blink 294
bloom filter
  about 198
  reference 199
blue-green deployment 187

Bower 143
BPG
  about 146
  reference 146
branch by abstraction 286
British Indian Ocean Territory (BIOT) 156
British Telecom (BT) network 164
broker
  advantages 244
Brotli
  about 140
  reference 140, 141
browsers
  Chrome 85, 86
  Firefox 87
BrowserStack
  reference 295
bundling 142

C

C# 6
  about 15
  asynchronous availability 17
  exception filters 16
  expression bodies 17
  null conditional operator 16
  string interpolation 15
C# 7
  about 17
  asynchronous improvements 21
  expression bodies 21
  literals 18
  out variables 19
  patterns 20
  references 19, 20
  tuples 18, 19
C#
  new features 14
cache busting 229
Cache Digests 199
caching
  about 148
  application layer caching 239
  avoiding 238
  database result set caching 241

K

Kestrel 192
key stretching 28
Kibana 91

L

lag 98
Language-Integrated Query (LINQ) 193
latency-based problems
  solutions 172
latency
  about 27, 98
  disk latency 98
  example 99
  network latency 98
Lempel-Ziv-Markov chain Algorithm
    (LZMA/LZMA2) 140
LibGD
  reference 147
Line of Business (LoB) applications 113
Lines of Code (LoC) 262
Linux 58, 236
Linux Containers (LXC) 65
lists 193
literals 18
load testing 283
Local Area Network (LAN) 30
locking
  about 216
  example 217, 218
logging
  about 265
  centralized logging 272
  error logging 265, 266
  integrated logging 269, 270, 271
Logstash
  reference 272
Long-Term Service Branch (LTSB) 41
lossless compression algorithms 140, 141

M

Mac 49
machine learning (ML) 305
Man in the Middle attack (MitM) 151

MapReduce 307
MassTransit
  reference 247
measurement 278
Message Authentication Code (MAC) 200
Message Digest 5 (MD5) 200
message queue (MQ)
  about 101, 241
  coffee shop analogy 242
  styles 243
Message Queuing (MQ) 99
messaging patterns
  about 243
  pub/sub 244, 245
  unicast 243, 244
microservices architecture
  versus monolith architecture 254, 255
Microsoft Developer Network (MSDN) 33
Microsoft Message Analyzer 89
Microsoft Message Queuing (MSMQ) 34, 243
Microsoft SQL Server (MS SQL) 178
Microsoft's Bond framework
  reference 207
MiniBench
  reference 194
minification 142, 143
Minimum Viable Product (MVP) 262
MiniProfiler
  about 79
  reference 79
MIT 33
Model-View-Controller (MVC) 191
monolith architecture
  versus microservices architecture 254, 255
Mozilla Public License (MPL) 246
mozjpeg
  reference 145
  URL 145
MQTT 246
multithreading 216

N

Nagios
  reference 297
Native Image Generator (NGen) 191

S